Edmund Spenser's Irish Experience

Edmund Spenser's Irish Experience

WILDE FRUIT AND SALVAGE SOYL

ANDREW HADFIELD

CLARENDON PRESS · OXFORD

1997

Oxford University Press, Great Clarendon Street, Oxford OX2 6DP

Oxford New York

Athens Auckland Bangkok Bogota Bombay
Buenos Aires Calcutta Cape Town Dar es Salaam
Delhi Florence Hong Kong Istanbul Karachi
Kuala Lumpur Madras Madrid Melbourne
Mexico City Nairobi Paris Singapore
Taipei Tokyo Toronto
and associated companies in
Berlin Ibadan

Oxford is a trade mark of Oxford University Press

Published in the United States
by Oxford University Press Inc., New York

British Library Cataloguing in Publication Data
Data available

Library of Congress Cataloging in Publication Data
Hadfield, Andrew.
Spenser's Irish experience: wilde fruit and savage soyl / Andrew Hadfield.
Includes bibliographical references (p.).
1. Spenser, Edmund, 1552?–1599—Homes and haunts—Ireland.
2. Poets, English—Early modern, 1500–1700—Biography. 3. Spenser,
Edmund, 1552?–1599—Knowledge—Ireland. 4. Spenser, Edmund,
1552?–1599. Faerie queene. 5. Epic poetry, English—Irish
influences. 6. British—Ireland—History—16th century.
7. Ireland—History—1558–1603. 8. Colonies in literature.
9. Ireland—In literature. I. Title.
PR2363.H23 1997 821'.3—dc21 [B] 96-40152

ISBN 0–19–818345–3

1 3 5 7 9 10 8 6 4 2

Typeset by Jayvee, Trivandrum, India
Printed in Great Britain
on acid-free paper by
Biddles Ltd.
Guildford and King's Lynn

FOR MY PARENTS
DAVID ARTHUR HADFIELD
KATHLEEN HILARY HADFIELD

Acknowledgements

THIS book was originally conceived as a D. Phil. thesis at the University of Ulster, Coleraine, supervised by Professor Robert Welch, 'a loose, baggy, monster', with the rather catchy title, 'The English Conception of Ireland, *c*.1540–*c*.1600, with special reference to the works of Edmund Spenser'. It was passed in 1988, but has taken nearly ten years to see the light of day in its complete form (although sections have appeared in article form over the years), for a whole host of reasons, academic and otherwise.

Any work which takes such a long time to complete inevitably incurs a host of debts to scholars who have helped the author in a variety of ways and it is my pleasure to be able to acknowledge these in print, at long last. My principal thanks must go to Bob Welch for encouraging me to undertake the project, thus saving me from my own half-baked ideas, and, in the course of my progress, providing enlightened and good-humoured supervision, and correcting numerous factual and stylistic errors. For reading parts of the typescript in its various forms as it evolved, my thanks go to Professor John Barnard, Michael Brennan, John Gillingham, Helen Hackett, Professor Brean Hammond, Professor Paul Hammond, Lesley Johnson, David Lindley, Diane Watt, and to my external examiner, John Pitcher, all of whom made valuable suggestions, as did the three anonymous readers for Oxford University Press. Special thanks go to Thomas Healy and Willy Maley, who read the whole typescript and saved me from numerous errors; those that remain are not their responsibility. Audiences at various institutions where I have given papers which have been incorporated into the final text have often provided stimulating and helpful criticism; I am grateful to audiences at University College, Cork; Birkbeck College, London; the London Renaissance Seminar; the University of Staffordshire; the University of Uppsala, Sweden; the University of Leeds; the University of Leicester; and Queen Mary and Westfield College, London; and to John Goodby, Tom Healy, David Cairns and Shaun Richards, the late Birgit Bramsbäck, Paul Hammond, Elaine Treharne, and Alan Stewart, for inviting me to speak on each occasion. Numerous colleagues I have worked with and encountered in various places have provided stimulating ideas and help with research: I would like to thank Brendan Bradshaw, Patricia Coughlan, John Dickie, Anne Fogarty, Bob Hunter, Douglas Jefferson, John McVeagh, Hiram Morgan, Andrew Mousley, Ken Rowe, Michael Smith, Diane Watt, and John Watts, who, I hope, know how much I have valued their advice.

The typescript of the book was completed while I was granted a semester's study leave by the Department of English, the University of Wales, Aberystwyth, so that I am grateful not only for the time spent away from my teaching and administrative duties, but also to my colleagues for making light of the burden I have placed upon them. I also owe a debt to the British Academy, who funded my research at both doctoral and post-doctoral level. The work was carried out in the libraries at the University of Ulster, Coleraine; the British Library; the National Library of Ireland; the National Library of Wales; the Brotherton Library, University of Leeds; and the Hugh Owen Library, University of Wales, Aberystwyth, and I am grateful for the helpful assistance I received from staff in all of them. Both Andrew Lockett, with whom I began the project at Oxford University Press, and Jason Freeman, with whom I have seen the book through the press, have been exemplary editors and thoroughly pleasant to work with.

My greatest debt goes to my family who have had to endure my truculence, egomania, and self-centredness for a long time. Alison, Lucy, Patrick, and Maud Hadfield all know how important their love and support has been over the years. I would also like to thank David and Mary Yarnold, not least for all the useful volumes they have passed my way. However, I have dedicated this work to my parents, David and Hilary, who have had to suffer such irritations, and done so with such good grace, for so long.

Some of the arguments developed in this book have already appeared in various forms in journals and edited collections. Sections of Chapters 2 and 6 appeared in 'Spenser, Ireland and Sixteenth-Century Political Theory', *Modern Language Review*, 89 (Jan. 1994), 1–18. A portion of Chapter 2 appeared as 'Was Spenser's *A View of the Present State of Ireland* Censored? A Review of the Evidence', *Notes and Queries*, 239 (Dec. 1994), 459–63. A version of Chapter 3 appeared as 'Briton and Scythian: Tudor Representations of Irish Origins', *Irish Historical Studies*, 28 (Nov. 1993), 390–408. Sections of Chapter 4 appeared in ' "The Sacred Hunger of Ambitious Minds": Spenser's Savage Religion', in Donna B. Hamilton and Richard Strier (eds.), *Religion, Literature* and Politics in Post-Reformation England, *1540–1688* (Cambridge: Cambridge University Press, 1996), 27–45. Sections of Chapters 4 and 6 appeared in 'The Trials of Jove: Spenser's Allegory and the Mastery of the Irish', *Bullan*, 2/2 (Winter/Spring 1996), 39–53. Sections of Chapter 5 appeared in 'Another Look at Irena and Serena', *Irish University Review* 26 (1996): *Special issue: Spenser in Ireland: The Faerie Queene, 1596–1996*, ed. Anne Fogarty, 291–302. A portion of Chapter 5 appeared in 'The Course of Justice: Spenser, Ireland and Political Discourse', *Studia Neophilologica*, 65 (1993), 187–96. I am grateful to the respective editors and the syndics of Cambridge University Press for permission to reproduce material in this book.

A.H.

Contents

Abbreviations

CI	*Critical Inquiry*
CSPI	*Calendar of State Papers, Ireland*
DNB	*Dictionary of National Biography*
EC	*Essays in Criticism*
EHR	*English Historical Review*
ELH	*English Literary History*
ELN	*English Language Notes*
ELR	*English Literary Renaissance*
FQ	*The Faerie Queene*, ed. A. C. Hamilton (London: Longman, 1977)
HJ	*Historical Journal*
HLQ	*Huntington Library Quarterly*
IHS	*Irish Historical Studies*
ISR	*Irish Studies Review*
JBS	*Journal of British Studies*
JCHAS	*Journal of the Cork Historical and Archaeological Society*
JEGP	*Journal of English and Germanic Philology*
JEH	*Journal of Ecclesiastical History*
JMRS	*Journal of Medieval and Renaissance Studies*
MLN	*Modern Language Notes*
MLQ	*Modern Language Quarterly*
MP	*Modern Philology*
NLH	*New Literary History*
N&Q	*Notes and Queries*
PAPS	*Proceedings of the American Philosophical Society*
PBA	*Proceedings of the British Academy*
PMLA	*Proceedings of the Modern Language Association of America*
PNR	*Poetry Nation Review*
P&P	*Past and Present*
TRHS	*Transactions of the Royal Historical Society*
PRIA	*Proceedings of the Royal Irish Academy*
RQ	*Renaissance Quarterly*
SAQ	*South Atlantic Quarterly*
SEL	*Studies in English Literature*
SHR	*Scottish Historical Review*
SP	*Studies in Philology*
Sp. Enc.	*The Spenser Encyclopedia*, ed. A. C. Hamilton (London: Routledge; Toronto: Toronto University Press, 1990)

Sp. Stud.	*Spenser Studies*
STC	A. W. Pollard and G. R. Redgrave (eds.), *A Short Title Catalogue of Books Printed in England, Scotland and Ireland and of English Books printed abroad, 1475–1640,* 2nd ed., 2 vols., revised and enlarged by W. A. Jackson and F. S. Ferguson, completed by Katherine F. Panzer (London: Bibliographical Society, 1976)
Tilley	Morris Palmer Tilley, *A Dictionary of Proverbs in England in the Sixteenth and Seventeenth Centuries* (Ann Arbor: University of Michigan Press, 1950)
TCBS	*Transactions of the Cambridge Bibliographical Society*
TLS	*Times Literary Supplement*
TP	*Textual Practice*
TSLL	*Texas Studies in Language and Literature*
TWASAL	*Transactions of the Wisconsin Academy of Sciences, Arts and Letters*
UTQ	*University of Toronto Quarterly*
Variorum	*The Works of Edmund Spenser: A Variorum Edition,* ed. Edwin Greenlaw *et al.,* 11 vols. (Baltimore: Johns Hopkins University Press, 1932–49)
YES	*Yearbook of English Studies*

Map of Ireland incorporating proper names mentioned in the text

Introduction:
Spenser, Colonialism, and National Identity

A T a conference of the English Association held during the First World War (1917), one of the speakers, John Bailey, told the following patriotic anecdote, intended to illustrate the intimate connection between reading English literature and virtuous action: '[Bailey] related a story of an officer who read the *Faerie Queene* to his men when they were in a particularly difficult situation. The men did not understand the words, but the poetry had a soothing influence upon them. Nothing better could be said of poetry than that.'[1] The officer's actions recall, perhaps deliberately, Sir Philip Sidney's argument in *An Apology for Poetry* that the poet was 'the right popular philosopher' whose 'sugared invention' moved 'men to take goodness in hand'.[2] One wonders exactly why *The Faerie Queene* was chosen by this anonymous officer; was it because of its soothing—some would say soporific—qualities,[3] or because it was considered a particularly suitable work for men undergoing military struggle?

If the former was the case, then there is a certain poetic justice if one continues the comparison with Sidney's *Apology*. Sidney rather snobbishly comments that Aesop's fables prove his point because their 'pretty allegories, stealing under the formal tales of beasts, make many, more beastly than beasts, begin to hear the sound of virtue from these dumb speakers' (p. 109), a description which matches not only the

---

[1] Cited in Brian Doyle, *English and Englishness* (London: Routledge, 1989), 28. I am grateful to Tim Woods for this reference.

[2] Sir Philip Sidney, *An Apology for Poetry*, ed. Geoffrey Shepherd (Manchester: Manchester University Press, 1965), 109, 103. Subsequent references are given in the text in parentheses. Sidney's text opens with a military anecdote. I owe this point to Willy Maley.

[3] A frequent criticism of Spenser's verse; see C. S. Lewis, *English Literature of the Sixteenth Century, Excluding Drama* (Oxford: Oxford University Press, 1954), 391. A. C. Hamilton has argued that '*The Faerie Queene* is not meant to be understood but to be possessed': 'Our New Poet: Spenser, "well of English undefyld" ', in Judith M. Kennedy and James A. Reither (eds.), *A Theatre for Spenserians* (Manchester: Manchester University Press, 1973), 101–23, at 101.

allegorical poem itself, but also the incomprehension of the soldiers under fire, able to face the perils of war through the 'cultural mystique' endowed by the qualities 'inherent in the *national* literature' (my emphasis).[4] The soldiers' reported reactions to the effects of literature can also be read as an inversion of the transformation of men into beasts by Circe, a story which Spenser used in one of the most frequently read and popular episodes in the poem, the destruction of the Bower of Bliss (see below, pp. 163–4).[5]

If the latter was what Bailey's officer had in mind, then his use of Spenser was both highly appropriate—probably well beyond his intentions—and deeply ironic. As Edward Said has recently commented in his study of the intimate relationship between English literature and the imperial history of England: 'it is generally true that literary historians who study the great sixteenth-century poet Edmund Spenser, for example, do not connect his bloodthirsty plans for Ireland, where he imagined a British army virtually exterminating the native inhabitants, with his poetic achievement or with the history of British rule over Ireland, which continues today.'[6] Said's analytical framework is a necessary antidote to a tradition which has often taken the Englishness of English literature for granted. However, the easy use of the term 'British' may hide a multitude of sins in that it rigidly separates Ireland from a mainland Britain which, in this context at least, is assumed to be united and homogeneous, existing from the sixteenth century to the present.[7] For the anonymous officer, Spenser is the poet of nation, for Said, he is the poet of empire.

Such separations are in themselves intensely problematic, particularly as regards sixteenth-century Ireland within the English-dominated British Isles. Where nations start and stop will never be a settled question. It will never be possible to determine exactly what forms of difference a nation will be prepared to include and what will have to be castigated as the alien 'other' against which such a body will seek to

    [4] Doyle, *English and Englishness*, 27.

    [5] Stanzas from the episode are cited as examples of Spenser's great gift for depicting 'sweetness and beauty' in R. W. Church's biography of Spenser for the Macmillan English Men of Letters series (1879), an important influence on the formation of the canon of English literature taught and on the ways in which it was read; see pp. 144–7. Yeats's edition of Spenser for the Golden Poets series (1906) contained extracts from the episode: see George Bornstein, 'Yeats, William Butler', *Sp. Enc.*, 738–9.

    [6] *Culture and Imperialism* (London: Vintage, 1993), 5.

    [7] A problem which has confronted other recent writers, notably Seamus Heaney in his poem, 'An Open Letter' (1983); see the discussion in Neil Corcoran, *A Student's Guide to Seamus Heaney* (London: Faber & Faber, 1986), 40–1.

define itself, not least because the boundaries between the two antithetical categories are inevitably fluid. As Homi K. Bhabha has argued, the nation must constantly be written and rewritten: 'The scraps, patches, and rags of daily life must be repeatedly turned into the signs of a national culture, while the very act of the narrative performance interpellates a growing circle of national subjects.'[8] Simply writing down the character of the nation alters a complex reality which only ever exists in the imaginations of those who wish either to belong or remain outside.[9]

Given this insurmountable ambiguity and given also the problematic relationship between the state of Englishness and Britishness in the sixteenth century (see Ch. 3), it is hard to cast Spenser as either the good poet of nation or the bad poet of empire. One of the central arguments of this book is that Spenser's status as an English poet in Ireland is not only crucial to an understanding of his work, but also stands as a demonstration that texts are inevitably caught up within the histories of nations and empires, both in terms of their inception and of their reception. History is doubly articulated in that the history which actually happened and which led to or caused the present that we live in (a history which is complicated by the significance of writing as one of its constituent elements), can only be known through the way in which it is written in the present, a problem elided by Said's conflation of these two histories in the phrase, 'which continues today'. Are they obviously the same history? Certainly the territories (nations?) have changed as Ireland itself has split into the Irish Republic and Northern Ireland, or 'the six counties', depending on one's view of history.[10]

I want to argue that Spenser's *A View of the Present State of Ireland* and *The Faerie Queene* are vitally important works within the complex history of Britain. They are, as Said alleges, works of imperialism; but they are also works which attempt to articulate a sense of a national identity in exile. The problem is that the experience of exile and the meeting of cultures inevitably altered the pristine Manichean divide a national identity demanded. As Benedict Anderson has recently argued, straightforward divisions between cultures simply do not happen. Even the representation of the 'native' is fraught with difficulty:

---

[8] 'DissemiNation: Time, Narrative, and the Margins of the Modern Nation', in id. (ed.), *Nation and Narration* (London: Routledge, 1990), 291–322, at 297.

[9] See *Imagined Communities: Reflections on the Origins and Spread of Nationalism* (London: Verso, 1983), ch. 1.

[10] A reading which also leaves out the complex history of Anglo-Scottish relations. Scotland, *pace* Said, was not absorbed within Britain when Spenser was writing.

For the native is, like colonial and creole, a white-on-black negative. The native-ness of natives is always unmoored, its real significance hybrid and oxymoronic. It appears when Moors, heathens, Mohammedans, savages, Hindoos, and so forth are becoming obsolete, that is, not only when, in the proximity of real print-encounters, substantial numbers of Vietnamese read, write, and perhaps speak French but also when Czechs do the same with German and Jews with Hungarian. Nationalism's purities (and thus also cleansings) are set to emerge from exactly this hybridity.[11]

The creation and homogenization of the 'native' as a cultural unity results from a threat to the supposedly monolithic construction of the identity of the hegemonic colonizer, so that no one identity—colonial, creole, native—can really be separated off as pure, whatever the precise political situation of relative dominance and subordination. The asser-tion of one people's supremacy over another will inevitably alter both dominant and subordinate groups, a truism which demonstrates the impossibility of separating nation formation and colonial/imperial expansion.[12] Anderson's generalization would seem to refer neatly to the anxieties of the colonial class to which Spenser belonged, the New English, caught between a host of competing and intersecting identities, and consequently worried that unless they defined their own identity in an aggressive way it would disappear before their very eyes. Hence the very easy polarity of 'native' and 'colonizer' betrays the existence of a more complex history.

This can be read in terms of two of the dedicatory sonnets appended to the first edition of *The Faerie Queene*.[13] The seventh of these is dedi-cated to the queen's cousin, Thomas Butler, tenth earl of Ormond and Ossory, a controversial figure who exploited his grant of the palatinate of Tipperary (which meant that he could circumvent many Irish and English laws), who often resorted to force in disputes with his neighbours, and whose loyalty was suspected over his erratic leadership of the Crown forces in Ireland.[14] Most importantly of all, Ormond was a member of the incumbent colonial group, the Old English, whose

[11] Benedict Anderson, 'Exodus', *CI* 20 (1994), 314–27, at 316. For the opposite view, see Abdul R. JanMahomed, 'The Economy of Manichean Allegory: The Function of Racial Difference in Colonialist Literature', in Henry Louis Gates, Jr. (ed.), *'Race', Writing, and Difference* (Chicago: Chicago University Press, 1986), 78–106.

[12] For further discussion, see Terry Eagleton, Fredric Jameson, and Edward W. Said, *Nationalism, Colonialism, and Literature* (Minneapolis: University of Minnesota Press, 1990).

[13] On the textual history of the sonnets, see L. G. Black, '*The Faerie Queene*, Commendatory Verses and Dedicatory Sonnets', *Sp. Enc.* 291–3.

[14] On Ormond see *DNB* entry; Ciaran Brady (ed.), *Worsted in the Game: Losers in*

ancestors had come over with the Anglo-Normans in the twelfth century, so that his seemingly privileged relationship with the queen was much resented by the upwardly mobile New English who came to Ireland on the back of the renewed Crown interest under the Tudors.

In the sonnet Spenser refers to his epic poem as the 'wilde fruit' of 'salvage soyl'. It is the product of a 'faire . . . land' in which there is 'not one *Parnassus*, nor one *Helicone* | Left for sweete Muses to be harboured' because Ireland has been 'through long wars left almost waste, | With brutish barbarisme . . . ouerspredd'. However, where Ormond has his 'braue mansione':

> There in deede dwel faire Graces many one.
> And gentle Nymphes, delights of learned wits,
> And in thy person without Paragone
> All goodly bountie and true honour sits,
> Such therefore, as that wasted soyl doth yield,
> Receiue dear Lord in worth, the fruit of barren field.

(lines 9–14)

The message can be seen to depend upon a clever sleight of hand; the giving of culture, *The Faerie Queene*, to Ormond, is portrayed as dependent upon his success in spreading English civility, yet also as an independent creation of the poet's, the 'fruit' which must be harvested if the bad nature of Ireland is to be civilized. It suggests that *The Faerie Queene* serves an Orphic function in its ability to transform the wilderness left by the natives; that it is at once congruent with a political authority and simultaneously aware of a potential to undermine what it ostensibly relies upon.

In a sense, this is what could be said to be happening in the sonnet, as Spenser's work can be read as militantly New English and contains a number of hostile attacks upon the Old English. The first editor of *A View*, Sir James Ware, commented in 1633 that, had Spenser written the work in the 1630s, 'he would have omitted those passages which may seeme to lay either any particular aspersion upon some families, or generall upon the Nation', showing that Spenser's ideological position did not escape early readers.[15] A straightforwardly ironic reading of the poem is made difficult because the same metaphors are used in the dedicatory sonnet—the tenth in the sequence—to Arthur, Lord Grey de

Irish History (Dublin: Lilliput, 1989), ch. 4; Richard Bagwell, *Ireland under the Tudors*, 3 vols. (London: Longman, 1885–90), vols. ii and iii, *passim*.

[15] Ware's Preface, repr. in *Variorum*, x. 530–2; quotation p. 532.

Wilton, Spenser's ertstwhile patron and one of the Tudor Lord Deputies most frequently praised by the New English as one who understood their position. However, Ormond and Grey were not simply representatives of different colonial classes, but also bitter rivals. Grey replaced Ormond as leader of military operations in Munster in the early 1580s, only to be recalled after Ormond and other Old English magnates had successfully lobbied the queen at court, claiming that Grey's brutality at Smerwick had led to the war being prolonged. Ormond was subsequently reinstated.[16]

Spenser pledges to leave in Grey's 'noble hands', 'Rude rymes, the which a rustick Muse did weaue | In sauadge soyle, far from Parnasso mount'. While it is easy enough to observe the contrast made between the savagery of the native Irish and the civilized sophistication of the English colonists in these two sonnets, more significant is the ambiguity or unease they express.[17] Once the identities of the two figures are known, the sonnets draw attention to a fracturing of Englishness in Ireland rather than its unity, and the difficulty, not the ease, of drawing up distinctions. The sonnet to Ormond in particular registers the fragile and precarious way in which a national identity is constructed and boundaries are drawn up between the inside and the outside, a problem which the very existence of the sonnet itself is witness to.

What these two sonnets point out is that, as has long been recognized by theorists of colonialism, the identity of the colonizer is transformed too so that the attempt to unite Britain under an English suzerainty renders Englishness at odds with itself, or, more accurately, its resulting hybrid selves.[18] Spenser's work has for too long been subsumed under the deceptive category of English literature—although it is worth noting that the recent *Field Day Anthology of Irish Writing* includes him as

[16] Nicholas Canny, 'Ireland: The Historical Context', *Sp. Enc.* 404–7, at 405–6.

[17] As Thomas Healy has recently noted, 'The precariousness of civilisation haunts *The Faerie Queene*': *New Latitudes: Theory and English Renaissance Literature* (London: Edward Arnold, 1992), 98. For a comprehensive survey of English representations of the Irish as barbarous, see Joseph Th. Leerssen, *Mere Irish and Fíor-Ghael: Studies in the Idea of Irish Nationality, its Development and Literary Expression Prior to the Nineteenth Century* (Amsterdam: Benjamens, 1986). See also Walter J. Ong, 'Spenser's *View* and the Tradition of the "Wild" Irish', *MLQ* 3 (1942), 561–71; Seamus Deane, *Civilians and Barbarians* (Derry: Field Day, 1983).

[18] See Homi K. Bhabha, 'Signs Taken for Wonders: Questions of Ambivalence and Authority under a Tree Outside Delhi, May 1817', in id., *The Location of Culture* (London: Routledge, 1994), 102–22; Bill Ashcroft *et al.* (eds.), *The Post-Colonial Studies Reader* (London: Routledge, 1995), pt. 6. See also Trinh T. Minh-ha, 'The Undone Interval', in Iain Chambers and Lidia Curti (eds.), *The Post-Colonial Question: Common Skies, Divided Horizons* (London: Routledge, 1996), 3–16, at 9–11.

Irish[19]—a classification which admirably proves Homi Bhabha's contention that 'Being obliged to forget becomes the basis for remembering the nation'.[20] Constructing a monolithic English tradition, not least a unified literary tradition, involves the assumption of a history and racial memory which never really existed.[21]

Spenser is not an easy writer to classify in terms of identity, and the following chapters will attempt to argue the case that his work revolves around the question of identity, individual and national, painfully aware that borders exist which can all too easily be transgressed and always need to be policed. His writing would also seem to provide evidence to support Benedict Anderson's contention that 'early conceptions . . . of nation-ness' developed in '*creole* communities' and that the experience of separation from one's homeland was the key factor in exciting interest in the question of identity.[22] The case could have been made by resorting to a variant on Fredric Jameson's thesis of the 'political unconscious' whereby history presses upon the narrative within which it is retextualized as an 'absent cause', whatever the problems with Jameson's argument.[23] However, one of my principal contentions is that not only does Spenser's writing make its interest in the problems of Britishness, Englishness, and Irishness quite clear, but it also advertises and promotes such an explicit focus as one of the key elements of his literary work (which is not to assert that Spenser is always in control of his material and that knowing his intentions will always unlock the mystery of the text).[24] *The Faerie Queene* opens with a book concerning the discovery of the identity of St George, the patron saint of England, but ends with a book which follows the adventures of a British knight,

[19] Nicholas Canny and Andrew Carpenter (eds.), 'The Early Planters: Spenser and his Contemporaries', in Seamus Deane (ed.), *The Field Day Anthology of Irish Writing*, 3 vols. (Derry: Field Day Publications, 1991), i. 171–234, at 171.

[20] 'DissemiNation', 311.

[21] Robert Crawford, 'The Scottish Invention of English Literature', in id., *Devolving English Literature* (Oxford: Clarendon Press, 1992), ch. 1. See also Roy Porter (ed.), *Myths of the English* (Cambridge: Polity Press, 1992).

[22] *Imagined Communities*, 52.

[23] Fredric Jameson, *The Political Unconscious: Narrative as Socially Symbolic Act* (London: Methuen, 1981), 102. For a cogent critique of Jameson's assumptions, see J. A. Berthoud, 'Narrative and Ideology: A Critique of Fredric Jameson's *The Political Unconscious*', in Jeremy Hawthorn (ed.), *Narrative: From Malory to Motion Pictures* (London: Edward Arnold, 1985), 101–15.

[24] A coherent overview is provided by Annabel Patterson, 'Intention', in Frank Lentricchia and Thomas McLaughlin (eds.), *Critical Terms for Literary Study* (Chicago: Chicago University Press, 1990), 135–46.

Britomart.[25] The ostensible hero is Arthur, legendary king of Britain, but the second edition of the poem ends—whichever extant version is accepted—with the triumph of chaos over civilization, allegorized as a figure which originated in Ireland (see Ch. 6). As I will argue, numerous narrative cruxes invite the reader to consider the problem of political and personal identity so that the question of the narrative's allegorical development cannot be separated from either the individual or political situation of that reader. In other words, there is no question of a choice being made between textuality and material reality; in fact, I will argue, this is one of the key messages of *The Faerie Queene*. The reality of the author's Irish experience demands to be placed at the forefront of attempts to read Spenser and it is something of a scandal that critics have been reluctant to attempt this task in any systematic or sophisticated manner until relatively recently.[26]

Spenser's literature is experimental in terms of both form and content, as might be expected from a writer in his position.[27] As Richard Helgerson has argued, Spenser did not simply attempt to fashion his readers as gentlemen, but also tried to create a role for himself as a significant cultural force.[28] One of the problems of reading English Renaissance literature is that one is never sure who most texts were written for or who actually read them.[29] This difficulty is especially acute in the case of Spenser, given his relatively isolated location (although an Irish existence did not necessarily mean intellectual banishment for an

[25] An argument I develop elsewhere in 'From English to British Literature: John Lyly's *Euphues* and Edmund Spenser's *Faerie Queene*', in Brendan Bradshaw and Peter Roberts (eds.), *British Identity and British Consciousness* (Cambridge: Cambridge University Press, forthcoming).

[26] My assertion is not absolutely correct and requires some qualification; while the text of the *Variorum* edition testifies to the vast quantity of work dealing with Spenser's life between the two world wars, much of it concerning his Irish career, little of this intensive labour, impressive though it undoubtedly is, goes beyond the antiquarian or biographical. Less acceptable is the general neglect of such study after the Second World War, so that the assumption of an English Spenser can be seen as a much more recent phenomenon.

[27] See Paul Alpers, 'Style', *Sp. Enc.* 674–6. For further discussion, see below, p. 116.

[28] *Self-Crowned Laureates: Spenser, Jonson, Milton and the Literary System* (Berkeley: University of California Press, 1983), ch. 2. See also Patrick Cheney, *Spenser's Famous Flight: A Renaissance Idea of a Literary Career* (Toronto: Toronto University Press, 1993).

[29] See Louis B. Wright, *Middle-Class Culture in Elizabethan England* (Chapel Hill: University of North Carolina Press, 1935); Elizabeth L. Eisenstein, 'The Expanding Republic of Letters', in id., *The Printing Revolution in Early Modern Europe* (Cambridge: Cambridge University Press, 1983); Andrew Hadfield, 'Introduction: the Nation and

Englishman), seemingly limitless ambition, and avant-garde writing strategies. While the letter to Raleigh would suggest that the poem was addressed to a male reader, the gentleman whom the poem was intended to fashion, in other places the poem's narrator seems to address a woman reader, specifically, the queen.[30] Clearly this is not simply a question of gender politics, but also a question of the implied audience of the poem, and the projected role of the reader. Moreover, in addition to being a sign of the anxious status of the literary text in the sixteenth century, it is also an indication of the simultaneously fluid and obsessive relationship between text, author, and reader, one which both *Colin Clouts come home againe* and *The Faerie Queene* foreground.[31]

As has frequently been pointed out, Spenser's dialogue *A View of the Present State of Ireland* has an uncertain status as a text and often relies upon similar tropes and metaphors to those which are used in the poetry (in the case of certain terms such as 'salvage' and 'sacred' this would seem too deliberate to be accidental). Just as the two dedicatory sonnets to Ormond and Grey challenge—perhaps deliberately and provocatively—the notion that literary and political discourses can be isolated and separated so too does the overlap between *A View* and Spenser's longer poems. Each could be said to fold over or into each other, at crucial moments dependent on identical figures, but always signifying their independence from the other form of writing.

The category of writing which is read as 'literature' is always inescapably double. A text acquires a status as literature by dint of being read in the appropriate manner—an inevitably circular argument—in the process signalling its simultaneous difference from and similarity to other forms of writing. This tricky paradox is articulated brilliantly by Jacques Derrida, a reader sensitive to the problems of history and form. Derrida has argued that 'What we call literature (not *belles-lettres* or poetry) implies that license is given to the writer to say everything he

Public Literature in the Sixteenth Century', in id., *Literature, Politics and National Identity: Reformation to Renaissance* (Cambridge: Cambridge University Press, 1994), 1–22.

[30] See Maureen Quilligan, *Milton's Spenser: The Politics of Reading* (Ithaca, NY: Cornell University Press, 1983); Simon Shepherd, *Spenser* (Hemel Hempstead: Harvester, 1989), ch. 2; John Watkins, *The Specter of Dido: Spenser and Virgilian Epic* (New Haven: Yale University Press, 1995). More generally, see Culler, 'Reading as a Woman', in id., *On Deconstruction: Theory and Criticism after Structuralism* (London: Routledge, 1983), 43–64.

[31] The classic study is Stephen Greenblatt, *Renaissance Self-Fashioning: From More to Shakespeare* (Chicago: Chicago University Press, 1980). See also Greenblatt, 'Psychoanalysis and Renaissance Culture', in Patricia Parker and David Quint (eds.), *Literary Theory/Renaissance Texts* (Baltimore: Johns Hopkins University Press, 1986), 210–24.

wants to or everything he can, while remaining shielded, safe from all censorship, be it religious or political'.[32] However such a bold, utopian hope needs to be set against Derrida's counter-argument that literature is also an institution with a complex history.[33] Derrida suggests that:

The name 'literature' is a very recent invention. Previously, writing was not indispensable for poetry or *belles-lettres*, nor authorial property, nor individual signatures . . . The set of laws or conventions which fixed what we call literature in modernity was not indispensable for poetic works to circulate . . . If the institutional or socio-political space of literary production as such is a recent thing, it does not simply surround works, it affects them in their very structure . . . The principle . . . of 'being able to say everything', the socio-juridico-politico guarantee granted 'in principle' to literature, is something which did not mean much, or not that, in Graeco-Latin culture and *a fortiori* in a non-Western culture. Which does not mean that the West has ever respected this principle: but at least here or there it has set it up as a principle.

Having said that, even if a phenomenon called 'literature' appeared historically in Europe, at such and such a date, this does not mean that one can identify the literary object in a rigorous way. It doesn't mean that there is an essence of literature. It even means the opposite.[34]

According to Derrida, literature exists as an ideal and as an institutional historical reality, the two circling around each other in a symbiotic relationship. The failure of the ideal of a 'free' literature ironically guarantees its survival in the face of a hostile series of institutional attacks, a paradox registered in Spenser's representation of the punishment of Bonfont (*FQ* v. ix. 25–6). The key point is not the reality of the functioning of the utopian hope, but the fact of its existence at all. Literature is at once a completely different category of writing from discourses of law, politics, medicine, education, ethics, and yet it is constituted by just such a variety of forms of discourse.[35] Derrida notes elsewhere, 'Every text *participates* in one or several genres, there is no genreless text, there is always a genre and genres, yet such participation never amounts to

[32] ' "This Strange Institution Called Literature": An Interview with Jacques Derrida', in *Acts of Literature*, ed. Derek Attridge (London: Routledge, 1992), 33–75, at 37. See also 'Before the Law', ibid. 181–220, at 214–16.

[33] Cf. Theodore Adorno, *Aesthetic Theory*, trans. C. Lenhardt (London: Routledge, 1984), 47–8. Adorno argues that art must 'want to be and must be squarely Utopian . . . while at the same time it should not be Utopian so as not to be found guilty of administering comfort and illusion', a description which could be applied to *The Faerie Queene*. See also 'Reconciliation under Duress', in Ernst Bloch *et al.*, *Aesthetics and Politics*, trans. Ronald Taylor *et al.* (London: Verso, 1977), 151–76.

[34] *Acts of Literature*, 40–1.

[35] See R. A. York, *The Poem as Utterance* (London: Methuen, 1986), introduction.

belonging'.[36] Every text has to be recognized and categorized before it can be read; and yet the very idea of literature announces the hope of a freedom from ideological constraints while recognizing that such a freedom could only occur if discourse were to end. Literature is at once saturated with ideology and distanced from the morass of ideological writing.[37] To a large extent this overlap and division represent the distinction between *A View* and *The Faerie Queene*, the former obliged to obey the 'rules' of political discourse and intervene in the public sphere (however that intervention may take place), the latter distanced, contradictory, and uncertain where it belongs. Against the certainty of such a neat distinction one should bear in mind that *A View* exists as that most literary of forms, the dialogue, and Spenser places *The Faerie Queene* in the line of 'Poets historical' ('A Letter of the Authors'), reinforcing Derrida's point that generic forms are not easy to isolate.[38]

In this book it is not my aim to cover every single allusion to Ireland or passage where Ireland is mentioned in the text.[39] Rather, I hope to argue that avoiding the Irish or British context of the poem involves the perpetuation of an Anglocentric distortion. More generally, I hope to persuade readers that Spenser should not be left to specialists—although I have no wish at all to denigrate their work—precisely because his writing poses serious questions for students of colonialism and national identity, whether of the British Isles or elsewhere, as diverse recent writers have recognized.[40] Spenser cannot be read—and never should have been read—as a straightforwardly English writer.[41]

[36] 'The Law of Genre', in Derrida, *Acts of Literature*, 221–52, at 230.
[37] Pierre Machery, *A Theory of Literary Production*, trans. Geoffrey Wall (London: Routledge, 1978), 51–3.
[38] 'A Letter of the Authors', *FQ*, pp. 737–8.
[39] Interested readers should also consult Pauline Henley, *Spenser in Ireland* (Cork: Cork University Press, 1928); Roland M. Smith, 'Spenser's Tale of the Two Sons of Milesio', *MLQ* 3 (1942), 547–57; id., 'Spenser, Holinshed, and the *Leabhar Gabhala*', *JEGP* 43 (1944), 390–401; Healy, *New Latitudes*, 98–101; Richard A. McCabe, 'Edmund Spenser, Poet of Exile', *PBA* 80 (1991, publ. 1993), 73–103; Willy Maley, *Salvaging Spenser: Colonialism, Culture and Identity* (London: Macmillan, 1997). I am grateful to Dr Maley for allowing me to see his book in typescript.
[40] See, e.g. Seamus Heaney, 'Bog Oak', in *New Selected Poems, 1966–1987* (London: Faber & Faber, 1990), 19–20; Said, *Culture and Imperialism*, 266, 268; Scott Wilson, *Cultural Materialism: Theory and Practice* (Oxford: Blackwell, 1995), 64–82; Angus Calder, *Revolutionary Empire: The Rise of the English-Speaking Empires from the Fifteenth Century to the 1780s* (London: Cape, 1981), 36–7, 93–4, *passim*; W. J. McCormack, *The Battle of the Books* (Gigginstown: Lilliput, 1986), 13, 32; Robert Welch, *The Kilcolman Notebook* (Dingle: Brandon, 1994).
[41] An error committed even by such a trenchant commentator on Irish politics and

His work is defined by the Tudors' attempt to expand their boundaries and unify a nebulously conceived ideal of Britain, as well as exploit and subdue other nations and cultures.[42] At the same time, Spenser's works participate in and reflect upon that enterprise in an active way, as Spenser himself participated in English colonial expansion via his career as a government official in Ireland. Whether Spenser's writings as I have analysed them point to a continuity with modern political experience or stand as a mark of historical difference, I leave to the reader to decide.[43] What cannot be denied is the legacy of the action in which Spenser took part, which still marks out the geopolitical boundaries of the British Isles.[44]

literature as Tom Paulin: see *Ireland and the English Crisis* (Newcastle: Bloodaxe Books, 1984), 47–8.

[42] Calder, *Revolutionary Empire*, bk. 1; A. L. Rowse, *The Expansion of Elizabethan England* (London: Macmillan, 1955); K. R. Andrews, *Trade, Plunder and Settlement: Maritime Enterprise and the Genesis of the British Empire, 1480–1630* (Cambridge: Cambridge University Press, 1984).

[43] For opposing reflections on this problem with regard to 'early modern' texts, see Greenblatt, 'Psychoanalysis and Renaissance Culture'; Thomas Healy, 'Selves, States, and Sectarianism in Early Modern England', *English*, 44 (1995), 193–213, at 211. A perceptive reflection on the problem is provided by Brian Walker, '1641, 1689, 1691 and All That: The Unionist Sense of History', *Irish Review*, 12 (1992), 56–64.

[44] See David Cairns and Shaun Richards, *Writing Ireland: Colonialism, Nationalism and Culture* (Manchester: Manchester University Press, 1988), ch. 1. See also Brian Friel, *Making History* (London: Faber & Faber, 1989).

I

The Contexts of the 1590s

Throughout his literary career, Edmund Spenser (1552?–99) encouraged his readers to identify him with his *alter ego*, Colin Clout, who appeared sporadically in his poetry.[1] In 1595 Spenser published a poem with his pseudonym in the title, *Colin Clouts come home againe*, which was presented in the brief dedicatory preface to Sir Walter Raleigh as a fictionalization of the author's recent visit to England (1589–90): 'I acknowledge my selfe bounden unto you, for your singular fauours and sundrie good turnes to me at my late being in England.' The poem is dated 'From my house of *Kilcolman* the 27. of December. 1591'. Before the reader has even started the poem, it becomes clear that the author does not consider England as his home, but Ireland.

Colin Clouts come home againe contains Colin's extensive description of his visit to 'Cynthia's land' (line 288) to the assembled gathering of shepherds before the necessity of work calls them away: 'All loth to part, but that the glooming skies | Warnd them to draw their bleating flocks to rest' (lines 954–5).[2] Hobbinol, one of the shepherds concerned, welcomes Colin home, but complains, 'how great a losse | Had all the *shepheards nation* by thy lacke?' (lines 16–17, my emphasis). In the letter to Raleigh appended to the first edition of *The Faerie Queene*, which had appeared in the previous year (1590), Spenser had stated that he had based one of his representations of the Faerie Queene on Raleigh's portrayal of Queen Elizabeth as Cynthia in 'The Ocean to Cynthia': 'For considering she beareth two persons, the one of a most royall Queene or Empresse, the other of a most vertuous and beautifull Lady, this latter part in some places I doe expresse in Belphoebe, fashioning her name according to your owne excellent conceipt of Cynthia

[1] See John D. Bernard, *Ceremonies of Innocence: Pastoralism in the Poetry of Edmund Spenser* (Cambridge: Cambridge University Press, 1989), *passim*.

[2] For commentary on the poem see Sam Meyer, *An Interpretation of Edmund Spenser's Colin Clout* (Cork: Cork University Press, 1969); Nancy Jo Hoffman, *Spenser's Pastorals: The Shepheardes Calender and 'Colin Clout'* (Baltimore: Johns Hopkins University Press, 1977); David R. Shore, '*Colin Clouts come home againe*', *Sp. Enc.* 173–7.

(Phoebe and Cynthia being both names of Diana), (p. 737). The poem
situates the author, via a fictionalized persona, as an inhabitant of Ireland who belongs as part of an Irish community ('the shepheards
nation'), which is clearly separated from England ruled by Elizabeth
('Cynthia's land').

This national difference is explored throughout the poem. Colin
explains how he listened to the song of 'The shepheard of the Ocean'
(Raleigh) (line 66) who laments the 'great unkindnesse' and 'usage
hard | Of *Cynthia* the Ladie of the sea, | Which from her presence fault-
lesse him debard' (lines 165–7). This inspires Colin to reflect on his
'lucklesse lot | That banisht had my selfe, like wight forlore, | Into that
waste, where I was quite forgot' (lines 181–3). This would seem to
imply a fierce attachment to his motherland by the poet/persona and
reluctance to remain marginalized in Ireland far from the action of the
English court surrounding the queen. However, a few lines later, when
Colin is describing the journey over the Irish Sea, he comments, 'So
farre that land our mother us did leave' (line 227), which would seem to
set up another explicit opposition between the safe land which nur-
tures Colin (Spenser) and Raleigh (the shepherd of the ocean) like a
(good) mother, and the dangerous *femme fatale* figure of the queen,
who has already unfairly dismissed the shepherd who takes her name.
The stability of the (female) land is contrasted with the instability of
the sea, represented as an attractive but dangerous rival for the men's
affections.[3]

When Colin describes their arrival in England/Cynthia's land, Cuddy
asks, 'What land is that thou meanest . . . | And is there other, then
whereon we stand?' (lines 289–90). He is ridiculed by the more sophisticated Colin ('thous a fon [fool]', line 292), but the question emphasizes
the vast gulf between different groups of Elizabeth's subjects. Although
she had been addressed as, 'Queen of England, France, and Ireland' in
the first edition of *The Faerie Queene*, and, after the Act declaring her
father, Henry VIII, king of Ireland (18 June 1541), she could claim to be
the legal sovereign of the whole of Ireland, the poem makes it clear
that in some of her dominions, Elizabeth was unknown and could
hardly rule personally.[4] The use of names from Spenser's earlier poem

[3] Cynthia is thus linked to the figure of Proteus in *The Faerie Queene*, who drags
Florimell into his undersea kingdom (III. viii. 29–42). Proteus is named as one of Cynthia's
marine shepherds; *Colin Clout*, lines 248–51. See Supriya Chaudhuri, 'Proteus', *Sp. Enc.*
560–1.
[4] On the act establishing Henry VIII as king, see Steven G. Ellis, *Tudor Ireland:
Crown, Community and the Conflict of Cultures, 1470–1603* (Harlow: Longman, 1985),

The Shepheardes Calender (1579)—Colin Clout, Cuddy, Hobbinol—
signals a transposition from the pastoral of rural England to that of rural
Ireland, making the disclaimer in the preface to Raleigh all the more
significant: 'with your good countenance protect against the malice of
euill mouthes, which are alwaies open to carpe at and misconstrue my
simple meaning'. *Colin Clouts come home againe* can be read to mean,
quite simply, that the poet considered himself no longer straightforwardly English, but a loyal (?) servant of the queen in a land where her
authority counted for little.

In his response to Cuddy, Colin heaps praise on rural England as an
ideal pastoral landscape in contrast to the rural Ireland where 'the shepheardes nation' live:

> Both heauen and heauenly graces do much more
> (Quoth he) abound in that same land, then this.
> For there all happie peace and plenteous store
> Conspire in one to make contented blisse:
> No wayling there nor wretchednesse is heard,
> No bloodie issues nor no leprosies,
> No griesly famine, nor no raging sweard
> No nightly bodrags nor no hue and cries;
> The shepheardes there abroad may safely lie,
> On hills and downes, withouten dread or daunger:
> No rauenous wolues the good mans hope destroy,
> Nor outlawes fell affray the forest raunger.
>
> (lines 308–19)

Colin represents an Ireland which is replete with danger, metaphorical
('leprosies') and actual ('famine'), pointedly contrasted to rural England, where the authority of the queen stretches forth unproblemat-
ically. The world of the poem is patently at odds with that reconstructed
by Michael MacCarthy-Morrogh, the historian of the Munster Plantation, where Spenser lived from the mid-1580s, who argues that moving
to south-west Ireland was 'less an emigration, more a migration within
an acknowledged unit'.[5]

After Colin has heaped praise on the poets (lines 376–455), and the
ladies at court (lines 464–583), as well as Cynthia herself, Thestylis asks
the obvious question:

139–40; Nicholas P. Canny, *From Reformation to Restoration: Ireland, 1534–1660*
(Dublin: Helicon, 1987), 41.

  [5] Michael MacCarthy-Morrogh, *The Munster Plantation: English Migration to
Southern Ireland, 1583–1641* (Oxford: Clarendon Press, 1986), 280.

> Why *Colin*, since thou foundst such grace
> With *Cynthia* and all her noble crew:
> Why didst thou ever leaue that happie place,
> In which such wealth might unto thee accrew?
> And back returnedst to this barrein soyle,
> Where cold and care and penury do dwell:
> Here to keep sheepe, with hunger and with toyle,
> Most wretched he, that is and cannot tell.

(lines 652–9)

Colin answers that he cannot cope with the corrupt life at court and that after seeing its 'enormities' chose instead 'back to my sheep to tourne' (line 672). He warns against those who would seek out its pleasures in hope of advancement because they will not be able to cope with its competitive malice. In lines which anticipate the ending of *The Faerie Queene*, Book VI, when the Blatant Beast rampages abroad threatening to engulf the delicate fiction the poem has laboured to establish (VI. xii. 38–41), Colin contrasts the 'deceitfull wit', 'leasings lewd', and 'fained forgerie' (lines 693, 695–6) of court speech to the poetry he can produce in exile: 'Ne is there place for any gentle wit, | Unlesse to please, it selfe it can applie' (lines 707–8).

There are advantages as well as disadvantages to the state of exile in Ireland. While conditions may be hard, there is liberty and freedom to write what one wants without having to serve a patron; not least, one suspects, because Ireland could provide an adequate income for Englishmen bold enough to enter the colonial world of Ireland.[6] Not only was Spenser able to buy a substantial estate which would never have come his way in England (the Kilcolman estate contained 4,000 acres), but he also became related to the richest man in Ireland, Richard Boyle, first earl of Cork (1566–1643), when he married for the second time to his kinswoman, Elizabeth Boyle, in June 1594.[7] One might also ask, who is supposed to be responsible for the fact that some of the queen's subjects do not know who she is? Colin does poke fun at Cuddy, who also fails to

---

[6] On the conditions of writing and patronage in Elizabethan England, see Michael G. Brennan, *Literary Patronage in the English Renaissance: The Pembroke Family* (London: Croom Helm, 1988); for one reading of Spenser's career in Ireland, see Richard Rambuss, *Spenser's Secret Career* (Cambridge: Cambridge University Press, 1993).

[7] See Ray Heffner, 'Spenser's Acquisition of Kilcolman', *MLN* 46 (1931), 493–8; Willy Maley, *A Spenser Chronology* (Basingstoke: Macmillan, 1994), 50, 64–5. On Richard Boyle, see Nicholas P. Canny, *The Upstart Earl: A Study of the Social and Mental World of Richard Boyle, First Earl of Cork, 1566–1643* (Cambridge: Cambridge University Press, 1982); Terrence Ranger, 'Richard Boyle and the Making of an Irish Fortune, 1588–1614', *IHS* 39 (Mar. 1957), 257–97. For Spenser's acquisition of other lands, see Frederic Ives

THE CONTEXT OF THE 1590S

realize that there is another world outside his own, but such ignorance cannot reflect well upon the monarch who is portrayed ambiguously in the poem: on the one hand she is said to be virtuous and deserving of the most extravagant praise; on the other she is shown to be capricious in her treatment of the undoubtedly loyal shepherd of the ocean, unable—or unwilling—to stem the flood of vice which emanates from her corrupt court, and ignorant of the good shepherds exiled in Ireland.

What *Colin Clouts come home againe* would appear to register is the development of an alternative Englishness in Ireland, one which represents the interests of the English and their queen better than those who actually possess authority and are able to influence policy. The centre has shifted to the margins.[8] The poem represents the English in Ireland as caught between the twin evils of hostile natives and neglectful metropolitan authorities, both of whom threaten their efforts to establish good government, the classic feelings of the colonizers.[9] The English in Ireland stand alone as guardians of an English identity which has been lost from the easy lives of the English in England; the identity which Colin/Spenser attempts to fashion is double. In one sense the Englishness of 'the shepheardes nation' is more English than the English, being a return to first principles lost at court and taken for granted in the country; in another, being in exile and facing hostile foes necessitates the creation of a new identity in terms of what has been left behind and what now appears as alien, neither recognizable as contemporary English nor purely different, a form of hybridity.[10]

Spenser had come to Ireland in 1580 as private secretary to Arthur, Lord Grey de Wilton, the new Lord Deputy, a hard-line Protestant who had been suggested for the position as early as 1572, but was rejected because it was felt that his aggressive anti-Catholic stance might lead to trouble.[11] It is possible that Spenser had visited Ireland earlier,

Carpenter, 'Spenser in Ireland', *MP* 19 (1922), 405–19; P. M. Buck, Jr., 'New Facts Concerning the Life of Edmund Spenser', *MLN* 19 (1904), 237–8.

[8] For a related argument concerning contemporary literature, see David Gervais, *Literary Englands: Versions of 'Englishness' in Modern Writing* (Cambridge: Cambridge University Press, 1993), afterword.

[9] See Albert Memmi, *The Colonizer and the Colonized*, trans. Howard Greenfield (New York: Orion Press, 1965), 1.

[10] See Homi K. Bhabha, 'The Other Question: Stereotype, Discrimination and the Discourse of Colonialism', in id., *The Location of Culture*, 66–84.

[11] See Richard A. McCabe, 'The Fate of Irena: Spenser and Political Violence', in Patricia Coughlan (ed.), *Spenser and Ireland: An Interdisciplinary Perspective* (Cork: Cork University Press, 1989), 109–25. For Grey's views, see Arthur Lord Grey de Wilton, *A Commentary of the Services and Charges of William Lord Grey de Wilton*, ed. Sir Philip

employed by the earl of Leicester, as Irenius claims to have witnessed the execution of the rebel Murrogh O'Brien at Limerick.[12] It is likely that Spenser was with Grey when he massacred the Spanish and Italian troops who had occupied the Fort d'Oro at Smerwick in November of that year, after they had surrendered, causing a scandal not just in Ireland but also at the English court, one which may well have led to Grey's recall.[13] Spenser defends Grey's actions in both *A View of the Present State of Ireland* and *The Faerie Queene*, v. xi–xii. Fittingly enough, the land which was confiscated as a result of the Desmond Rebellion (1579–83)—of which the massacre at Smerwick was a significant incident—went to establish the Munster Plantation after 1584, where Spenser made his fortune, until, he too, was overcome by force during the Nine Years War in 1598.[14] Between 1580 and 1584 Spenser held a variety of administrative and secretarial posts in Dublin, Kildare, and Wexford; in leasing the dissolved House of Friars, known as New Abbey, Co. Kildare, Spenser was described as 'Gent.', implying a significant rise in social status since his departure from England.[15] Sometime in 1584 Spenser left for Munster, to become Deputy to the Clerk of the Council of Munster, Lodowick Bryskett (c.1542–1612), who included Spenser as one of the participants in his Italianate dialogue, *A Discourse of Civil Life* (1606), supposedly the representation of a colloquy held at his house near Dublin in 1582.[16] Bryskett's dialogue is an adaptation of various Italian courtesy books: principally that of Giraldi's *Ecatommiti* (which Bryskett largely translates from), but also

de Malpas Grey Egerton (London: Camden Society, 1847). The information on Spenser's life in the following paragraphs relies upon Maley, *Spenser Chronology*; Alexander C. Judson, *The Life of Edmund Spenser* (Baltimore: Johns Hopkins University Press, 1945) (*Variorum*, xi) *FQ*, 'Chronological Table', pp. viii–xii.

[12] See Lisa Jardine, 'Encountering Ireland: Gabriel Harvey, Edmund Spenser, and English Colonial Ventures', in Brendan Bradshaw, Andrew Hadfield, and Willy Maley (eds.), *Representing Ireland: Literature and the Origins of Conflict, 1534–1660* (Cambridge: Cambridge University Press, 1993), 60–75, at 61, 71. See also Paul E. McLane, 'Was Spenser in Ireland in Early November, 1579?', *N&Q* 204 (1959), 99–101; Maley, *Spenser Chronology*, 6–7. An opposite view is provided in Donald Bruce, 'Spenser's Irenius and the Nature of Dialogue', *N&Q* 237 (1992), 355–7.

[13] For details, see Alfred O'Rahilly, *The Massacre at Smerwick (1580)* (Cork: Cork University Press, 1938); *Variorum*, x. 524–30.

[14] For details, see MacCarthy-Morrogh, *Munster Plantation*, 1–4; Ciaran Brady, 'Faction and the Origins of the Desmond Rebellion of 1579', *IHS* 22 (1981), 289–312.

[15] More evidence of Spenser's secretarial career is provided in Henry R. Plomer, 'Edmund Spenser's Handwriting', *MP* 21 (1923), 201–7; Raymond Jenkins, '*Newes Out of Munster*: a Document in Spenser's Hand', *SP* 32 (1935), 125–30.

[16] *A Discourse of Civil Life* (London, 1606), ed. Thomas E. Wright, San Fernando Valley State College Renaissance Editions, 4 (Northridge, Calif.: 1970), 6, 26.

that of Piccolomini and Stefano Guazzo's *Civil Conversation*, which is referred to in *The Faerie Queene*, Book VI.[17] Spenser did not lack intellectual companions in Ireland, particularly those who were interested in the same Italianate culture as he was.[18]

In the mid-1580s it is likely that Spenser accompanied both Sir John and Sir Thomas Norris, who served as President of Munster and colonel of the forces in Munster, on their military expeditions to Ulster and Connaught, as well as their attendance of the Irish Parliament in Dublin in 1585 and 1586 and the relatively frequent Munster Councils in Cork and Limerick. In the autumn of 1588, or possibly later, Spenser occupied the estate of Kilcolman on the Munster Plantation, where he lived for the rest of his life. In 1589 he travelled to England with Sir Walter Raleigh and had an audience with the queen, to whom he may have presented *The Faerie Queene*, which was dedicated to her when it was published in 1590. Spenser was also involved in prolonged law suits with the 'Old' English Lord Roche who had already written to the queen complaining that the undertakers on the Munster Plantation were not only illegally seizing his lands but threatening his tenants, stealing his cattle, and beating his servants. Spenser and other undertakers presented a series of counter-complaints. In 1591 Spenser was granted a pension of £50 a year by the queen, and his volume of *Complaints* was finally published. In 1594 he married Elizabeth Boyle, the courtship and marriage being fictionally dramatized in *Amoretti and Epithalamion*, published together the following year. In November, 1596 the second edition of *The Faerie Queene* was published, containing Books IV–VI, which led to complaints from King James VI of Scotland regarding the portrait of his mother in Book V. In 1597 he purchased the castle and lands of Renny in south Cork for his youngest son, Peregrine, Elizabeth, as well as Buttevant Abbey. In 1598 *A View* was entered into the Stationers' Register in April and in September, with Tyrone's Rebellion at its peak, Spenser was nominated as sheriff of Cork by the Privy Council as 'a man endowed with good knowledge in learning and not unskillful as without experience in the service of the wars'.[19] However, in October Kilcolman was sacked and burnt by rebels, killing a 'little child new born',

---

[17] See Thomas E. Wright, 'Lodowick Bryskett', *Sp. Enc.* 119; Peter Burke, *The Fortunes of the Courtier: The European Reception of Castiglione's Cortegiano* (Cambridge: Polity Press, 1995), 53; John Leon Lievsay, *Stefano Guazzo and the English Renaissance, 1575–1675* (Chapel Hill: University of North Carolina Press, 1961), 83–8, 96–9.

[18] For brief biographies of Spenser's circle in Munster, see Maley, *Spenser Chronology*, 85–108.

[19] Cited ibid. 72.

according to Ben Jonson.[20] After taking refuge in Cork, Spenser and his wife fled to Westminster, where he probably delivered his last work, 'A Briefe Note of Ireland', to the Privy Council. Spenser died in January 1599 'for lack of bread', again according to Jonson. He was buried in Westminster Abbey, near Chaucer, the funeral being paid for by his last patron, Robert Devereux, second earl of Essex. A funeral monument was erected in 1620. In 1609 the first folio edition of *The Faerie Queene* was published, including the fragment of a seventh book, 'Two Cantos of Mutabilitie'.

Spenser's life in Ireland does not mark him out as a particularly unusual Elizabethan writer. There are numerous other examples of English writers going to Ireland out of necessity or desire: Thomas Churchyard, Barnaby Googe, Barnaby Rich, Lodowick Bryskett, Geoffrey Fenton, Sir Walter Raleigh, John Derricke, and Sir John Davies; all were connected to the Elizabethan civil service or military, often both.[21] One should also bear in mind the fortunes of the Sidney family and their Irish connections, given Sir Henry Sidney's role as perhaps the most successful of Elizabeth's Lord Deputies, as well as that of the Protestant polemicist, John Bale.[22] Spenser's experience marks him out as a member of the 'New' English who emigrated to Ireland after 1534, but principally in Elizabeth's reign, to take up relatively lucrative positions in the civil service, as army regulars or soldiers of fortune, or to acquire land on one of the schemes for colonizing Ireland.[23] The New English were to be distinguished from 'the descendants of the medieval English colony, who, though refusing to become Protestant, had remained loyal

[20] Cited in R. M. Cummings (ed.), *Edmund Spenser: The Critical Heritage* (London: Routledge, 1971), 136. For the historical background, see A. J. Sheehan, 'The Overthrow of the Plantation of Munster in October, 1598', *The Irish Sword*, 15 (1982–3), 11–22.

[21] See the relevant entries in the *DNB*; Andrew Hadfield and Willy Maley, 'Introduction: Irish Representations and English Alternatives', in Bradshaw *et al.* (eds.), *Representing Ireland*, 1–23, at 14.

[22] On Sidney, see Ciaran Brady, *The Chief Governors: The Rise and Fall of Reform Government in Tudor Ireland, 1536–1588* (Cambridge: Cambridge University Press, 1994), ch. 4; on Bale, see Andrew Hadfield, 'Translating the Reformation: John Bale's Irish *Vocacyon*', in Bradshaw *et al.* (eds.), *Representing Ireland*, 43–59; Steven G. Ellis, 'John Bale, Bishop of Ossory, 1552–3', *Journal of the Butler Society*, 3 (1984), 283–93.

[23] On Tudor colonial schemes in Ireland, see Robert Dunlop, 'The Plantation of Leix and Offaly', *EHR* 6 (1891), 61–96; id., 'Sixteenth-Century Schemes for the Plantation of Ulster', *SHR* 22 (1924–5), 50–60, 115–26, 199–212; David B. Quinn, 'The Munster Plantation: Its Problems and Opportunities', *JCHAS* 71 (1966), 19–40; Hiram Morgan, 'The Colonial Venture of Sir Thomas Smith in Ulster, 1571–5', *HJ* 28 (1985), 261–78; MacCarthy-Morrogh, *The Munster Plantation*.

to the crown'.[24] Ireland could be seen to house two competing colonial communities, both largely contained within the Pale around Dublin; in the definitions of contemporary Irish historians, New English (*Nua Ghaill*) and Old English (*Sean Ghaill*), both keen to establish themselves as the obvious rulers of Ireland at the expense of their rivals, until, with the gradual emergence of the former faction as victorious, the latter started to side with the native (Old) Irish (*Gaedhil*) in a fractious alliance against the New English and Crown forces, culminating in the events surrounding the 1641 rebellion.[25] Spenser's neighbours, John Barry and David Roche, the latter the son of Spenser's rival claimant for his estate, both came out in open rebellion in 1597.[26]

Such divisions and alliances are easy to describe with confidence as abstract historical phenomena, but in reality they were often quite fluid. Geoffrey Keating (1570–?1644?), the apologist of Irish Ireland, was descended from an Anglo-Norman family, a common occurrence amongst the first settlers in the twelfth century;[27] Spenser's own son, Sylvanus, successfully sued his mother for the possession of Kilcolman, indicating how quickly families could split up over property in Ireland; one of his grandsons, William Spenser, actually became a Catholic, and had to appeal to Cromwell to secure his inheritance.[28] Such a phenomenon, that of 'degeneration' or, 'going native', was legislated against from the Norman invasion of Ireland onwards, most notably in the

---

[24] T. W. Moody, 'Early Modern Ireland', in T. W. Moody, F. X. Martin, and F. J. Byrne (eds.), *A New History of Ireland*, iii. *Early Modern Ireland, 1534–1691* (Oxford: Clarendon Press, 1976), pp. xxxix–lxiii, at p. xlii.

[25] The literature on identities in early modern Ireland is extensive: see e.g. Roy Foster, 'Prologue: Varieties of Irishness', in id., *Modern Ireland, 1600–1972* (London: Penguin, 1988), 3–15; Colm Lennon, *Richard Stanihurst, the Dubliner, 1547–1618* (Dublin: Irish Academic Press, 1981); id., *The Lords of Dublin in the Age of Reformation* (Dublin: Irish Academic Press, 1989); Nicholas P. Canny, 'Identity Formation in Ireland: The Emergence of the Anglo-Irish', in Nicholas P. Canny and Anthony Pagden (eds.), *Colonial Identity in the Atlantic World, 1500–1800* (Princeton: Princeton University Press, 1987), 159–212; T. C. Barnard, 'Crises of Identity among Irish Protestants, 1641–85', *P&P* 127 (1990), 39–83. On the 1641 rebellion, see Brian Mac Curta (ed.), *Ulster, 1641: Aspects of the Rising* (Belfast: Institute of Irish Studies, Queen's University, 1993).

[26] Maley, *Spenser Chronology*, 74.

[27] See Brendan Bradshaw, 'Geoffrey Keating: Apologist of Irish Ireland', in Bradshaw *et al.* (eds.), *Representing Ireland*, 166–90; Bernadette Cunningham, 'Seventeenth-Century Interpretations of the Past: The Case of Geoffrey Keating', *IHS* 25 (1986), 116–28. On the tendency of the Anglo-Norman lords to accept Irish customs and lifestyle, see Robin Frame, *English Lordship in Ireland, 1318–61* (Oxford: Clarendon Press, 1982), *passim*; James Lydon (ed.), *The English in Medieval Ireland* (Dublin: Royal Irish Academy, 1984).

[28] W. H. Welpy, 'Edmund Spenser: Some New Discoveries and the Correction of Some Old Errors', *N&Q* 146 and 147 (1924), 445–7, 35; Henley, *Spenser in Ireland*, 194–6, 206–7.

Statutes of Kilkenny (1366)—which forbade contact between the English and Irish via marriage or trade, banned the use of Irish laws or participation in Irish culture by the English, and ruled that the king's
subjects speak only English, effectively splitting the country into two
discrete regions—and the 'Act for the English Order, Habit and Language' (1537), which deplored a 'certain savage and wild kind and manner of living' amongst the king's subjects in Ireland and demanded that
all conform to English social practices.[29] The cross-cultural transformation of the Old English in Ireland is obsessively documented by New
English sixteenth-century commentators as a realization of their worst
fears and, also, a means of deliberately discrediting the Old English as
more culpable than the native Irish in their resistance to English rule.
Barnaby Rich argued that English recusants in Ireland were worse than
the ignorant 'mere' Irish because they should have known better.[30] John
Derricke, in his poetic depiction of the Irish, described how the natural
tendency of the Irish kern (literally a foot-soldier, but clearly standing—
metonymically—for the native Irish) was to seek out the savage wildness
of his original life, however civilized the influences to which he had been
exposed.[31] Richard Beacon's *Solon his Follie* (1594) devotes a considerable amount of space to the question of 'a corruption of manners' and
how to deal effectively with the problem, using Ireland as a test case for
a general theory.[32] Spenser's *A View* affords the problem a similarly
extensive treatment and is far more specific in its recommendations, as
Irenius manages to convince Eudoxus that the 'English Irish' are much
more of a problem than the native Irish and deserve the greater oppro-
brium. Both have usurped the prerogative of the Crown in adopting Irish
habits and customs, and practices of land tenure:

theareuppon woulde appeare firste how all those greate Englishe Lordes do
Claime those greate services what seigniories they usurpe what wardeshippes they
take from the Quene what Landes of hers they Conceale and then howe those
Irishe Captaines of Countries have encroched uppon | the Quenes freholders and

---

[29] See Michael Richter, *Medieval Ireland: The Enduring Tradition* (Basingstoke:
Macmillan, 1983), 166–7; Ann Rosalind Jones and Peter Stallybrass, 'Dismantling Irena:
The Sexualising of Ireland in Early Modern England', in Andrew Parker *et al.* (eds.),
Nationalisms and Sexualities (London: Routledge, 1992), 157–171, at 157–8.
[30] *A New Description of Ireland* (London, 1610), ch. 4.
[31] *The Image of Ireland* (London, 1581), pt. 1.
[32] *Solon his Follie* (Oxford, 1594), bk. 2, chs. 17–20, bk. 3, ch. 11, *passim*. See also
Fynes Moryson, *Shakespeare's Europe*, ed. Charles Hughes (London: Sherratt & Hughes,
1903), 218–21 *et passim*.

Tennantes how they have translated the Tenures of them from Englishes houldinge unto Irishe *Tanistrye*.[33]

The linguistic metaphor, 'translate', serves to highlight the significance of the 1537 Act, and point to language as an index of wider practices. Significantly, the English Eudoxus is far more indignant and eloquent than the normally dominant Irenius on the culpability of the English, the rhetorical repetitions and parallels serving to emphasize his anger:

as for the greate men which had suche grauntes made them at first by the Kinges of Englande it was in regarde that they shoulde kepe out the Irishe and defende the kinges righte and his subiectes. | But now seinge in steade of defendinge them they Robb and spoile them and in steade of kepinge out the Irishe they doe not onelye make the Irishe theire Tennantes in those Landes and thruste out the englishe, but allso they themselues become meere Irishe with marryinge with them fosteringe with them, and Combyninge with them againste the Quene . . . for sure in mine opinion they are more sharpelye to be chasticed and reformed then the rude Irishe whiche beinge verie wilde at the firste are now become somwhat more Civill when as these from Civillitye are growne to be wilde and mere Irishe. (p. 209)[34]

Irenius concurs that the Old English 'doe nede a sharper reformacion then the Irishe for they are muche more stubborne and disobedient to lawe and governement then the Irishe be, and more malicious againste the Englishe that dailye are sente ouer' (p. 210). Spenser would appear to be mounting a virulent attack on his rivals for colonial power and attempting to blame them for Ireland's current ills.

The Old English, of course, fought back in a series of submissions sent directly to the Privy Council, arguing that they were the best suited to govern Ireland and that the forms of government they had evolved, rather than the aggressive solutions often advocated by the New English would enable a peaceful transformation from a divided to a united country.[35] A significant coup for the cause of the Old English was the inclusion

[33] Edmund Spenser, *A View of the Present State of Ireland*, in *Variorum*, x, pp. 39–231, at p. 208. All subsequent references to this edition in parentheses in the text. On tanistry, see Ch. 2 n. 24. On English perceptions of the practice, see David Beers Quinn, *The Elizabethans and the Irish* (Ithaca, NY: Cornell University Press, 1966), 16.

[34] On the Irish custom of 'fostering' children out to other families, see Quinn, *Elizabethans and the Irish*, 84–5; Moryson, *Shakespeare's Europe*, 196, 233–5; Anne Laurence, 'The Cradle to the Grave: English Observation of Irish Social Customs in the Seventeenth Century', *Seventeenth Century*, 3 (1988), 63–84, 75–8.

[35] See 'Roland White's "The Disorders of the Irishry" (1571)', ed. Nicholas Canny, *Studia Hibernica*, 19 (1979), 147–60; id., 'Roland White's "A Discourse Touching Ireland" (c.1569)', ed. Nicholas Canny, *IHS* 20 (1977), 439–63; Anon., 'A Treatise for the Reformation of Ireland, 1554–5', ed. Brendan Bradshaw, *The Irish Jurist*, 16 (1981), 299–315; id., *The Irish Constitutional Revolution of the Sixteenth Century* (Cambridge: Cambridge University Press, 1979).

of Richard Stanihurst's 'Description of Ireland' in the first edition of
Holinshed's *Chronicles* (1577), which argued that the best solution was
for a continuation of current policies which effectively divided Ireland
into two sections containing the English and Gaelic Irish. Stanihurst
claims that the true guardians of Englishness are the Old English:

> The inhabitants of the English pale have beene in olde time so much addicted to
> their civilitie, and so farre sequestered from barbarous savagenesse, as their
> onelie mother toong was English. And trulie, so long as these impaled dwellers
> did sunder themselves as well in land as in language from the Irish: rudenesse
> was daie by daie in the countrie supplanted, civilitie ingraffed, good lawes estab-
> lished, loialtie observed, rebellion suppressed, and in fine the coine of a yoong
> England was like to shoot in Ireland.[36]

Stanihurst argues the case for the Old English against the Gaelic Irish,
who are savage and barbarous, and the New English, who are vulgar
and ignorant of their own culture. To illustrate this last point, he tells an
anecdote concerning an English peer who is sent to Wexford as a com-
missioner and is able to pick up some odd words and phrases from various 'countrie clowns'. Feeling pleased with himself, he boasts to his
friends that he has acquired Irish quite easily, 'supposing that the blunt
people had prattled Irish, all the while they jangled English', clearly
unable to recognize his own language so corrupt has his usage of it
become.[37] Later in his life, Stanihurst praised the English-speakers in the
Pale as preserving 'among them the pure and pristine tongue' of English,
rather than 'That strange and florid English, currently fashionable,
which plunders from foreign languages'.[38] Just as Spenser wished to
advocate a conception of Englishness in exile in *Colin Clouts come
home againe* superior to that preserved in England itself, so too did
Stanihurst, making the use of pristine English the badge of Old English
virtue.[39] In *A View*, Irenius rather haughtily dismisses Stanihurst as a
poor historian taken in by idle Irish myths through his credulity in
believing the Egyptian origin of the Irish battle-cry, '*Ferragh Ferragh*'

[36] 'Description of Ireland', in Raphael Holinshed, (ed.), *Chronicles of England, Scotland and Ireland* (1577, rev. and expanded 1587), 6 vols., vol. vi, *Ireland* (London: J. Johnson, 1807–8), 4. For analysis, see Willy Maley, 'Spenser's Irish English: Language and
Identity in Early Modern Ireland', *SP* 91 (1994), 417–31, at 418–21.
[37] 'Description of Ireland', 4.   [38] Cited in Lennon, *Richard Stanihurst*, 144.
[39] For further analysis see also Andrew Hadfield, 'English Colonialism and National
Identity in Early Modern Ireland', *Eire-Ireland*, 28/1 (Spring 1993), 69–86, at 74–7. On
Irish English, see Alan Bliss, 'The Development of the English Language in Early Modern
Ireland', in Moody *et al.* (eds.), *A New History of Ireland*, iii. 546–60.

(p. 104) (derived from 'Pharoah')—significantly enough, a story concerning the use of language.

Spenser too placed a strong emphasis on language as the main agent of change from one culture to another, as would seem apparent from his use of the metaphor 'translate' for cultural practices.[40] Irenius argues that the chief cause of English 'degeneration' is speaking Irish: 'And firste I haue to finde faulte with the Abuse of language that is for the speakinge of Irishe amongest the Englishe which as it is unnaturall that anye people shoulde love anothers language more then theire owne soe is it verye inConvenient and the Cause of manye other evills' (p. 118). This has occurred because the English have intermarried with the Irish and accepted their child-rearing practices, fostering children out to wet-nurses:

The which are two moste daungerous infeccions for firste the Childe that suckethe the milke of the nurse muste of necessitye learne his firste speache of her, the which beinge the firste that is envred to his tongue is ever after moste pleasinge unto him In so muche as thoughe he afterwardes be taughte Englishe yeat the smacke of the first will allwaies abide with him and not onelye of the speche but *allsoe of the manners and Condicions* . . . So that the speache beinge Irishe the harte muste nedes be Irishe for out of the abundance of the harte the tonge speakethe [my emphasis]. (p. 119)[41]

Irenius conceives of a dialectical process whereby speech both introduces and reinforces a development already started in the infant's life via fostering; the belief that the influence of the mother tongue cannot be eradicated implies that subsequent efforts will be doomed to failure.[42]

Despite the differences in emphasis and content, all these analyses owe much to the writings of Gerald of Wales, the most significant 'English' writer on Ireland from the twelfth century to the Renaissance (see below, pp. 92–5). Gerald made the problem of 'degeneration' a central focus of his analysis of Ireland:

[40] On Spenser's knowledge of Irish, see J. W. Draper, 'Spenser's Linguistics in *The Present State of Ireland*', MP 17 (1926), 111–26; id., 'More Light on Spenser's Linguistics', MLN 41 (1926), 127–8; F. F. Covington, Jr., 'Another View of Spenser's Linguistics', SP 19 (1922), 244–8; Roland M. Smith, 'The Irish Background of Spenser's *View*', JEGP 42 (1943), 499–515.

[41] Cf. the comments of William Gerard; 'Notes of his report on Ireland, May 1578', *Analecta Hibernica*, 2 (1931), 93–291, at 122.

[42] Cf. Edmund Campion's comments in *Two Bokes of the Histories of Ireland* (*c*.1570), ed. A. F. Vossen (Assen: Van Gorcum, 1963), p. 20, bk. 2, ch. 10, where he argues that education will transform the situation straightforwardly. Campion claimed that Irish was a language so mixed and corrupt that even native speakers found it difficult to learn (bk. 1, ch. 4).

people are so concerned not with what is honourable, but all of them only with what is expedient . . . so strongly has the pest of treachery grown and put in roots here; so natural through long usage have bad habits become; to such an extent are habits influenced by one's associates, and he who touches pitch will be defiled by it; that foreigners coming to this country almost inevitably are contaminated by this, as it were, inborn vice of the country—a vice that is most contagious.[43]

Gerald, through his reading of Old Testament history, argued that the Irish deserved to be conquered because they had fallen so far from civilized and religious values: 'You will never find that any race has ever been conquered except when their sins demanded this as a punishment.'[44] Gerald provided a picture of the Irish which was echoed throughout sixteenth-century chronicles, accounts, political analyses, and government reports on the Irish. He argued that 'although they are fully endowed with natural gifts, their external characteristics of beard and dress, and internal cultivation of mind, are so barbarous that they cannot be said to have any culture'. The Irish lived 'like beasts', and Gerald listed a series of cultural traits in order to justify his opinion. He criticized Irish habits of riding bareback and going naked into battle, although he conceded that they were often effective fighters, being 'quicker and more expert than any other people in throwing'.[45] He claimed that they had not progressed at all from 'the primitive habits of pastoral living' and were too lazy to cultivate crops efficiently despite the natural fertility of the land: 'The wealth of the soil is lost, not through the fault of the soil, but because there are no farmers to cultivate even the best land.'[46] They were also too lazy to produce flax or wool or to practise any mechanical art because 'they think that the greatest pleasure is not to work, and the greatest wealth is to enjoy liberty'.[47] They were 'ignorant of the rudiments of the Faith', failing to 'attend God's church with due reverence'. They did not honour marriage, or avoid incest, and in some places 'debauch, the wives of their dead brothers'. As a

[43] *The History and Topography of Ireland*, trans. J. J. O'Meara (Harmondsworth: Penguin, 1951), 108–9.

[44] *Expugnatio Hibernica (The Conquest of Ireland)*, ed. and trans. F. X. Martin and A. B. Scott (Dublin: Royal Irish Academy, 1978), 233.

[45] Cf. Quinn, *Elizabethans and the Irish*, 40–1, *passim*.

[46] Ibid. 70–1, *passim*; Moryson, *Shakespeare's Europe*, 195. This was a commonplace of colonial literature; see Bernard W. Sheehan, *Savagism and Civility: Indians and Englishmen in Colonial Virginia* (Cambridge: Cambridge University Press, 1980), 51–2; H. C. Porter, *The Inconstant Savage: England and the North American Indian, 1500–1660* (London: Duckworth, 1979), 100–2, 277–8.

[47] Moryson, *Shakespeare's Europe*, 193, 198; Campion, *Two Bokes of the Histories of Ireland*, 15–16.

result, these unions often produced 'beings contrary to [Nature's] ordinary laws', as a punishment from God, examples of which Gerald collects throughout his text.[48] They were notoriously treacherous, never keeping their word, being 'neither strong in war, nor reliable in peace'. Overall, 'This is a filthy people, wallowing in vice'.[49] Despite some skills, such as music, the Irish were 'barbarous' because they were such a remote people who needed civilizing influences: 'they are so removed in these distant parts from the ordinary world of men, as if in another world altogether and consequently cut off from well-behaved and law-abiding people, they know only of the barbarous habits in which they were born and brought up, and embrace them as another nature',[50] precisely what Spenser argued.

Fynes Moryson's (1566–1617) compendious history of his travels throughout Europe, North Africa, and the Near East (1591–7), *An Itinerary Containing his Ten Yeeres Travell* (1617), which singles out the Irish and the Turks as the least civilized nations he has encountered and includes his account of his service as Lord Mountjoy's secretary in 1600 during the Nine Years War, contains a significant anecdote illustrating one generalized English perception of the Irish in the sixteenth century.[51] During his campaign in Ireland, Mountjoy marched towards the north, where he had information that Tyrone was hiding. On the way, he fought with the rebels in Leix, killing many chieftains and spoiling their corn as, according to Moryson, he had planned.[52] Despite this preconceived aim, Moryson pauses in his narrative to comment:

Our Captaines, and by their example (for it was otherwise painefull) the common souldiers, did cut downe with their swords all the Rebels corne, to the value of ten thousand pound and upward, the onely meanes by which they were to live, and to keepe their Bonaghts (or hired souldiers). It seemed incredible, that by so barbarous inhabitants, the ground should be so manured, the fields so orderly fenced, the Townes so frequently inhabited, and the high waies and paths so well beaten, as the Lord Deputy here found them. The reason whereof

---

[48] *History and Topography of Ireland*, 106, 118. On Irish sexual vices and perverse unions, see ibid. 69–76. See also Barnaby Rich, *A Short Survey of Ireland* (London, 1609); Edward M. Hinton (ed.), 'Rych's "Anatomy of Ireland" [1615], with an account of the author', *PMLA* 55 (1940), 73–101, at 82–6.

[49] *History and Topography of Ireland*, 106–7. Campion, *Two Bokes of the Histories of Ireland*, 22, 25; Moryson, *Shakespeare's Europe*, 233–6; id., 'A Description of Ireland', in *Ireland under Elizabeth and James I*, ed. Henry Morley (London, 1890), 411–30, at 426–7.

[50] Gerald, *History and Topography of Ireland*, 101–3.

[51] On Moryson's life see Charles Hughes's introduction to Moryson, *Shakespeare's Europe*; *DNB* entry.

[52] *An Itinerary Containing His Ten Yeeres Travell* (1617), 4 vols. (Glasgow: MacLehose, 1907), ii. 328. See Ch. 2 n. 48 below.

was, that the Queenes forces, during these warres, never till then came among them.[53]

This is an odd moment in the narrative, where for once the Irish are represented as civilized and the English forces as destructive barbarians. Moryson admits that what he has witnessed challenges his preconceived ideas of the Irish as savages, a perception of them he is keen to write on at great length elsewhere in his account of his travels. The last sentence is shrouded in irony, because later Moryson provides some horrific descriptions of the effects of famine, which were a direct result of the brutal military tactics employed to defeat the rebels:

the famine was so great . . . the common sort of Rebels were driven to unspeakable extremities . . . Captaine Trevor & many honest Gentlemen lying in the Newry can witnes, that some old women of those parts, used to make a fier in the fields, & divers little children driving out the cattel in the cold mornings, and comming thither to warme them, were by them surprised, killed and eaten, which at last was discovered by a great girle breaking from them by strength of her body, and Captaine Trevor sending out souldiers to know the truth, they found the childrens skulles and bones, and apprehended the old women, who were executed for the fact.[54]

The Irish are here represented as the ubiquitous savages of Western literature; the story resembles numerous first-hand accounts of man-eating from the Americas, especially in its description of the discovery of the remnants of the cannibal meal, rather than the act itself, as witness to the fact.[55] Yet, put alongside the earlier passage, it becomes obvious that the division between the two peoples is not as absolute as Moryson would wish to assert elsewhere in his narrative, and there is a tacit admission that his perceptions of the Irish may owe much to false propaganda (compare Spenser's comments on the Munster famine below, p. 66–7).

The incident deserves comparison with one of Gerald's many anecdotes, concerning the 'sly reply of the archbishop of Cashel', and placed strategically just after Gerald's discussion of Irish character and vices. Gerald recalls how he and other clerics were complaining about the deficiencies of the Irish church and 'blaming the prelates for the terrible enormities of the country', when the archbishop 'gave a reply which cleverly got home':

---

[53] *Itinerary*, ii. 330. Mountjoy himself records the incident: *CSPI (1600)*, 338.
[54] *Itinerary*, iii. 282.
[55] See Peter Hulme, *Colonial Encounters: Europe and the Native Caribbean, 1492–1797* (London: Methuen, 1986), 80–1.

It is true . . . that although our people are very barbarous, uncivilized, and savage, nevertheless they have always paid great honour and reverence to churchmen, and they have never put out their hands against the saints of God. But now a people has come to the kingdom which knows how, and is accustomed, to make martyrs. From now on Ireland will have its martyrs, just as other countries.[56]

Gerald quotes the reply with minimal comment, appearing to acknowledge that the danger is always present that the civilizers will come to resemble those they wish to define themselves against, the savage, a stubborn reality which will emerge in the process of violently transforming the other into the self. English representations of Ireland nervously recognized this problem; Gerald admits that the Archbishop's words 'cleverly got home', yet asserts that they 'did not rebut my point' (about Irish vices), which may well have been true, but the response did open up a whole series of unwelcome possibilities for English writers.

Although not mentioned in *A View*, much of Spenser's analysis of Irish customs would seem to owe a great deal to Gerald, whether directly or indirectly is hard to determine (see John Hooker's complaint below, pp. 93–5).[57] There is a long analysis of Irish farming, which, *pace* Moryson's observations, attempts to demonstrate that the Irish rely exclusively on pastoral forms of existence rather than systematic agricultural production. According to Irenius, the Irish follow herds of cattle around the countryside establishing small encampments (booleys, *buaile*) as they go, a practice known as transhumance. Such a lifestyle makes it hard to control the itinerant population and encourages outlaws, who can blend in and out of the non-permanent settlements. The opportunities provided by such a cultural practice are also dangerous, leading to the lack of discipline Gerald criticized:

the people that live thus in these Bollies growe thearby the more Barbarous and live more licentiouslye then they Could in townes . . . for theare they thinke themselues haulfe exemted from lawe and obedience and havinge once tasted fredome doe like a steare that hath bene longe out of his yoke grudge and repine ever after to Come under rule againe. (p. 98)

According to Irenius, booleying also prevents the proper use of the land, as do Irish practices of land leasing, which cede too much power to landlords, enabling them to dismiss tenants at a year's notice and quarter themselves on them whenever they see fit, customs enshrined in Irish

[56] *History and Topography of Ireland*, 115–16. For comment, see Robert Bartlett, *Gerald of Wales, 1146–1223* (Oxford: Clarendon Press, 1982), 37.
[57] See, however, Smith, 'Spenser, Holinshed, and the *Leabhar Gabhala*', 399.

(Brehon) law.[58] The result is that tenants have no incentive to improve their land or cultivate extensive crops because they fear that either they will be moved out and on, or that the extra effort will simply go to line the landlord's pockets. The power of landlord over tenant and the latter's uncertainty of tenure also encourages resistance to the English Crown:

the evill which Comethe thereby is greate for by this meane both the landlorde thinketh that he hath his Tenant more at Comaunde to followe him into what accion soeuer he shall enter and allsoe the Tenant beinge lefte at his libertye is fitt for euerie variable occacion of Change that shalbe offered by time and so muche allsoe the more readye and willinge is he to runne thereinn. (p. 134)

A View also contains harsh criticisms of Irish religion and religious practice. Although Spenser is concerned to attack the Catholic faith of the Irish, it is arguable that his comments on their barbaric practices mark a tradition that does not postdate the Reformation, but looks back to Gerald and the twelfth century.[59] Irenius comments that he does not need to discuss Irish religion at length because its character is straightforward: 'they are all Papistes by their profession but in the same so blindelye and brutishly enformed for the moste parte as that ye woulde rather thinke them *Atheists* or infidles', because 'not one amongest a hundred knowethe anye grounde of religion anie article of his faithe but Cane perhaps saie his pater noster or his *Ave marye* without anie knowledge or understandinge what one worde thereof meaneth' (p. 136). The point is that the Irish are not simply Catholics but savage Catholics, outside the boundaries of civilization as well as the faith, so that they become the inverse of the loyal citizen, the atheist, outside the moral codes which restrain deviant urges.[60] Irenius' language seems to match Gerald's disdain for a people whose habits are (literally) beyond the Pale. Although their ignorance is not their fault, the Irish are almost too revolting to contemplate:

But neuerthelesse since they drunke not from the pure springe of life but onelye tasted of suche trobled waters as weare broughte unto them the druggs thereof haue bred great Contagion in theire Soules the which dailye encreasinge And beinge still Augmented with theire owne lewde lives and filthie Conuersacion

[58] For definitions, see Quinn, *Elizabethans and the Irish*, 52.
[59] See John Gillingham, 'The English Invasion of Ireland', in Bradshaw *et al.* (eds.), *Representing Ireland*, 24–42; Brendan Bradshaw, 'Sword, Word and Strategy in the Reformation of Ireland', *HJ* 21 (1978), 475–502, at 502.
[60] Cf. the most celebrated use of the term when applied by Thomas Kyd and Richard Baines to Christopher Marlowe: J. B. Steane, *Marlowe: A Critical Study* (Cambridge: Cambridge University Press, 1964), 7–10, 363–4.

hathe now bred in them this generall disease that Cannot but onelye with verye
stronge purgacions be Clensed and Carryed awaie. (pp. 137–8)

The people have become an infection which needs to be cured before the
land can be saved. Just as their habits and general mode of life are dirty,
so are their minds.[61] Just as Gerald praises the natural qualities of the
Irish, but dwells upon the defects of their society which transforms them
into barbarians, thus sanctioning Henry II's imposition of order, so does
Spenser proclaim their ignorant innocence while likening the situation
to a disease which requires drastic treatment.

Elsewhere in *A View* Irenius is actually able to praise, albeit somewhat indirectly, the Irish propensity for religion. Eudoxus asks how the
Irish are to be converted; Irenius explains that religion cannot be
imposed upon the Irish but will require a time of peace and stability to
become established. However, 'if that the ancient godlie fathers which
first Conuerted them beinge infidels to the faithe weare able to pull them
from Idolatrye and Paganisme to the trewe belief in Christe . . . how
muche more easely shall godlie teachers bringe them to the trewe understandinge of that which they allreadye professe'. The problem is that
there is a huge discrepancy between Catholic priests and Protestant
ministers in Ireland; the one 'spare not to Come out of Spaine from
Rome from Reymes by longe toile and dangerous travell hither wheare
they knowe perill of deathe', the other are 'Idle ministers . . . havinge the
livinges of the Countrye offered them without paines without perill' are
reluctant to be 'drawen forthe from theire warme nestes . . . to loke out
into godes haruest, which is even readie for the sickle'. Irenius suggests
that instead, 'it is expediente that some discrete ministers of theire owne
Cuntrymen be firste sente amongeste them which by theire milde per-
swacions and instruccions as allso by theire sober liffe and Conuersacion maie drawe them firste to understande and afterwardes to imbrace
the doctrine of theire salvacion' (pp. 221–2).

The passage can be related in design to the description of the skilful
Irish bards who, although misguided in their aims, serve as a stick with
which to beat the English neglect of the art of poetry. Here, English
ministers are seen as complacent and self-interested, unwilling to care
for their flocks, a stock image of the established church presented by the

---

[61] See also Rich, *New Description of Ireland*, 'To the Reader', and ch. 3; Fynes
Moryson's description of the naked Cork girls grinding corn ('Description of Ireland',
424–6). More generally, see Mary Douglas, *Purity and Danger: An Analysis of Pollution
and Taboo* (London: Routledge, 1966).

'puritan' wing and one commonly found in Spenser's poetry.[62] In contrast, the Catholic priests are seen as energetic, successful, and respected, willing to die for their cause. It is further notable that Irenius recommends that the first attempts to convert the Irish—which can only be carried out when the English have reconquered Ireland and imposed their will upon the island—must be made by the Irish themselves. The context and phrasing would imply that Irenius does mean the native Irish ('theire owne Cuntrymen') who, like the priests of presumably diverse nationalities entering Ireland on dangerous missions, will draw the people to them. Irenius suggests that one of the reasons for this predicted success is his faith in the 'Conuersacion' of the clean-living Irish Protestant ministers; at the start of *The Faerie Queene*, Book VI, the book of courtesy, the narrator defines courtesy as a virtue which stems from the court, forming the 'roote of ciuill conuersation' (VI. i. 1).[63] Such a juxtaposition would suggest that here, despite the seeming thrust of the argument and wealth of examples contained in *A View*, the Irish are portrayed as more cultivated, reasonable, and civil than their English counterparts.

This particular representation of the native Irish resembles that of Edmund Campion written in the early 1570s, when he observed that, although the Irish were all too often addicted to 'lycentiousnes and evill custome', 'there is daily triall of good natures amonge them'. Campion argued that education had a power 'to make or marre', and that many Irish had been 'reclaymed and to what rare giftes of grace and wisdome they doe have aspired', in contrast to the frequently brutish English who 'degenerated'.[64] In essence, Spenser and Campion are following a fundamental ambiguity in representations of the 'savage' in Western literature, an ambiguity also present in Gerald's representations of the Irish.[65] On the one hand, the good naked savage could be brought up to the level of the civilized if educated correctly; on the other, the bad naked savage threatened the very bonds of civilized society and had to be destroyed, or

[62] John N. King, *Spenser's Poetry and the Reformation Tradition* (Princeton: Princeton University Press, 1990), chs. 1–2.
[63] Catherine Bates, *The Rhetoric of Courtship in Elizabethan Language and Literature* (Cambridge: Cambridge University Press, 1992), 151–72; Lievsay, *Stefano Guazzo*, 20–1.
[64] *Two Bokes of the Histories of Ireland*, 19–20.
[65] See Hayden White, 'The Noble Savage: Theme as Fetish', in Fredi Chiapelli (ed.), *First Images of America: The Impact of the New World on the Old* (Berkeley: University of California Press, 1976), 121–35; Hulme, *Colonial Encounters*, ch. 2; Nicholas P. Canny, 'The Ideology of English Colonisation: From Ireland to America', *William and Mary Quarterly*, 30 (1973), 575–98.

assigned to a menial role; what, in terms of Spanish debates concerning the New World, could be described as 'natural slavery'.[66] The former group were often used to criticize the vices of the corrupt, decadent Old World, as in More's *Utopia* and Montaigne's essay 'Of the Cannibals'; the latter to affirm the superiority of the civilized as well as their worst fears concerning man's inherent bestiality.[67]

It is hardly surprising that the Old English, keen to persuade the metropolitan court that they were the best suited to govern Ireland and so avoid a military reconquest which would enhance the claims of their rival colonial élite, should tend to take a more generous view of the chances of reforming the native Irish, nor that the New English should generally take the opposite view.[68] Such perceptions were also current among the New English, especially in tracts aimed at persuading English colonists to emigrate over the Irish Sea, a technique pioneered by Sir Thomas Smith, for his spectacularly unsuccessful attempt to colonize the Ards Peninsula (1572–3).[69] One specifically relevant example is Robert Payne's *A Brief Description of Ireland*, published in 1590 but dated as written in 1589. Payne was an agricultural writer of some standing and had become an undertaker on the Munster Plantation with twenty-five of his neighbours. He had gone on ahead to Munster and his treatise was his report back to them to persuade them to follow him. The tract contains lavish praise of the opportunities for English colonists in Ireland, depicting Ireland as a land of utopian abundance: 'the commodities of the countrie are many moe then eyther the people can well use or I recite.' Payne provides a series of shopping lists for the would-be colonists, going so far as to provide prices and values: 'Their soile for the most part is very fertil, and apte for Wheate, Rye, Barly, Peason, Beanes,

[66] The literature on savagery is extensive. Opposing interpretations of the evidence are provided in Sheehan, *Savagism and Civility*; Karen O. Kupperman, *Settling with the Indians: The Meeting of English and Indian Cultures in America, 1580–1640* (London: Dent, 1980). See also Margaret Hogden, *Early Anthropology in the Sixteenth and Seventeenth Centuries* (Philadelphia: Pennsylvania University Press, 1971). On 'natural slavery', see Anthony Pagden, *The Fall of Natural Man: The American Indian and the Origins of Comparative Ethnology* (Cambridge: Cambridge University Press, 1982), 39.

[67] Anthony Pagden, 'The Savage Critic: Some European Images of the Primitive', YES 13 (1983), 32–45; Stephen Greenblatt, 'Learning to Curse: Aspects of Linguistic Colonialism in the Sixteenth Century', in Chiapelli (ed.), *First Images of America*, 561–80.

[68] See Bradshaw, (ed.), ' "A Treatise for the Reformation of Ireland" '; id., *The Irish Constitutional Revolution of the Sixteenth Century*, ch. 9; Nicholas Canny, *The Formation of the Old English Elite in Ireland*, O'Donnell Lecture (Dublin: National University of Ireland, 1975), 14–16.

[69] David Beers Quinn, 'Sir Thomas Smith (1513–77) and the Beginnings of English Colonial Theory', PAPS 89 (1945), 543–60, at 550–4; Mary Dewar, *Sir Thomas Smith: A Tudor Intellectual in Office* (London: Athlone, 1964), ch. 14.

Oates, Woade, Mather, Rape, Hoppes, Hempe, Flaxe and all other graines and fruites that England any wise doth yeelde'; 'A barrell of Wheate or a barrel of bay Salt contayning three bushels and a halfe of Winchester measure, is sold there for iiii. s. Malt, Peason, Beanes, for ii. s. viii. d. Barly for ii. s. iiii. d. Oates for xx. d. a fresh Sammon worth in London x. s. for vi. d. xxiiii.'; 'There be great store of wild Swannes, Cranes, Pheasantes, Partriges, Heathcocks, Plouers, greene and gray, Curlewes, Woodcockes, Rayles, Quailes, & all other fowles much more plentifull then in England.'[70] Ireland, in Payne's description, has all the advantages of England and more besides.

Payne's account of the native Irish is designed to offset English fears. The work opens with an exhortation to the reader not to believe everything he or she has heard: 'Let not the reportes of those that haue spent all their owne and what they could by any meanes get from others in England, discourage you from Ireland.' Payne admits that there are bad colonists who 'haue wrought a generall discredite to all English men', 'the worsser sorte of undertakers', who 'haue done much hurte in the countrie'.[71] But, in reality, the English have little to fear from the Irish. He divides the people into three categories: 'the better sorte are very ciuill and honestly given' and inclined to husbandry, 'although as yet unskilful'; the kerns, who are, as Payne admits, 'warlike men', yet 'most of that sorte were slayne in the late warres' so they make up the least number of the native Irish; and the 'third sorte . . . a very idle people, not unlike our English beggars, yet for the moste parte, of pure complexion and good constitution of bodie'. Payne says little of these, but his judgement that the better sort err in not making 'that idle sort giue accompt of their life', strikes an ominous note, especially as he declines to note their numbers.[72]

[70] *A Brief Description of Ireland* (1590), ed. Aquilla Smith (Dublin: Irish Archaeological Society, 1841), 6–7. Such utopian descriptions are common in colonial pamphlets and tracts; see e.g. *The First Three English Books on America*, ed. Edward Arber (Birmingham, 1885), 22, 67, 87–9, 150, 156, *et passim*; Thomas Hariot, 'A briefe and true report of the new found land of Virginia' (1588), in Richard Hakluyt, *The Principal Navigations, Voyages, Traffiques and Discoveries of the English Nation* (1599), 8 vols. (London: Everyman, 1907), vi. 164–96, at 166–86.

[71] *Brief Description*, 3, 7. Cf. the letter 'To the Adventurers, Favourers, and Welwillers of the enterprise for the inhabiting and planting of Virginia', which introduces Hariot's 'brief and true report', which complains of 'slanderous and shamefull speeches bruted abroad by many that returned from thence' (p. 165). Hariot's report was published two years before Payne's tract. On the exhortationary designs of Hariot's text, see Stephen Greenblatt, 'Invisible Bullets', in id., *Shakespearian Negotiations: The Circulation of Social Energy in Renaissance England* (Oxford: Clarendon Press, 1988), 21–65, at 31.

[72] *Brief Description*, 3–4.

His extended description of 'the better sorte' is clearly intended to reassure other would-be colonists unsure whether to take up residence in Munster:

Most of them speake good English and bring up their children to learning. I saw a Grammar schoole in *Limbrick*, one hundred, & threescore schollers, most of them speaking good and perfit English, for that thay haue used to conster the Latin into English. They keepe their promise faithfully, and are more desirous of peace then our English men, for that in time of warres they are more charged, And also they are fatter praies for the enemie, who respecteth no person. They are quicke witted and of good constitution of bodie; they reforme them selues dayly more and more after the English manners: nothing is more pleasing unto them, then to heare of Good Iustices placed amongst them . . . They are obedient to the laws, so that you may trauel through all the land without any danger or iniurie offered of the verye worst Irish, and be greatly releeued of the best.[73]

Payne emphasizes the desire of the Irish to be English, so that Ireland is presented as an alternative England, as MacCarthy-Morrogh suggested was the case in his account of English migration to Ireland, with English law functioning as at home. But to read the text simply as an accurate description of a reality is to ignore its specific propagandist function and deliberate construction of a bucolic world at odds with the violent pastoral of Spenser's *Colin Clouts come home againe* (which raises the perennial problem of evidence, whether literature is, in fact, less elaborately constructed and easier to decode than many eye-witness accounts.)[74] Payne's account is indeed far more nervous than its fulsome praise of the Irish would indicate. The suggestion that the Irish 'are fatter praies for the enemie' highlights one of Payne's central aims, to convince English readers that the Irish were not keen to formulate an alliance with the Spanish, a pressing fear after the Armada (1588), when it was feared that Ireland could serve as a bulwark for a Spanish invasion of Britain. Nearly all of the many Spanish troops shipwrecked in Ireland after the failure of the operation were summarily dealt with.[75] The pamphlet can be classed as a contribution to the 'Black Legend', the

---

[73] *Brief Description*, 3–4.

[74] See Natalie Zemon Davis, *Fiction in the Archives: Pardon Tales and their Tellers in Sixteenth-Century France* (Stanford: Stanford University Press, 1987), introduction. For a strong, possibly naïve, case for the use of literature as straightforward evidence, see Tom Dunne 'A Polemical Introduction: Literature, Literary Theory and the Historian', in id. (ed.), *The Writer as Witness: Literature as Historical Evidence*, Historical Studies 16 (Cork: Cork University Press, 1987).

[75] See Evelyn Hardy, *Survivors of the Armada* (London: Constable, 1966); T. P. Kilfeather, *Ireland: Graveyard of the Spanish Armada* (Dublin: Anvil, 1967); Grenfell Morton, *Elizabethan Ireland* (London: Longman, 1971), ch. 8.

widespread use of anti-Spanish propaganda, in its attempt to portray English colonialism as benevolent and Spanish as malevolent.[76] Payne suggests that 'the better sort doe deadly hate the Spaniardes' and that most have read accounts of 'their monsterous cruelties in the west Indians', probably meaning the works of Bartolomé de Las Casas, one of which, the *Brevissima Relacion*, had recently been translated as *The Spanish Colonie, or Brief Chronicle of the Acts and Gestes of the Spaniards in the West Indies* (1583), and further popularized via a reference in Richard Hakluyt's *Discourse concerning Western Planting*, the following year.[77]

Nevertheless, Payne's text sits uncomfortably on the fence with regard to questions of Irish loyalty: 'no doubte there are some Traytors in Ireland. I woulde I coulde truely say there were none in England.'[78] In the penultimate paragraph, he turns away from detailing the manifold advantages of Ireland to deal with the stubborn problem of the Desmond Rebellion, the event which led to the foundation of the Plantation. Payne writes of a rumour that Sir William Stanley, the former sheriff of Cork, who had defected to the Spanish during the Dutch Wars, would return to Ireland with the Spanish and that 'the Irish people who loued him wil take his part'. However, Payne argues,

suppose that hee doe come. what is hee to the last greate Earell of Desmonde, who had greater followers then Sir Willam is, and the King of spayne his purse more plentifull then he can haue it? yet did not the said Desmonde bring his countrie to that meserie that one did eate another for hunger, and himselfe with all his posteritie and followers to utter ruinne. Can the Irish so soon forget such a great distrease, and be drawen into the like action with a meaner man? surely no. . . . I thinke it be true that the Irish would gladlye haue their publicke masse againe: but they had rather continewe it in corners, then to heere it openlye in fetters and chaines as the poore Indianes do.[79]

The argument shifts uneasily from a denial that things could ever be as

---

[76] See William S. Maltby, *The Black Legend in England: The Development of Anti-Spanish Sentiment, 1558–1660* (Durham, NC: Duke University Press, 1971). See also Walter Raleigh, *The Discovery of the Large, Rich and Beautiful Empire of Guiana* (1595), in *Selected Writings*, ed. Gerald Hammond (Harmondsworth: Penguin, 1986), 76–123, at 100–1, 114–15.

[77] Maltby, *The Black Legend in England*, 13. On Las Casas, see Pagden, *Fall of Natural Man*, chs. 3–4. On English use of Spanish precedents in colonizing Ireland see Nicholas P. Canny, *The Elizabethan Conquest of Ireland: A Pattern Established, 1565–76* (Hassocks: Harvester, 1976), 133–4.

[78] *Brief Description*, 5.

[79] Ibid. 12–13. On Sir William Stanley (1548–1630), see *DNB* entry; Bagwell, *Ireland under the Tudors*, iii. 161–3.

bad again because there will never be such a concentration of forces in the area and the terrible effects of the rebellion will prevent the pragmatic majority from such desperate actions (see Spenser's description of the same famine below, pp. 66–7), to an admission that it is only the threat of such consequences which stands between order and rebellion. In other words, a reversal of Payne's earlier claims that the Irish were overwhelmingly in favour of English rule and were fast becoming Anglicized. It was Payne's fears rather than his hopes that were to be realized in the 1590s.

The importance of language as the primary agent of cultural transformation is again in evidence in Payne's tale of the dutiful scholars at the Limerick grammar school being strategically placed at the start of his treatise. His attempt to represent the majority of the Irish as keen to use English, contrasts with the vision of another planter, William Herbert (1553?–1593), whose occupation of an Irish estate in Munster roughly coincided with that of both Payne and Spenser. Three treatises by Herbert were collected among the State Papers in the late 1580s, one of which, 'A Description of Munster' (1588), made a strong case for the use of Irish in attempts to convert the natives to both Anglicized behaviour and Protestantism. Herbert argued that the reform of the Irish should take place in three interrelated ways: via religion, which would also teach them, 'loyalty to Her Majesty'; via the spread of English justice, 'whereby they may repose the safety of their lives, lands, and goods'; and via the social and linguistic influence of the English, 'in a courteous demeanour, affability of speech, and care of their well doing, ever expressed towards them by such English gentlemen as shall inhabit and govern amongst them'. Herbert explains that he has already taken steps to achieve these goals and, to complete the first aim, has 'been careful in those parts wherein I am, to have them taught the truth in their natural tongue, to have the Lord's prayer, the Articles of the Creed, the Ten Commandments, translated into the Irish tongue; public prayers in that language, with the administration of the sacraments and other ecclesiastical rites, which in a strange tongue could be to them but altogether unprofitable'.[80]

Such sentiments would seem to place Herbert as a 'good colonist', who tried to mitigate the excessive harshness of English rule through a sympathetic identification with the needs of the Irish, and his work has

---

[80] *CSPI (1586–8)*, 527–39, at 532–3. On Herbert's life, see *DNB* entry; Sir William Herbert, *Croftus Sive De Hibernia Liber*, ed. Arthur Keaveney and John A. Madden (Dublin: Irish Manuscripts Commission, 1992), introduction, pp. ix–xvii.

been favourably contrasted to the more brutally Anglocentric statements of some of his contemporaries.[81] However, one should note a
potential contradiction even in this seemingly benign political analysis:
on the one hand Herbert is quite happy to teach the Irish in Irish, but on
the other, he hopes that they will benefit from the 'affability of speech'
of the English gentlemen on the Munster Plantation who, presumably,
speak little or no Irish. It is quite clear from the context of Herbert's
remarks that the use of Irish is a contingency plan: the list of texts translated—the articles of the Creed, the Ten Commandments, the Lord's
Prayer and other public prayers, the sacraments and other rites—illustrates that the translation provided is from English into Irish, not an
attempt to provide an Irish equivalent of the English. There is no question of replacing English with Irish. In other words, Herbert only has
faith in the use of Irish because he believes that the message can survive
the medium, in contrast to Spenser's or Sir William Gerrard's fear that
Irish speech 'made the man Irish' and hence opposed to Anglicization
(for Gerrard, see below, p. 62).

   Herbert's lengthy Latin treatise, *Croftus Sive De Hibernia Liber*
(*c*.1591), a careful and stylistically elaborate analysis of how Ireland
should be governed, which owes much to wide reading in Classical and
contemporary European political thought, shows Herbert in a different
light, even though it contains the same plea for the use of Irish (p. 97).[82]
Herbert adopts the 'absolutist' stance which denies the rights of subjects
ever to resist their sovereign: 'Tyranny exercised by a prince or supreme
magistrate can be ended or punished by God alone. All other remedies
whatsoever are either unholy or foolish' (p. 67), although elsewhere he
frequently cites Machiavelli (pp. 75, 77, 87, 93), in English political
thought a dubious republican thinker.[83] Herbert argues that good

---

[81] On the 'good colonist', see Memmi, *Colonizer and Colonized*, 19–44. For
favourable interpretations of Herbert, see Ciaran Brady, 'Spenser's Irish Crisis: Humanism and Experience in the 1590s', *P&P* iii (1986), 17–49, at 24–5; Brendan Bradshaw,
'Robe and Sword in the Conquest of Ireland', in Claire Cross *et al.* (eds.), *Law and Government under the Tudors: Essays Presented to Sir Geoffrey Elton on his Retirement*
(Cambridge: Cambridge University Press, 1988), 139–62, at 140–52. In contrast, see
Nicholas Canny, 'Edmund Spenser and the Development of an Anglo-Irish Identity', *YES*
13 (1983), 1–19, at 10–11.

[82] The introduction to the parallel text by Keaveney and Madden is invaluable, especially as regards Classical sources used. They suggest that it was prepared for publication:
Croftus, pp. xviii–xix. Subsequent references to this text are given in parentheses in the
text.

[83] For an extended discussion see Quentin Skinner, *The Foundations of Modern Political Thought*, 2 vols. (Cambridge: Cambridge University Press, 1978), vol. ii, chs. 7–9;
Penry Williams, *The Tudor Regime* (Oxford: Clarendon Press, 1979), 351–9.

government in Ireland requires not only 'a complete and efficient type of government', but also 'the exalted power and fortune of the chief magistrate' ('in summi magistratus potentia et fortuna excelsa') (pp. 89–91). This viceregal figure must protect 'the king's power, which is the fount and origin of justice and judgement', from injury (p. 113), and should attempt to achieve this by means of persuasion: 'the chief magistrate should strive for and wholeheartedly devote himself to acquiring and retaining the goodwill of his subjects . . . He will gain goodwill by clemency, kindness and friendliness or affability' (p. 89). Nevertheless, his primary duty is to uphold the spread of English law. Herbert heaps praise upon Henry VIII and Elizabeth, who have passed 'salutary laws . . . to destroy and stamp out these uncivilised manners, rites, dress and these hostile and barbarous customs'. He concludes that, had such laws been established and observed earlier, then the families of those who came over from England would not have 'degenerated to the point where they have rejected not only their ancestral institutions, their innate concept of who they are and their very nature, but also their *manner of speech* and their way of life' (pp. 81–3, my emphasis).

It is interesting to note how quickly and easily Herbert slips from one form of political analysis or discourse to another which would appear to cut across, even contradict, what he has been arguing. Irish is to be used and tolerated, but its use by English colonists serves as a sign of their degeneration ('degenerationes', 'degenerasse': Herbert uses both noun and verb in succeeding sentences), showing how insidious was an anthropological language derived from Gerald. Herbert continues his analysis with an attempt to show that, far from being unique, essential, and 'bound up with Ireland's safety and, prosperity' (p. 83), as some Irish claim, their social practices are simply the common behaviour of barbarous, uncivilized people as noted by Cicero, Suetonius, Pliny, and other Classical authorities (pp. 83–5).

Herbert is prepared to sanction the most brutal measures in order to eliminate such behaviour:

Yet, if the Irish are not disposed by any laws, persuasion or examples to embrace from the heart a way of life distinguished by the best principles and ordinances but decide, whenever any opportunity is offered, to fall back and relapse into their old habits and vices, then I avow and predict with quite as much truth as force that some king of England and Ireland, of great prudence and power, prompted by political considerations and designs, will disperse that entire race and will extirpate all the inhabitants there who have lapsed into the habits and customs of the Irish. (pp. 85–7)

Herbert does distance himself to an extent from such violence by representing this outcome as an inevitable result of others' failures and nothing to do with himself; but his disapproval is a moot point, given his stress on viceregal authority. Towards the end of the tract, Herbert lists ways that the monarch can transform the country and includes, 'the transplantation of inhabitants from one province to another' (p. 113), in itself a drastic measure unlikely to have been carried out within the boundaries of England, and the cause of immense suffering when enforced in the 1650s.[84]

Herbert's major solution to the problem of Irish intransigence is the establishment of colonies, which is hardly surprising given his situation on the Munster Plantation. Herbert's stress on the need to spread the rule of English law, but also establish colonies of Englishmen in Ireland, points out the constitutional anomaly which Ireland had become within the expanding territorial domains of the English monarch who held sway over the greater part of the British Isles and an empire.[85] In Ciaran Brady's words:

On the one hand there was a perception of the island, more prescriptive than real, as a culturally undifferentiated society, a polity with a constitution similar to England's, in other words, a kingdom as defined by the 1541 act for 'the kingly title'. Yet there was a second assumption, more adventitious perhaps but more real, that Ireland was a colony with opportunities for gain and advancement for those who were willing to adventure for them.[86]

In the same way, the Irish were regarded as akin to the natives of the New World or other 'savage' peoples, as well as ordinary 'domestic' subjects under the rule of English law, part of the 'nation' (however that be defined) and/or part of the empire.[87] Herbert argues that the estab-

[84] See Foster, *Modern Ireland*, 107–14; T. C. Barnard, *Cromwellian Ireland: English Government and Reform in Ireland, 1649–1660* (Oxford: Oxford University Press, 1975), 10–12; John P. Prendergast, *The Cromwellian Settlement of Ireland*, 3rd edn. (Dublin: Mellifont, 1922).

[85] Michael Hechter, *Internal Colonialism: The Celtic Fringe in British National Development, 1536–1966* (Berkeley: University of California Press, 1975), pt. 2; Hugh Kearney, 'The Making of an English Empire', in *The British Isles: A History of Four Nations* (Cambridge: Cambridge University Press, 1989), ch. 7.

[86] Ciaran Brady and Raymond Gillespie (eds.), *Natives and Newcomers: The Making of Irish Colonial Society, 1534–1641* (Dublin: Irish Academic Press, 1986), introduction, 16–17.

[87] See e.g. Karl S. Bottigheimer, 'Kingdom and Colony: Ireland in the Westward Enterprise, 1536–1660', in K. R. Andrews *et al.* (eds.), *The Westward Enterprise: English Activities in the Atlantic and America, 1480–1650* (Liverpool: Liverpool University Press, 1979), 45–64; Nicholas Canny, 'The Marginal Kingdom: Ireland as a Problem in the First British Empire', in Bernard Bailyn and Philip D. Morgan (eds.), *Strangers Within the Realm: Cultural Margins of the First British Empire* (Chapel Hill: University of North Carolina Press, 1991), 35–66; Andrew Hadfield, 'The Naked and the Dead: Elizabethan Perceptions

lishment of colonies will help to 'do away with and completely destroy the habits and practices of the natives', who will 'put on and embrace the habits and customs of the colonists'; a process equal and opposite to that taking place at that time, with the English 'degenerating' into the Irish. The logic used is that, once the English exist in sufficient numbers within the realm, change can be enforced and the natives manipulated to follow the colonists' lead rather than vice versa, and Ireland will come to be English: 'once you have removed those things which can alienate hearts and minds, they will both become united, first in habits, then in mind' (p. 81).

Herbert, like Spenser, regards the New English as saviours of a degenerate Ireland, infected by the vices of the natives and badly run from the mother country (despite his fulsome praise for Elizabeth, pp. 117–19). Herbert argues that the English authorities must surrender political control to those in Ireland, the colonial government of the New English:

The combined prudence of the council and the authority of the governor need not be so reined in and curbed that they must always depend on directions from England. In the greatest troubles, these directions, because of storms, tempests and a variety of circumstances, can make their appearance and arrive so unseasonably that opportunities for action and advantages slip away and escape, and in consequence the greatest difficulties follow. (pp. 115–17)

This is an argument for the devolution of power, which would seem to contradict Herbert's stress elsewhere on the absolute rights of monarchs, but is in line with his championship of the rights of magistrates. Herbert praises the provincial councils which have administered 'the more remote parts [of Elizabeth's dominions], namely Wales and the northern province' (p. 73), and recommends that the government of Ireland be based on these lines.[88] In the section which argues for the significant role of the Lord Deputy, Herbert also emphasizes the vital role of the magistrates in any sound body politic:

A government must indeed be equipped with the necessary arteries, sinews and veins. These are the higher and lower magistrates so that through them the living breath and blood of the laws and ordinances can penetrate and refresh all parts of the state. Otherwise the state must be considered weak, crippled and moribund, rather than full of life, flourishing and happy. (p. 91)

of Ireland', in Michèle Willems and Jean-Pierre Maquerlot (eds.), *Travel and Drama in Shakespeare's Time* (Cambridge: Cambridge University Press, 1996), 32–54, at 40–1, 48–9.

[88] On these councils, see Williams, *Tudor Regime*, 227–9; John Guy, *Tudor England* (Oxford: Oxford University Press, 1988), 355–6.

Herbert's political opinions are not clear: was he simply a confused and contradictory figure, as his modern editors suggest, 'a cultivated but unimaginative gentleman', whose critical acumen is leaden despite his obviously wide reading? (p. xli) Or is *Croftus*, a carefully written and learned text, designed to flatter and gain influence, secretly trying to have power devolved to the New English colonists in Ireland under the guise of royalist politics? The example of *Croftus* would seem to imply that it is by no means an easy task to separate the republican sheep from the absolutist goats.

It should also be noted that there is only one extant manuscript of the text itself, unlike other roughly contemporary texts such as Spenser's *A View* where a number of manuscripts survive (see below, p. 79). There is also a manuscript translation into English, which was probably undertaken between 1603 and 1610 (for details, see *Croftus*, pp. xlii–xlvii). It is not at all clear how widely Herbert's opinions could have circulated; but the careful state of the manuscript suggests that Herbert hoped to have the text published, and the fact that he chose to write in Latin would further suggest that he was seeking an international audience, as well as a national one (pp. xviii–xix). Alternatively, it might imply that Herbert felt the need to disguise his text, dressing it up as a general treatise on European politics, when its real aim was to influence a select few into devolving power to the New English. Although such speculations require further evidence, they do indicate that publishing any political work on Ireland in the late sixteenth century was not a straightforward task, as the history of *A View* demonstrates.

This problem, alongside several others, links *Croftus* to another major treatise on Ireland written on the Munster Plantation, Richard Beacon's *Solon his Follie, or a political discourse touching the reformation of commonweals conquered, declined or corrupted* (1594), as many commentators have noted.[89] Beacon's treatise was published in Oxford, not London, which was unusual and may well have been an attempt to avoid censorship. The work is in the form of a dialogue between Epimenides, a semi-legendary Greek prophet and poet, who lived in the sixth century BC, Pisistratus, a moderate tyrant (who plays a subordinate role in the dialogue), and Solon, the statesman and law-giver who was a leading general in the Athenian attempt to capture Salamina from

---

[89] Brady, 'Spenser's Irish Crisis: Humanism and Experience', 24–5; Bradshaw, 'Robe and Sword', 152–4; Canny, 'Edmund Spenser and the Development of an Anglo-Irish Identity', 8; Canny and Carpenter (eds.), 'The Early Planters', 172–3. Subsequent references to *Solon* are given in parentheses in the text.

the Megara.[90] the work, which owes a vast amount to Machiavelli's political writings, is clearly written to mask its underlying intention and it is by no means obvious until it is actually read that it deals with Ireland at all (which may tell us something about Elizabethan censorship or, at least, Beacon's conception of it).[91] The prefatory letter 'To Her Most Sacred Majestie', argues that Ireland is now subdued, faction has been ended, famine replaced by plenty, cities have been established, the wild and cruel life of the Irish has been civilized and that, although the cost to the queen has been great, she has achieved greater glory than Brutus did in founding Rome (fo. 3), thus letting the initiated who have bothered to open the book into the secret that *Solon his Follie* is an analysis of contemporary Ireland. The measures Beacon recommends are remarkably similar to those advocated by other planters like Herbert and Spenser (see *Solon*, ch. 2).[92] The disputants consider various types of commonwealth which have declined, and conclude that commonwealths which have decayed completely cannot be reformed by laws alone, even though the law must be used whenever possible: the possibility of reforming a state depends upon there being an authority to enforce such reform (*Solon*, chs. 3, 5). To this end, the law must be suspended in times of war, and pity for the plight of any rebels stamped out, because the safety of the state must be considered before everything else (fos. 16–17). Epimenides heaps praise upon the conduct of Lord Grey and Sir Richard Bingham, who were able to instil into the Irish 'a fear to offend, bred in the hearts of the people by the true discipline of laws', thus making it possible to reform the country (fo. 8). Corrupt laws have to be removed; in Salamina there are many, coyne and livery, tanistry, the harbouring of rebels with impunity, inadequate punishments for murder (fo. 21). Five means of achieving this are recommended: the establishment of proper authority; obtaining the goodwill of the people; persuasion; force; and the use of magistrates to suppress disobedience (fo. 22). The problem is that, although there are good laws established in Salamina, they are not obeyed and strong magistrates are needed to enforce them (fo. 58–9). The final chapters of the dialogue consider the ways in which the decline of a commonwealth can be halted: a number of military

[90] For details on all three as historical figures, see Sir Paul Harvey (ed.), *The Oxford Companion to Classical Literature* (Oxford: Oxford University Press, 1984).

[91] On Beacon's debt to Machiavelli, see Sydney Anglo, 'A Machiavellian Solution to the Irish Problem: Richard Beacon's *Solon his Follie*', in Edward Cheney and Peter Mack (eds.), *England and the Continental Renaissance: Essays in Honour of J. B. Trapp* (Woodbridge: Boydell & Brewer, 1990), 153–64.

[92] Canny, 'Edmund Spenser and the Development of an Anglo-Irish Identity', 8.

tactics are recommended, many taken from Machiavelli's *Arte of Warre* and *The Prince*. These include keeping provinces separate as the Romans achieved in Macedonia (and the governors failed to achieve in Ireland when Shane O'Neill was able to build up a huge force, as were the Burkes and O'Rourkes), preventing rebels from speaking to the people and executing those corrupted thereby, refusing to let the people take up arms under any circumstances, and taking hostages and pledges (fos. 95–102).

Solon his Follie concludes, rather like *Croftus Sive De Hibernia Liber*, with a statement that Salamina (Ireland) will be best reformed if colonies of English are sent over who will establish military garrisons in times of war, administer the laws in times of peace, and generally help to inspire the Irish to become English (fos. 107–14). Epimenides lists the benefits of colonization, which are that it is a bloodless means of making the conquered country obey the superior civilization of the conqueror, the situation in the fictional Salamina (fo. 113).[93] The colonists will serve as a garrison when required; pay a yearly rent to the governor; seek out conspiracies when necessary; and, function as beacons (a pun the author makes) to spread civilization and its laws. Such colonies need to be strong and populous, and so should be established on rich and fruitful lands. It is also important for Beacon that they be held for the life of the colonist only, so that the prince can rely on the loyalty of the tenant in question (and gain the profits on the death of the tenant), reward loyal subjects, and guard against various bad practices (intermarriage, leasing to natives) (fos. 110–12).

Solon his Follie would also seem to be a plea for the cause of the New English with their demands that strong government be devolved to the colonists (magistrates) in Ireland. The text makes a case that, under normal circumstances, Ireland will function well if it has an adequate judiciary and civil service to run the country on its own, away from England. However, in times of crisis—for Beacon, the time when the book was published, on the eve of the Nine Years War—such methods must be suspended in favour of brutal martial law. Beacon's extensive and obvious use of Machiavelli implies that his text is more transparently transgressive than Herbert's, hence, perhaps, the need for disguise. Beacon's casting of the Athenian tyrant, Pisistratus, in a role which appears to have little function beyond introducing Epimenides to Solon could be

---

[93] Beacon's discussion owes much to Niccolò Machiavelli; see *The Discourses*, trans. Leslie J. Walker and Brian Richardson, ed. Bernard Crick (Harmondsworth: Penguin, 1970), bk. 2, chs. 6–10.

read as a criticism of tyrannical government at home.[94] Elsewhere, during the discussion on how to prevent commonwealths declining, the disputants conclude that a conqueror needs to win over the hearts of the people in the newly acquired territory, and that this will flock to him if the tyrannical nobility are humbled and a better life is promised for the ordinary citizens. Such conclusions would seem to rely on Machiavelli's argument that 'A man who becomes prince with the help of the nobles, finds it more difficult to maintain his position than one who does so with the help of the people'. The further conclusion, that in conquered corrupted states it is necessary to impede the nobility and help the people in order to remove tyranny (fos. 81–2), would also seem to rely on Machiavelli's continuation of his case:

The people are more honest in their intentions than the nobles are, because the latter want to oppress the people, whereas thay want only not to be oppressed. Moreover, a prince can never make himself safe against a hostile people: there are too many of them. He can make himself safe against the nobles, who are few . . . a prince must always live with the same people, but he can well do without the nobles, since he can make and unmake them every day, increasing and lowering their standing at will.[95]

Beacon emphasizes the need to defend the ordinary native Irish against the oppressions of their masters, defending loyal subjects from rebels, handing out favours in deserving cases, and establishing Irish tenants as English freeholders (fos. 83–5), which serves to support his use of Machiavelli as a means of forming an alliance between New English colonists and Irish tenants against the oppressions of the Irish nobility and Old English (who are frequently attacked in the text (fos. 18, 42, 93, *passim*)).

Solon his Follie can clearly be read as a forceful colonial text; but it is also possible that the masked colonial writing has an ancillary function in equating the exploited Irish subjects with their English counterparts, thus using the doubly displaced geographical location in order to represent the colonizing state itself. Beacon's tart criticisms of tyranny could be seen to rebound on English as well as Irish society: Barnaby Rich noted twenty years later, 'thos wordes that in Englande would be brought wythin the compasse of treason, they are accounted wyth us in Ireland for ordynary table taulke'.[96]

---

[94] A reading hinted at but refused in the extract published in Deane (ed.), *Field Day Anthology*, 203.

[95] *The Prince*, trans. George Bull (Harmondsworth: Penguin, 1961), 68.

[96] Hinton, 'Rych's "Anatomy of Ireland" ', 91.

Beacon and Herbert were two among many figures associated with Ireland who were clearly interested in Italian culture and, specifically, Italian civic humanism and republicanism.[97] Sydney Anglo has noted that 'there are astonishingly few political treatises built substantially upon the foundation of [Machiavelli's] writings', so the appearance of so much Machiavellianism in an Irish context should strike us as significant.[98] As Lisa Jardine has indicated, Spenser's early acquaintance with Classical colonial theory and Machiavelli would almost certainly have come via his mentor, Gabriel Harvey, who participated in a series of debates on such matters with Sir Thomas Smith, author of *De Republica Anglorum* and originator of a series of disastrous colonial schemes in the Ards Peninsula, which ultimately led to the death of his son. Also present was Sir Humphrey Gilbert, one of the principal Elizabethan colonizers and explorers, who was on active service in Ireland between 1566 and 1570, where he ruthlessly suppressed the Fitzmaurice rebellion.[99] Geoffrey Fenton, the translator of Francesco Guicciardini's *History of the Wars of Italy* (1579), another significant document of Florentine thought—albeit rather less republican in emphasis than Machiavelli's writings—also served in Ireland on the Munster Plantation, and held the post of Principal Secretary from 1580, when he travelled over just before Lord Grey took up his Lord Deputyship, until his death in 1608.[100] Fenton was the father-in-law of Sir Richard Boyle, the first earl of Cork, who married Fenton's daughter Catherine in 1600, which meant that both Fenton and Spenser, who married Elizabeth Boyle in 1594, belonged to the same family, albeit at slightly different times. Boyle kept a copy of Fenton's translation as one of his most treasured possessions.[101]

Sir Walter Raleigh, Spenser's friend and neighbour on the Munster Plantation, used Machiavelli heavily in his *Maxims of State* and *The History of the World*, as well as being closely associated with others who appear to have been familiar with his writings, such as Thomas Hariot.[102] There was also the Essex circle, which was known to contain

---

[97] The background is provided in Skinner, *Foundations of Modern Political Thought*, vol. i, chs. 4–6.

[98] Anglo, 'A Machiavellian Solution to the Irish Problem', 154–5.

[99] Jardine, 'Encountering Ireland', 60–75.

[100] On Fenton's life, see *DNB* entry; Maley, *Spenser Chronology*, 93. On the contrast between Guicciardini and Machiavelli, see Denys Hay, *The Italian Renaissance in its Historical Background* (Cambridge: Cambridge University Press, 1961), 176–7; Skinner, *Foundations of Modern Political Thought*, 155–6, 161.

[101] See Canny, *Upstart Earl*, 6, 28.

[102] See Muriel Bradbrook, *The School of Night: A Study in the Literary Relationships of Sir Walter Raleigh* (Cambridge: Cambridge University Press, 1936), 72–3; Felix Raab,

many who were familiar with such writings, including Henry Cuffe (1563–1601), Essex's secretary and 'evil genius' who, like his master, was executed after his master's rebellion in 1601.[103] It is no accident that Essex's creation of a mass of knights as a power base for this rebellion, occurred in Ireland.[104] Sir John Harington (1561–1612), the queen's god-son, was one of these knights. Harington translated Ariosto's *Orlando Furioso* (1591), a work which had an undoubted influence on *The Faerie Queene*, and, when Essex visited Hugh O'Neill, earl of Tyrone, to organize a truce, Harington presented a copy to the earl, who not only got Harington to read him some extracts but 'solemnly swore his boys should read all the book over to him'.[105] The exchange illustrates how close the two sides could appear at times, part of a shared culture rather than diametrically opposed polarities, the civilized and the barbarian.[106]

In addition, there was Lodowick Bryskett, whose *A Discourse of Civil Life* (1606), was purportedly a record of a meeting of various English intellectuals in Ireland in 1582, including Spenser, Archbishop Long, the primate of Armagh, and Sir Thomas Norris, and which is one of the first sources to mention *The Faerie Queene* in its early stages. Spenser is described as 'very well read in Philosophie, both morall and naturall', but declines to contribute much to the debate on virtue—although he does make a minor intervention later on—because he has 'already undertaken a work tending to the same effect, which is in *heroical verse*, under the title of a *Faerie Queene*, to represent all the moral vertues'.[107] The treatise is dedicated to Lord Grey, a further tribute to his high standing amongst the New English. On the third day of the dialogue,

The English Face of Machiavelli: A Changing Interpretation, 1500–1700 (London: Routledge, 1965), 70–3. On Hariot and Raleigh, see John W. Shirley, 'Sir Walter Raleigh and Thomas Hariot', in id., (ed.), *Thomas Hariot: Renaissance Scientist* (Oxford: Oxford University Press, 1974), 16–35; Greenblatt, 'Invisible Bullets', 22–5.

[103] On Cuffe, see *DNB* entry. Henry Cuffe's kinsman, Hugh, was an undertaker on the Munster Plantation; see MacCarthy-Morrogh, *Munster Plantation*, 138–9. I owe this reference to Willy Maley.

[104] See G. B. Harrison, *The Life and Death of Robert Devereux, Earl of Essex* (London: Cassell, 1937), chs. 13–15; Robert Lacey, *Robert, Earl of Essex, An Elizabethan Icarus* (London: Weidenfeld & Nicolson, 1971), ch. 24. On Spenser's relationship to Essex, see Ray Heffner, 'Spenser's *View of Ireland*: Some Observations', *MLQ* 3 (1942), 507–15, at 509.

[105] John Harington to Justice Carey, Oct. 1599, in N. M. McLure (ed.), *The Letters and Epigrams of Sir John Harington* (Philadelphia: Pennsylvania University Press, 1930), 76–9.

[106] For further comment see Andrew Hadfield and John McVeagh (eds.), *Strangers to that Land: British Perceptions of Ireland from the Reformation to the Famine* (Gerrards Cross: Colin Smythe, 1994), ch. 7.

[107] Bryskett, *Discourse of Civil Life*, 26.

which mainly concerns the behaviour of the virtuous individual and the *summum bonum*, a troop of soldiers arrives, and the conversation leads on to praise of the Lord Deputy's actions in stopping the rebellions of the natives and foreign enemies. Sir Robert Dillon thanks Grey for sowing the seed with the hope of a good harvest later so that Ireland may hope to enjoy well-ordered government in the future as other commonwealths do. The company walk off up the hill, which is now decreed safe because the rebels have been rooted out and conspiracies discovered, until a servant calls them in for dinner.[108] The treatise reminds its readers how fine is the line between civilization and anarchy.

Despite such cultural complexities, shifting frontiers, and political sophistication, the last example illustrates in what fraught and dangerous times Spenser was writing. With the outbreak of the Nine Years War in 1594, when Hugh O'Neill launched the most serious offensive yet against English rule in Ireland, which finally threatened to transform the situation there into an international crisis, the Munster planters had to face the threat they had been anticipating. The first records of English being killed occur in 1594 and there was increasing hostility until the Plantation was largely destroyed in the uprising of 1598. Many Irish reoccupied the land that had been confiscated, but the Plantation was largely rebuilt after the defeat of O'Neill at Kinsale (1601) and his eventual surrender in 1603, just days after the death of Elizabeth.[109]

In such circumstances it is hardly surprising that the nature of treatises written on the Munster Plantation changed in both tone and content. Most take the form of desperate pleas for urgent military aid and are not prepared for publication (again, hardly surprising). A typical example is 'A Supplication of the blood of the English most lamentably murdered in Ireland, Cryeng out of the yearth for revenge', deposited among the State Papers in November or December 1598. The tract opens in apocalyptic vein:

ffrom the face of that disloyall and rebellious yearthe of Irland, Crieth the bloode of yo^re Ma:^ties subiects, whose bodyes dismembred by the tyranie of traytors, devowred by the merciles Iawes of ravenous woolves, humblie Craveth at the hands of yore sacred Ma:^tie (unto whom god hath comitted the sword of Iustice to punishe the offender, and upon whom he hath imposed a care and charge for the mainten[a]nce and defence of the innocent) To revenge the monstrous rapes of many poore forlorne widdowes, and the bloody murders of many yo^re

---

[108] Bryskett, *Discourse of Civil Life*, 157–9.
[109] MacCarthy-Morrogh, *Munster Plantation*, 132–3; Sheehan, 'Overthrow of the Plantation of Munster'.

faithfull subiects: And wthall, to provide for the safetie and securitie of those soules that yet remayne, and heare after shall by yo^{re} grace be placed, among those malicious and wicked sonns of Edom, amonge that faithlesse, unmercifull, Idolatrows, and unbelevinge nation of the Irish.[110]

The similarities to the world of *Colin Clouts come home againe* are significant, both in terms of the reference to the Irish wolves surrounding the embattled English colonists and of the distant queen who has become cut off from those who are truly loyal. The author, whom the editor of the treatise suggests was 'a late Elizabethan ideologue, probably a cleric' (p. 9), establishes a straightforward division between 'them' and 'us', using the intimacy of an appeal to the queen through the second person singular possessive pronoun, exhorting her to intervene. On the one side are 'yo^{re} Ma:^{ties} subiects', 'yo^{re} faithfull subiects', and, elsewhere, 'yo^{re} naturall and true subiects', the New English; on the other, 'ravenous woolves', 'that faithlesse, unmercifull, Idolatrows, and unbelevinge nation of the Irish'. The division of Ireland into two nations enshrined in the Statutes of Kilkenny has returned with a vengeance.

The 'Supplication' does preserve a clear continuity with previous works in reserving particular bile for the 'degenerate' Old English:

They were in the former tymes, as wee are now, meere Englishe in habite, in name, in nature. They nowe retaine nothinge of that they were but the bare name. Our apparell is scorned of them; o^{re} nature hated; o^{re} selves abhorred . . . the first descent, is become soe Irishe as that he hath quite forgotte himselfe to be Englishe; whose children will spitt at the sight of an Englishe man. what a change may yee thinke soe many ages, soe many generations, hath wroughte in yore English-Irishd sweete hartes? what difference (I praye yee) doe yee finde between the O Roorkes and Garaldins, betweene the O Moores and the Iacyes, betwene the O mulveanies and the Purcells, the Supples, and the McShees; Are they not neere hande all rebells to god, their prince, and their contry? Is there lesse hatred towards us in the one then in the other? Is there any more love, any more humanytie, any more conscience, any more religion in the one then in the other? They are nowe all one: *there is no difference.* (pp. 38–9, my emphasis)

Ireland is split into two implacably opposed factions, the English and the Irish, between whom there is every difference.

Spenser's own contribution to this genre, the three State Papers which are collected together as 'A Brief Note of Ireland', bears many resemblances to the 'Supplication', although its status as part of the Spenser

---

[110] 'A Supplication of the blood of the English most lamentably murdered in Ireland, Cryeng out of the yearth for revenge' (1598), ed. Willy Maley, *Analecta Hibernica*, 36 (1994), 1–90, at 13. Subsequent references are given in parentheses in the text.

canon is uncertain.[111] The second—and most substantial—piece, addressed 'to the Queen', opens, 'Out of the ashes of disolacon and wastnes of this your wretched Realme of Ireland. vouchsafe moste mightie Empresse our Dred soveraigne to receive the voices of a fewe moste unhappie Ghostes', the repetition of 'moste' highlighting the vast gulf between the powerful but distant queen and her suffering subjects in exile, who thus serve as a guilty politico-historical conscience which returns to haunt her.[112] The 'Brief Note' adds little to either Spenser's other comments elsewhere or the general body of work written by the English in Ireland in late Elizabethan times; like the 'Supplication' it eventually becomes a straightforward plea for immediate military action. The final tract, 'Certaine pointes to be considered of in the recovery of the Realme of Ireland', of which there is least doubt over Spenser's authorship, argues that a resolution must be made 'to subdue Ireland wholly with stronge force' after a proclamation has been issued giving a general pardon for ten or twelve days. Spenser notes, 'Great force must be the instrument but famine must be the meane for till Ireland be famished it can not be subdued'. As in the 'Supplication', Ireland is rigidly divided into two 'nations': 'there can be no sounde agreement betwene twoe equall contraries viz: the English and Irish' (pp. 244–5). Although Spenser makes great play of the pun 'sa(l)vage' in both his poetry and prose, indicating that the Irish 'other' needs to be redeemed as well as eliminated, such paradoxes are cast aside in the face of imminent destruction, and old dualisms inexorably reaffirmed.[113]

[111] See Ciaran Brady, 'A Brief Note of Ireland', *Sp. Enc.*, 111–12; Jean R. Brink, 'Constructing *A View of the Present State of Ireland*', *Sp. Stud.* 11 (1990, publ. 1994), 203–28, at 219; V. B. Hulbert, 'Spenser's Relation to Certain Documents on Ireland', *MP* 34 (1936/7), 345–53.

[112] 'A Brief Note of Ireland', in *Variorum*, x. 233–45, at 236. Subsequent references are given in parentheses in the text. On haunting and 'hauntology', see Jacques Derrida, *Spectres of Marx: The State of the Debt, the Work of Mourning, and the New International*, trans. Peggy Kamuf (London: Routledge, 1994), ch. 1.

[113] Cf. the essays in Stephen Greenblatt, *Marvelous Possessions: The Wonder of the New World* (Oxford: Clarendon Press, 1991). See also my review, *TP* 7 (1993), 103–9.

2

'That they themselves had wrought': The Politics of *A View of the Present State of Ireland*

PROBABLY the most influential twentieth-century critic of Edmund Spenser's poetry has been C. S. Lewis. Lewis, his opinions perhaps later bolstered by the New Critical dominance of the post-war years, was not keen to have readers delve into the historical background of Spenser's work which had been so painstakingly researched by the editors of the *Variorum* edition, finally completed in 1949. Lewis sought to move his readers away from topical references to current events in *The Faerie Queene* and towards the more significant and eternal themes of secular and divine love. Specifically, Lewis did not want his readers to explore the Irish background to Spenser's romantic epic and alleged that Ireland had corrupted Spenser's imagination, a judgement in line with that of W. B. Yeats, who regarded Spenser as fatally divided between his role as colonial official and vocation as a symbolic poet.[1] Lewis's attitude implies that poetry and politics should be kept separate. If they mix, the result is bad poetry which students should not bother to study. The circular logic of the argument serves to protect canonical literature from contemporary political events; if the latter intrude, then the work is defective and so needs to be removed from the canon: Lewis suggested that Book V of *The Faerie Queene* be kept hidden because of its unsuitable Irish subject-matter.[2]

This is a familiar story, which, none the less, should not be forgotten, especially if one wishes, as I do, to argue that Spenser's Irish experience

---

[1] C. S. Lewis, *The Allegory of Love: A Study in Medieval Tradition* (Oxford: Oxford University Press, 1936), 349; W. B. Yeats, 'Edmund Spenser', in id., *Essays and Introductions* (London: Macmillan, 1961), 356–83.
[2] On this general process see e.g. Catherine Belsey, *Critical Practice* (London: Methuen, 1980), chs. 1–2. For a recent argument, see Tracey Hill, 'Humanism and Homicide: Spenser's *A View of the Present State of Ireland*', *ISR* 4 (Autumn 1993), 2–4.

cannot just be seen as an aspect of Spenser's later poetry, but was a
constant preoccupation which both invades and haunts the texts. It is
difficult to gauge how instrumental Lewis has been in determining how
The Faerie Queene has been taught in university English departments
throughout the world and in preventing a serious consideration of
Spenser's Irish residence as at all relevant to his poetry (even though, to
all intents and purposes, he made Ireland his home after 1580, possibly
earlier).[3] Certainly in the period which stretches from the end of the
Second World War to the 1980s very little of the huge amount of
research devoted to Spenser seeks to situate him within the important
and vigorous political debates concerning Ireland carried out between
the various interested parties, despite the fact that he wrote one of the
longest and most sophisticated essays on Ireland during Elizabeth's
reign, *A View of the Present State of Ireland* (c.1596).[4] It was apparently
written in order to persuade those in authority to take the bull by the
horns, send over a huge army, and crush Irish resistance to the spread of
English authority so that Ireland could be transformed into a land
peopled by loyal subjects, profitable to the Crown at long last.[5] *A View*
survives in numerous contemporary manuscripts and was clearly circulated among important statesmen. It was entered into the Stationers'
Register in 1598 but not published until 1633, and had a major influence
on subsequent Anglo-Irish relations throughout the next century. That
A View found its way into the State Papers would imply that Spenser's
work was taken seriously, even if his suggestions were not implemented.[6] This chapter will attempt to provide an analysis of the political world in which Spenser wrote, suggesting ways in which *A View*

[3] In a posthumously published—and less well known—essay Lewis appears to have
reversed his judgement, claiming that 'we can call *The Faerie Queene* an Irish product' and
that the poem 'should perhaps be regarded as the work of one who is turning into an Irish-
man' ('Edmund Spenser, 1552–99', in *Studies in Medieval and Renaissance Literature*, collected by Walter Hooper (Cambridge: Cambridge University Press, 1966), 121–45, at 125,
126). However, despite a series of comments dealing the Irish aspects of the poem (the
'quests and wanderings and inextinguishable desires' of the narrative sharing a 'real affin-
ity' with 'the soft, wet air, the loneliness, the muffled shapes of the hills, the heart-rending
sunsets', p. 126, Lewis regards Spenser's metamorphosis ('degeneration') as in its putative
stage, and the thrust of the argument is the importance of exile to Spenser's work. The
remainder of the essay considers Spenser within the tradition of English poetry.
[4] On the date of *A View*, see William C. Martin, 'The Date and Purpose of Spenser's
Veue', *PMLA* 47 (1932), 137–43; Rudolf Gottfried, 'The Date of Spenser's *View*', *MLN* 52
(1937), 176–80.
[5] See Ellis, *Tudor Ireland*, chs. 5–6; Brady, *Chief Governors*, for details of official
Tudor writing on Ireland.
[6] For a list of the manuscripts of *A View*, see *Variorum* vol. x, app. 3, pp. 506–7. On
the early history of the printed text, see F. R. Johnson, *A Critical Bibliography of the*

can—and should—be read, and demonstrate how Spenser's imagination was absorbed with the problems of governing Ireland. While one must never make the mistake of conflating poetry and political prose, each kind of Spenser's writing is best served when read in terms of the other.[7]

A View is written in the form of a dialogue between Eudoxus, an Englishman whose name might be glossed as 'good judgement' or 'of good repute, honoured', and Irenius, who lives in Ireland (his nationality is not given, but his views and situation would seem to mark him out as a member of the New English), and whose name might be rendered variously as 'man of peace', 'man of anger', or 'man of Ireland'.[8] The dialogue wastes no time with formalities or in presenting a fictionalized setting, but plunges straight into the argument, which would seem to highlight its seriousness and connote a desired verisimilitude.[9] The text falls into two roughly equal sections: the first, where Irenius outlines the abuses and cultural inferiority of the Irish, which necessitates their transformation into reasonable subjects; and the second, where the means of effecting this change are outlined.[10] Spenser's descriptions of Ireland and Irish life, his condemnation of the Irish people's pastoral mode of agriculture, and their heretical and primitive religion, incestuous intermarriage, mixed and corrupt genealogy, wasteful use of the resources at their disposal, laziness, filthiness, false learning, tendency to be violent, excessive grief at funerals, ridiculous land titles, inherently unstable society, lechery, and so on, are all familiar variations on a theme derived from Gerald, the common currency of English commentators on Ireland in the sixteenth century and beyond.

More significant is the question of how the political rhetoric of the text functions, what makes it different from other works which use the same materials, and how that distinction can be made. Analysis of A View has often concentrated on the problem of pigeonholing the text and trying to identify it as a specific type of work and its author as a specific type of writer. A highly influential model has been drawn up by

Works of Edmund Spenser Printed Before 1700 (Baltimore: Johns Hopkins University Press, 1933), 48–53.

[7] Raymond Jenkins, 'Spenser and Ireland', ELH 19 (1952), 131–42, at 132–4. See also McCabe, 'Edmund Spenser, Poet of Exile'.

[8] For speculation on the etymologies of the names see Variorum x. 276.

[9] Cf. the opening to Beacon's Solon his Follie, fos. 3–4, which establishes the Athenian setting of the dialogue which is to ensue.

[10] For an alternative division of the text, see Bruce Avery, 'Mapping the Irish Other: Spenser's A View of the Present State of Ireland', ELH 57 (1990), 263–79.

Brendan Bradshaw, who has claimed that two divergent approaches to the reformation of Ireland existed among English politicians and thinkers. These reflected, according to Bradshaw, a radical tension discernible in English Protestantism between an outlook derived from early sixteenth-century Erasmian humanism and one of stern, unbending Calvinism. Those in the former group believed that the dominant psychological faculty was the intellect and advocated persuasion as a means of facilitating reform, whether the object were the Turks or the wild Irish, whereas the more pessimistic Calvinists argued that the mind was controlled by the will and, therefore, only coercion could subdue a recalcitrant people. Spenser's proposals in A View, according to Bradshaw, are simply 'a variation on the theme of the disciplinary [i.e. Protestant] strategy' in their insistence that 'the sword was the necessary precursor of the word', violence was to come before evangelism. A View might 'deck itself out in the clothes of humanism'—its form as a dialogue—but 'the different voice with which [it] speaks is clearly distinguishable in [its] theory of government'.[11]

Erasmus' writings against the terrible consequences of war are well known and form one of the central concerns of his ethical and political works, The Colloquies, The Adages, The Education of a Christian Prince, The Handbook of the Christian Soldier, and The Complaint of Peace, to name but a small proportion of his prodigious output.[12] However, these powerful and diverse criticisms of bellicose and violent actions may well be irrelevant so far as English responses to Ireland are concerned. It is not likely that many sixteenth-century political thinkers perceived the struggle in Ireland in terms of international conflict, nor that they constructed their own relations to Turks and Irish in the same way, however similar representations of the two peoples might have

[11] Brendan Bradshaw, 'Sword, Word and Strategy', 482, 497. See also id., 'The Elizabethans and the Irish: A Muddled Model', Studies, 20 (1981), 38–50; id., 'Edmund Spenser on Justice and Mercy', Historical Studies, 16 (1987), 76–89. Bradshaw's thesis has clearly influenced that of his student Alan Ford in The Protestant Reformation in Ireland, 1590–1641 (Frankfurt: Peter Lang, 1985), as is recognized by Nicholas Canny in 'Protestants, Planters and Apartheid in Early Modern Ireland', IHS 98 (Nov. 1986), 105–15, at 107. See also Brady, 'Spenser's Irish Crisis: Humanism and Experience', 44–6.

[12] 'The Soldier and the Carthusian', in The Colloquies of Erasmus, trans. C. R. Thompson (Chicago: Chicago University Press, 1965), 127–33; 'Dulce Bellum Inexpertis', in M. M. Phillips, 'The Adages' of Erasmus: A Study with Translations (Cambridge: Cambridge University Press, 1964), 308–53; The Education of a Christian Prince, trans. M. M. Cheshire and M. J. Heath, in Complete Works, vol. xxvii, ed. A. H. T. Levi (Toronto: Toronto University Press, 1986), 199–288; The Handbook of the Christian Soldier, trans. C. Fantazzi, in Complete Works, vol. lxvi, ed. J. W. O'Malley (Toronto:

been.[13] As Alastair Fowler has pointed out: 'although *A View* frequently uses the term "war" and represents the Irish as incompletely conquered, Spenser seems not to have thought of the Irish rebellion as war in the legal sense. Thus the Spanish massacred at Smerwick were not "lawful enemies"; nor were the Irish "rebels and traitors" who received them.'[14] Irenius, defending the actions of Spenser's ertswhile patron, Arthur, Lord Grey de Wilton, when he massacred the Spanish and Italian troops stationed in the garrison, states that the envoys 'Came forthe to entreate that they mighte parte with theire Armours like souldiours, at leaste with theire lives accordinge to the Custome of warr and lawe of nacions'. Grey refused their request specifically because 'they Coulde not iuslye pleade either Custome of war or lawe of nacions, for that they weare not anie lawfull enemyes', because they did not fight under the banner of 'the Pope or the kinge of Spaine or any other', but were 'one-lye adventurours that Came to seke fortune abroade and serve in warrs amongest the Irishe whoe desired to entertaine them'. As a result they had forfeited their lives as 'Rebells and Traytours', and the mercy they sought was refused 'for terrour of the Irishe, who weare muche embouldened by those forreine succours' (*View*, 161–2).

Irenius is keen to place the Irish outside any discourse of war, such as Erasmus' *Complaint of Peace*, which condemned the 'just war' against the Turks.[15] For Spenser, the Irish and their allies are seen to exist within the boundaries of the state, as defined by Henry VIII's Act of Supremacy and assumption of sovereignty over Ireland, so are subject to the jurisdiction of the Crown rather than the laws of international conflict. They have no legal rights outside those granted by a state which classed them as rebels.[16]

Toronto University Press, 1988), 1–127; *The Complaint of Peace Spurned and Rejected by the Whole World*, ed. and trans. Betty Radice, in *Complete Works*, xxvii. 289–322.

[13] See the extensive comments in Moryson, *Shakespeare's Europe*, bk. 1, ch. 1, bk. 2, ch. 5.

[14] 'Spenser and War', in J. R. Mulryne and M. Shewing (eds.), *War, Literature and the Arts in Sixteenth-Century Europe* (Basingstoke: Macmillan, 1989), 147–64, at 158.

[15] *Complaint of Peace*, 314. The comparison is made by Bradshaw, 'Sword, Word and Strategy', 500. On theories of the 'just war' see Philippe Contamine, *War in the Middle Ages*, trans. M. Jones (Oxford: Blackwell, 1984), ch. 10; J. Barnes, 'The Just War', in Anthony Kenny *et al.* (eds.), *The Cambridge History of Later Medieval Philosophy from the Rediscovery of Aristotle to the Disintegration of Scholasticism, 1100–1600* (Cambridge: Cambridge University Press, 1982), 771–84.

[16] For an overview of the constitutional changes see Canny, *From Reformation to Restoration*, chs. 2–3. On the political theory of rebellion in the 16th c., see Skinner, *Foundations of Modern Political Thought*, vol. ii, chs. 3–4, 7–9.

It is possible, in fact, to claim that *A View* is a particularly Erasmian text. Erasmus was no simple pacifist, but argued that a prince needed to defend his kingdom when it was threatened, and sanctioned the assassination of tyrants, neither of which views conflicts with Spenser's understanding of the massacre at Smerwick.[17] This is not identical to saying that Spenser's work is Erasmian, in the sense that Spenser was consciously influenced by Erasmus' work when writing his dialogue, for such exercises in monolinear intellectual genealogy are all too often easy to 'prove' and fraught with theoretical and empirical dangers (which is not to discount the question of 'influence', merely to render it problematic as a heuristic category).[18] In a sense, that is the point I am trying to make: many texts share similar assumptions without necessarily being related in a straightforward manner; rather, the relationship is an intertextual one where each shares a series of underlying assumptions and means of representation without being consciously related to the other.[19] However, it would be surprising if Spenser had not been closely acquainted with Erasmus' writings, amongst the most frequently read, translated, and reprinted in sixteenth-century England, and a major source for the educational ideals of Richard Mulcaster, Spenser's headmaster at the Merchant Taylors' School.[20] Erasmian echoes and influences have frequently been detected in Spenser's poetry, but parallels with *A View* remain unexplored.[21]

Nevertheless, a more helpful way to analyse *A View* might be to examine its political rhetoric and style of argument, paying attention to its modes of analysis, the emphasis given to certain points, and the sophistication (or lack of it) of its construction as a dialogue, whether the text actually opens out towards a genuine debate between the characters, or whether its form, as well as the substance of its

---

[17] *Education of a Christian Prince*, 217, 282–6; *Tyrannicida*, ed. and trans. E. Fantham and G. Rummal, in *Complete Works*, vol. xxix (Toronto: Toronto University Press, 1989), 71–123, at 112–15.

[18] See Quentin Skinner, 'Meaning and Understanding in the History of Ideas', *History and Theory*, 8 (1969), 3–53; id., 'Motives, Intentions and the Interpretations of Texts', *NLH* 3 (1972), 393–408; Brady, 'Spenser's Irish Crisis: Humanism and Experience', 20.

[19] See Julia Kristeva, *Desire in Language: A Semiotic Approach to Art and Literature*, ed. Leon S. Roudiez, trans. Thomas Gora *et al.* (Oxford: Blackwell, 1981), 15; Roland Barthes, 'From Work to Text', in Josue Harari (ed.), *Textual Strategies: Perspectives in Post-Structuralist Criticism* (London: Methuen, 1980), 73–81, at 77.

[20] J. K. McConica, *English Humanists and Reformation Politics under Henry VIII* (Oxford: Oxford University Press, 1965). On Mulcaster see the entry in *DNB*; William W. Barker, 'Merchant Taylors' School', *Sp. Enc.*, 468–9; Judson, *Life of Spenser*, 15–18; Kenneth Charlton, *Education in Renaissance England* (London: Routledge, 1965), ch. 4.

[21] See William W. Barker, 'Erasmus, Desiderius', *Sp. Enc.*, 251–2.

arguments, is simply a masquerade.[22] The text opens with a discussion of the lack of headway English laws have made in Ireland and the stubborn Irish adherence to the native practices of Brehon Law and tanistry.[23] Eudoxus declares himself shocked by such Irish intransigence and asks: 'what remedye is theare then or meanes to avoide this Inconveniaunce for without firste Cuttinge of this daungerous Custome it semeth harde to plante anye sounde ordinaunce or reduce them to a Civill gouerment, | Since all theire ill Customes are permitted unto them.' Irenius disagrees that the task is so hard: the Act which made Henry king of Ireland gave him the same 'absolute power of Principalitye' that his 'famous progenitours and worthie Conquerors of that lande' had 'and theire [the Irish] Libertis weare in his fre power to appointe what tenures what lawes, what Condicions he woulde ouer them, which weare all his, againste which theare coulde be no resistaunce, or if theare weare he mighte when he woulde establishe them with a stronger hande'. Eudoxus objects that 'perhaps it semed better unto that noble king to bringe them by theare owne accorde to his obedience', that is, effecting 'a more voluntarye and loyall subieccion' and that Elizabeth might alter various laws to the same end. But Irenius objects: 'not soe. for it is not so easye nowe that thinges are growen into an habit and haue theire certaine Course to Change the Chanell and turne theire streames another waye' (pp. 52–3).[24]

Later on, in a passage which has frequently been analysed in recent articles on *A View*, Irenius asserts that Ireland can only be reformed via the use of the sword, whereas Eudoxus claims that the use of the 'halter' will suffice. It is easy to see that the violent, invasive redress implied by the political metaphors has been prepared for from the start of the tract: persuading the Irish to obey, as Eudoxus suggests in good 'humanist' fashion, is simply not a viable proposition.

This is a problem which Erasmus foresaw. In *The Education of a Christian Prince*, written for the 16-year-old future Charles V, whose

[22] See Brady, 'Spenser's Irish Crisis: Humanism and Experience', 41. More generally see Virginia Cox, *The Renaissance Dialogue: Literary Dialogue in its Social and Political Contexts, Castiglione to Galileo* (Cambridge: Cambridge University Press, 1992), ch. 9.
[23] 'Tanistry', the means whereby a chief of an Irish sept was elected; 'Brehon Law', native Irish legal practice, most notorious to English observers for punishing murder with no more than a fine. For further details see Kenneth Nicholls, *Gaelic and Gaelicized Ireland in the Middle Ages* (Dublin, Gill & Macmillan, 1972), chs. 2–3.
[24] See Juan E. Tazón Salces, 'Politics, Literature and Colonization: A View of Ireland in the Sixteenth Century', in C. C. Barfoot and Theo D'haen (eds.), *The Clash of Ireland: Literary Contrasts and Connections* (Amsterdam: Rodolphi, 1989), 23–36, at 31.

counsellor Erasmus had just become, the young prince is advised how to enact or amend laws:

Plato rightly warns that everything else must be tried, that no stone, as they say, should be left unturned, before the supreme penalty is invoked. To persuade men not to break the law, you must first use reasoned arguments, then, as a deterrent, the fear of divine vengeance against criminals, and in addition threats of punishment. If these are ineffective, you must resort to punishment, but of a comparatively light kind, more to cure the disease than to kill the patient. If none of this is successful, then at last the law must reluctantly cut the criminal off, like a hopeless, incurable limb, to prevent the infection spreading to the healthy part.[25]

Erasmus, then, was prepared to argue for strategies every bit as ruthless in their means of defending the legitimate authority of the godly ruler as Spenser. What *A View* claims is that things have become so turbulent and anarchic in Ireland that even radical reform is doomed to failure. A reconquest must establish the ground upon which reform can take place; at every point Eudoxus objects and tries to put the case for less harsh methods, but each time is forced to concede the inadequacy of his arguments. Erasmus also works out a sliding scale, a classification, of legal judgements, which includes the possibility that force must at some point replace the use of reason ('the law must reluctantly cut the criminal off').[26]

At times there are direct linguistic parallels between the two works, when each writer resorts to identical tropes to justify and explain respective arguments. The stock image of the prince as doctor to the wounded body of the state (a commonplace of sixteenth-century political writing), appears in both texts.[27] Erasmus uses the analogy to point out that prevention is better than cure:

A reliable and skilful doctor will not resort to amputation or cauterization if he can cure the disease by compresses or a draught of medicine, and will never fall back on them unless compelled by the illness to do so. In the same way, the prince will try all other remedies before resorting to capital punishment,

---

[25] *Education of a Christian Prince*, 266. On Erasmus' status at the time, see *Complete Works*, xxvii, 200.

[26] *Education of a Christian Prince*, sec. 6.22.

[27] See D. G. Hale, *The Body Politic: A Political Metaphor in Renaissance English Literature* (The Hague: Mouton, 1971); Thomas F. Mayer, *Thomas Starkey and the Commonweal: Humanist Politics and Religion in the Reign of Henry VIII* (Cambridge: Cambridge University Press, 1989), chs. 5–6. For an analysis of *A View*, see Eamon Grennan, 'Language and Politics: A Note on Some Metaphors in Edmund Spenser's *A View of the Present State of Ireland*', *Sp. Stud.* 3 (1982), 99–110, at 103–4. The most obvious source of

remembering that the state is one body; no one cuts off a limb if it can be restored to health in some other way.[28]

Spenser's use of the trope is similarly directed towards the recovery of an organic wholeness. Irenius suggests that it is impossible to spread the doctrine of the Reformation in Ireland 'amongst swordes' because 'instruccion in religion nedethe quiett times'. Eudoxus objects, perhaps shocked, that 'Correccion shoulde begine at the howse of god' and care of the soul is more important than care of the body. Irenius agrees that Eudoxus' generalization is correct, *except in this instance* ('but not in the time of reformacion'). Again, his strategy is to invoke the rationale of the uncanny, the exception to the established rules, based on his personal experience of Ireland. His counter-argument depends on a confidence in the non-fatal nature of the disease:

for if youe should knowe a wicked persone daungerouslye sicke havinge now bothe soule and bodye sore diseased, *yeat bothe recouerable*, woulde ye not thinke it ill advizement to bringe the preacher before the phisicion? for if his bodie weare neclected it is like that his Languishinge soule beinge Disquieted by his diseasefull bodye woulde utterlye refuse and lothe all spirituall Comforte, But if his bodye weare firste recured and broughte to good frame shoulde theare not then be founde best time to | Recure his soule allsoe: so it is in the state of a realme. (pp. 138–9, my emphasis).

Spenser's analogy might seem to be far more dubious than that of Erasmus and to beg a multitude of questions: are the illnesses referred to of independent causation? If not, did they occur simultaneously, or did one precipitate the other? Is it really true that diseased bodies would refuse spiritual comfort? When Irenius says that the diseases are recoverable, who knows this: the patient and the physician, or just the physician?[29] But it is clear that both writers ground their arguments in the same currency of political discourse and employ a commonly agreed series of figures. This might imply that, whatever the conscious divergence of belief between them (Protestant versus humanist), the logic of such shared analogies would lead to the same conclusion and posit similar notions of authority.

Spenser's judgement, that the Irish have become so wilful and savage that only a strong and brutal central power can hope to effect their

such a metaphorical comparison was Aristotle, *Politics*, trans. T. A. Sinclair (Harmondsworth: Penguin, 1962), bk. 5, chs. 3, 8.

[28] *Education of a Christian Prince*, 266–7.

[29] See Grennan, 'Language and Politics', 109–10; Brady, 'Spenser's Irish Crisis: Humanism and Experience', 40–2.

transformation to obedience and civility, is one which Irenius turns to again and again throughout the dialogue. In another much discussed passage in the middle of the text which marks the shift from the analysis of Ireland's ills to concrete proposals for its reform, Eudoxus reacts strongly to Irenius' dark hint that 'the reformacion muste nowe be with the strengthe of a greate power'. Surely, Eudoxus objects, 'that mighte be with makinge of good lawes and establishinge of newe statutes with sharp penalties and punishementes' because to alter 'the whole forme of the governement' may lead to disaster: 'ffor all inovacion is perillous in so muche as thoughe it be meante for the better yeat soe manye accidentes and fearfull eventes maye Come betwene as that it maye hazzarde the losse of the wholle.' Irenius agrees, 'all chaunge is to be shonned'. The point he is making is that Ireland breaks the rules of such accepted maxims of domestic government. One has to have 'practical' knowledge to supplement one's 'intellectual' knowledge in order to understand this; one has to be 'a man of Ireland':

where ye thinke that good and sounde lawes mighte amende and reforme thinges theare amisse, ye thinke surelie amisse. ffor it is vaine to prescribe lawes wheare no man carethe for kepinge them nor fearethe the daunger for breakinge them. But all the Realme is firste to be reformed and lawes are afterwardes to be made for kepinge and Continewinge in that reformed estate (p. 147).[30]

What Irenius is saying is in many ways quite obvious. No purpose is served in establishing laws if no one is going to obey them. The law has to be enforced by an executive power which authorizes it or it will not function. One might suggest that an aporia, a fundamental split, vitiates such legal discourse: the law is both a system of rules and ordinances (sense one), as well as the very power (authority) which makes them possible (sense two). Violence is both what the law needs to uphold it and what it seeks to suppress. The one presupposes the other and they cannot be prised apart as antitheses, a site of contradiction acknowledged in Spenser's treatment of the Legend of Justice in *The Faerie Queene*, Book V (see below, Ch. 5). Irenius' comments preface his argument that Ireland *must* be sudued by the sword; only when 'the evil that is of it selfe evill' (p. 148), that is, inimical to reform, has been destroyed will the nation be made good.

It is important to recognize that this need for executive power to

---

[30]   On the distinction between types of knowledge, see Michael Oakshott, 'Rationalism in Politics', in id., *Rationalism in Politics and Other Essays* (London: Methuen, 1962), 1–36.

effect Ireland's transformation is the key to the rhetorical strategies of *A View*'s often labyrinthine arguments: such authority sanctions the political discourse of the text and, consequently, serves as its vanishing-point. Eudoxus asks Irenius how the sword actually differs from the halter (the use of laws to reform Ireland), as he cannot understand the distinction made between the metaphors: 'Is not your waie all one with the former *in effecte* which yee founde faulte with save onelye this odds that I saide by the halter and ye saie by the sworde?' (my emphasis).[31] Irenius answers that such semantic niceties matter both theoretically and practically:

> theare is surelie greate when youe shall understande it. ffor by the sworde which I named I doe not meane | The Cuttinge of all that nacion with the sworde, which farr be it from me that euer I shoulde thinke soe desperatlye or wishe soe uncharatablie: but by the sworde I meante the *Royall power of the Prince* which oughte to stretche it selfe forthe in her Chiefe strengthe. (p. 148, my emphasis).

'The Royall power of the Prince' is what makes the metaphor of the sword possible; it stands as the master trope, free from the contingent nature of other analogies and representations. The 'sworde' must reassert its right to rule Ireland and clear the ground for the legal reform which cannot take place without its effective sanction. Irenius invokes a secular authority to validate what it is possible to say, around which all arguments must circle; yet this very locus of authority can only appear through the use of a commonly agreed series of figures which flesh it out. Vanishing-point of discourse the power of the prince may well be, but it has to reappear as a part of those political discourses it authorizes. There can be no simple escape from representation, which will always threaten to engulf any confidence in an assertion of stability and truth free from the play of language.[32]

Irenius' more detailed criticisms of the English common law as used in Ireland concern its implementation rather than its substance. He notes that 'no lawes of man, according to the straighte rule of righte, are iuste, but as in regarde of the evills which they prevente and the safe-tye of the Comon weale which they provide for' (p. 65), which makes the law something pragmatic and variable rather than absolute and per-manent (Irenius is considering sense one of the law); its duty is to fit the

---

[31] For a discussion of these political metaphors, see Ciaran Brady and Nicholas Canny, 'Debate: Spenser's Irish Crisis', *P&P* 120 (1988), 201–15.

[32] See Terence Cave, *The Cornucopian Text: Problems of Writing in the French Renaissance* (Oxford: Clarendon Press, 1979); Susanne Kappeler, *The Pornography of Representation* (Cambridge: Polity Press, 1986), 2–3.

people concerned. Irenius lists a series of specific reasons why the law does not work in Ireland: Irish jurors resolutely refuse to pass objective judgement at trials, simply perjuring themselves against the queen and the loyal English; land laws are abused so that land is concealed from the Crown; wardships are used to bring children up 'lewdlye and Irishe like' (p. 73); the granting of palatinates (areas exempted from normal legal restrictions) to various nobles has been a disaster as they have 'degenerated' and become Irish; and the ability of a felon to challenge the selection of jurors proposed for his trial often means that trials are postponed indefinitely.[33] Eudoxus' suggestions that Parliament could reform some of these flaws and that heavy penalties could persuade jurors to be loyal are rejected by Irenius; the Irish Parliament, according to Irenius, is composed of those who benefit from these practices, so loopholes that would be closed in England would remain open in Ireland and the malice of Irish jurors is so ingrained that correction is futile (pp. 65–75).[34]

Irenius' judgement that the English legal system has failed to work in Ireland had been made twenty years before by William Gerrard, the Irish Lord Chancellor, who similarly concluded that no justice would come to Ireland until it had been put to the (literal?) sword. He also placed little trust in the efficacy of the common law, and referred to a court in Trim as resembling 'an English penfold for cattle'. This was in a county, Meath, which 'in estimation and every charge doubleth any of the rest'. The trials themselves were conducted in an inadequate manner: 'There assembly to serve the Queen of the poorest apparelled, like English cottagers, or worse, no crier to attend; no show of a sheriff; the proceedings for the Queen to indict and arraign as "disorderous" . . . Her Majesty may perceive how high time it is to send over English officers.'[35]

Each analysis carries an importantly different emphasis. Gerrard, unlike Spenser, did have faith in the strength of the executive backed up

---

[33] The term 'palatinate' is said to derive from 'pale', 'a pale and defence to theire inner landes so as it is nowe Called the Englishe pale'. Irenius attacks the 'abuse of some bad ones' who used the palatinate of Tipperary as 'a receptacle to robb the reset of the Countries aboute it by meanes of whose priviledges none will followe theire stealthes' (p. 74). In the 1590s, the incumbent was the queen's cousin, the tenth earl of Ormond (1531–1614), elsewhere praised for his loyalty (p. 147) and to whom the seventh dedicatory sonnet attached to the first edition of *The Faerie Queene* was addressed.

[34] For an analysis of a contemporary trial, see Raymond Gillespie, *Conspiracy: Ulster Plots and Plotters, 1615* (Belfast: Ulster Society for Irish Historical Studies, 1987).

[35] 'Lord Chancellor Gerrarde's Notes of his Report on Ireland, May 1578', *Analecta Hibernica*, 2 (1931), 93–291, at 114.

by the army to force the people to obey the existing laws; but this was because he believed that Ireland was how Eudoxus would have it, amenable to the 'halter'. Irenius' radical departure is his seeming conclusion that princely authority must be re-established.[36]

Some commentators have argued that the logic of *A View* is confused, its arguments incoherent and contradictory. Two statements of Irenius are often cited as an example of the author's inconsistency. During an early stage of the debate, he claims that the 'lawes oughte to be fashioned unto the manners and Condicion of the people to whom they are mente and not to be imposed unto them accordinge to the simple rule of righte' (p. 54); ironically, a statement which sounds like a defence of customary law against the reception of Roman civil law, as keenly debated in England, but, in fact, is part of an argument against the use of the common law in Ireland.[37] Later he reverses his comments: 'sithens we Cannot now applie Lawes to fitt the people as in the firste institucion of Comon wealthes it oughte to be we will applie the people and fitt them to the Lawes as it moste Convenientlye maye be' (p. 199).[38]

To read the two comments against each other is to ignore that the text exists formally as a dialogue. *A View* is clearly of a different generic type to *The Faerie Queene*, but this does not mean that it can be treated as if the problems of reading that complex work simply do not apply to the prose text and statements can be removed from a narrative to speak as the author's true intention.[39] As Annabel Patterson has recently pointed out, the assumption that literary and historical texts can be regarded as wholly different species has resulted in some very confused interpretations of Spenser's attitudes towards Ireland.[40]

What Irenius actually says is that laws '*oughte* to be fashioned unto the manners and Condicion of the people' (my emphasis) and this proposition is made to suggest that Ireland poses a problem because, as

[36] See Ciaran Brady, 'The Road to the *View*: On the Decline of Reform Thought in Tudor Ireland', in Coughlan (ed.), *Spenser and Ireland*, 25-45.

[37] On this legal debate, see J. G. A. Pocock, *The Ancient Constitution and the Feudal Law: A Study of English Historical Thought in the Sixteenth Century*, rev. edn. (Cambridge: Cambridge University Press, 1987), chs. 1-2; W. S. Holdsworth, *A History of English Law*, 12 vols. (London: Methuen, 1924), iv. 217-93.

[38] Brady, 'Spenser's Irish Crisis: Humanism and Experience', 36-7. See also David J. Baker, ' "Some Quirk, Some Subtle Evasion": Legal Subversion in Spenser's *A View of the Present State of Ireland*', *Sp. Stud.* 6 (1986), 147-63.

[39] See John Breen, 'Imagining Voices in *A View of the Present State of Ireland*: A Discussion of Recent Studies Concerning Edmund Spenser's Dialogue', *Connotations*, 4 (1994/5), 119-32.

[40] 'The Egalitarian Giant: Representations of Justice in History/Literature', *JBS* 31 (1992), 97-132, at 99-102.

the people are beyond reform at present, any laws fashioned to fit the needs of the Irish will clearly fail to transform them. The use of 'oughte' points to the circularity of the argument. The reason that Irenius eventually asserts that laws do not need to be made anew, as he had initially suggested should be the case, is that doing so will only breed confusion, the English in Ireland desiring to obey the laws they already know and the Irish, under good government, being drawn to true obedience. The crux of the argument, once again, rests on the need for a central authority to impose itself upon Ireland. Although, '*it be in the power of the Prince*' (p. 199, my emphasis) to change the content of the laws, it is not necessary or desirable. Irenius asserts that faulty laws can now (after the sovereignty of the monarch has been firmly established) be redressed by Parliament, which will be made up of 'frehouldes of Englishe' and 'other Loyall Ireshmen' (p. 200). The very possibility of the exploitation of the law as a code depends upon its survival as an executive authority.

Irenius, whose analysis of Ireland's evils begins with a consideration of the laws (which are to be followed by discussions of customs and religion, p. 45), deliberately leaves the debate concerning the means of reforming Ireland and his proposals to effect this until the last section of the dialogue, constantly delaying the impatient Eudoxus, who is forced to concede that Irenius' seeming circumlocutions, concerning legal theory (p. 65) and the Scythian origin of the Irish (p. 82), show that he is in control of his material. Eudoxus exhibits signs of frustration at Irenius' meanderings when the latter starts to deal with the question of the relationship between the Irish and the Scots, exclaiming, 'I wonder *Irenius* wheather ye run so farr astraye for whilste we talke of Irelande me thinkes yee ripp upp the Originall of Scottlande'. When Irenius argues that he is dealing with both countries because 'Scotlande and Irelande are all one and the same', Eudoxus compounds his sarcasm: 'That semeth more straunge. ffor we all knowe righte well that they are distinguished with a great sea runninge betwene them' (p. 83). Yet, when Irenius has finished, Eudoxus' barbed humour, perhaps reminiscent of that found in such widely read humanist dialogues as Erasmus' *Praise of Folly* or More's *Utopia*, has melted away.[41] Not only does he confess that 'This rippinge up of Ancestries is verye pleasinge unto me and indede savorethe of good conceite and some readinge

---

[41]   On the influence of these works in 16th-c. England, see Arthur F. Kinney, *Humanist Poetics: Thought, Rhetoric, and Fiction in Sixteenth-Century England* (Amherst: University of Massachusetts Press, 1986), chs. 1–2.

withall' (p. 95), a tacit reversal of his earlier comment which places positive rather than negative emphasis on the verb 'to rip' as illuminating rather than pedantic, but he also explicitly endorses the use of the seemingly anecdotal or antiquarian aside as a vital part of their discussion: 'ye bringe your selfe *Iren*: verye well into the waye againe notwithstandinge that it *semethe ye weare never out of the waye*' (p. 97, my emphasis).[42] Eudoxus has been forced to develop his conception not only of Ireland and the means of governing it, but also his understanding of the ways in which political debate has to be carried out, in a reversal which parallels Irenius' revised conception of the application of the law. According to Irenius, Ireland is beyond the comprehension of the rational humanist schooled in the methods of civilized debate and armed with a thorough knowledge of civil and common law.[43] Irenius has to do things his way because he knows how; what Eudoxus initially dismisses as red herrings he later judges to be politically astute observations. Ireland demands 'local' knowledge.[44]

The implied reader of *A View* is manipulated into accepting Irenius' judgements, which is why, I would argue, it was written as a dialogue.[45] Eudoxus always takes the position of an educated English reader; his opinions and conclusions are reasonable given the information and knowledge at his disposal. But he has to submit that an English official who has lived in Ireland qualifies his assumptions at every point through his superior knowledge. Irenius not only knows what will function in Ireland, he organizes his knowledge in the most useful way. In this case (the discussion of the laws), a particular maxim of government is given early on (laws should fit the people), which serves as a thesis or provisional statement. Eudoxus does not challenge the wisdom of Irenius' organization of their discussion, only why the specific laws of England should not be introduced: 'I Cannot see how that maie better be then by the discipline of the Lawes of Englande' (p. 54). However,

---

[42] For an alternative assessment, see Patricia Coughlan, ' "Some secret scourge which shall come by her unto England": Ireland and Incivility in Spenser', in id. (ed.), *Spenser and Ireland*, 46–74, at 65–8.

[43] On 'humanism' and humanist education, see Maria Dowling, *Humanism in the Age of Henry VIII* (London: Croom Helm, 1986); Lisa Jardine and Anthony Grafton, *From Humanism to the Humanities: Education and the Liberal Arts in Fifteenth and Sixteenth Century Europe* (London: Duckworth, 1986).

[44] See Clifford Geertz, *The Interpretation of Cultures* (New York: Basic Books, 1982).

[45] On the use of the dialogue in Renaissance England, see Elizabeth Merrill, *The Dialogue in English Literature* (New York: H. Holt & Co., 1911); Katherine Wilson, *Incomplete Fictions: The Formation of English Renaissance Dialogue* (Washington, DC: Catholic University Press, 1985); Kinney, *Humanist Poetics*.

Irenius' insistence that they deal with other issues before tackling the problem of the law serves to answer the question. When Ireland's faults and defects have been described and Irenius' proposal that the Irish are so alien, so 'other', that only a fresh conquest can restore peace and harmony has been made, it is found that there is no need to change the laws or create new ones for Ireland, as the very act of making Ireland a governable place means that it will have to become like England. On one level, the text's logic works to assume that if Ireland is to be saved, then, as another contemporary treatise bluntly concludes, it will have to become 'mearely a West England'.[46] It is the very condition of absolute difference, between the savage and the civilized, which necessitates identity in the language of *A View*'s political discourse, because all the savage (Scythian) elements have to be purged. If the Irish were not so different, if they were not savage barbarians, then the laws could be made to fit the people, and a state of contingent 'otherness' tolerated. But as things stand, the Irish constitute a threat to the imperial majesty of the queen and her right to impose laws upon her land; no dialogue can take place between colonizers and colonized, nor can any alien presence be discreetly overlooked.[47] Hence the text seeks to locate, circumscribe, and exorcize: as Adorno once remarked of another time and another place, the philosophy of pure identity is death.[48]

The implicit terror of this position manifests itself in the notorious description of the Munster famine:

Out of euerie Corner of the woods and glinnes they Came Crepinge forthe uppon theire handes for theire Leggs Coulde not beare them, they loked like Anotomies of deathe, they spake like ghostes Cryinge out of theire graues, they did eate the dead Carrions, happie wheare they Coulde finde them, Yea and one another sone after, in so muche as the verye carkasses they spared not to scrape out of theire graves. And if they founde a plotte of water Cresses or Shamarocks theare they flocked as to a feaste for the time, yeat not able longe to Continue thearewithall, that in shorte space theare weare non allmoste lefte and a moste populous and plentifull Countrye sodenlye lefte voide of man or beaste. (p. 158)

The authoritarian logic of the passage is brought out in its conclusion: 'yeat sure in all that warr theare perished not manie by the sworde but

---

[46] Anon., ' "A Discourse of Ireland" (*circa* 1599): A Sidelight on English Colonial Policy', ed. David Beers Quinn, *PRIA*, 47 (1942), sect. C, pp. 151–66, at 166.

[47] On the Tudor claim to an imperial title, see Walter Ullman, ' "This Realm of England is an Empire" ', *JEH* 30 (1979), 175–203; Franklin Le Van Baumer, *The Early Tudor Theory of Kingship* (New Haven: Yale University Press, 1940).

[48] Theodor W. Adorno, *Negative Dialectics*, trans. F. B. Ashton (London: Routledge, 1973), 362.

all by the extreamitye of famine *which they themselves had wroughte*' (my emphasis). It is the Irish rebels, reduced to the lowest form of humanity, the negation of civilized, humanist man, cannibalizing each other and so becoming what they eat as they fall into graves in a seemingly endless cycle of *self-destruction*, who have to learn the lesson of war the hard way: 'dulce bellum inexpertis' (war is sweet to the ignorant), according to Erasmus' famous dictum.[49] They have threatened the power of the prince, the very basis of any legal and social order, and so have to pay the price.[50] Their devoured and devouring bodies form a pointed contrast to the continued existence of the body politic, something strengthened, almost nourished, by their self-consumption. The splendid irony of the passage is that what Irenius has argued so long and hard for in the dialogue, the sword, is not even needed because the Irish are represented as doing the government's work for it. It is the Irish rebels who should have taken heed of Erasmus' warnings, not the English: 'The Irish . . . have a long tradition of starvation and the British a scandalous tradition of ignoring it.'[51]

On this reading of *A View*, the implied reader is led to follow Irenius' arguments so that at the end of the dialogue, like Eudoxus, s/he is convinced of the necessity of sending over a huge army to reconquer Ireland, making it ready for reformation and the establishment of proper laws. More importantly still, perhaps, s/he should be convinced of the need for government officials in England to listen to the English in Ireland and be prepared to delegate authority to those, like Irenius, who know how to govern the savage land. *A View* sends out a multitude of signals that, as Nicholas Canny has argued, it is a militantly New English work.[52]

But the description of the famine is not quite so easy to deal with and allows the possibility that it can be read against the grain of this authoritarian political rhetoric. Spenser's earlier work would seem to

---

[49] On the taboo of 'cannibalism' see Sheehan, *Savagism and Civility*, 60–1; Sigmund Freud, *Totem and Taboo*, trans. anon. (London: Routledge, 1950), 140–6.

[50] 'It were better to conquere the enemie with famine, then with yron': one of Machiavelli's 'Generall rules of warre' in *The Arte of Warre*, trans. Philip Whitehorne (1560), repr. in The Tudor Translations 59, ed. W. E. Henley (London: David Nutt, 1905), 223.

[51] Maud Ellmann, *The Hunger Artists: Starvation, Writing and Imprisonment* (London: Virago, 1993), 11. See also the description of the starving children who devour the corpse of their mother in Moryson, *Itinerary*, iii. 282–3. Comment on this passage is extensive; see e.g. Jenkins, 'Spenser and Ireland', 132; Juan E. Tazón Salces, 'Some Ideas on Spenser and the Irish Question', *Revista canaria de estudios ingleses*, 16 (1988), 105–19, at 115–16.

[52] 'Edmund Spenser and the Development of an Anglo-Irish Identity', 15.

imply that he was no friend of absolutist politics within his native land. He had made a potentially dangerous defence of the suspended puritan Archbishop Grindal against Elizabeth's heavy-handed intervention in church matters in the May eclogue of *The Shepheardes Calender* (1579), which cast the archbishop as Algrind, hardly a taxing allegorical disguise;[53] he had been openly critical of the queen during her diplomatic marriage negotiations with Alençon in the same poem, suggesting that Elizabeth was neither listening to her subjects nor discharging her responsibility towards them;[54] he had probably managed to offend William Cecil, Lord Burghley, through satirizing his corrupt style of government in *Mother Hubberds Tale*, which may have led to the suppression of the volume of *Complaints* in 1580 (it was not published until 1591) and to Spenser's decision to pursue a career in Ireland;[55] his portrayal of Duessa as Mary Queen of Scots at her trial in *The Faerie Queene*, v. ix. 36–50, angered James VI of Scotland so much that he placed considerable pressure on the English Secretary in Scotland, Robert Bowes, that 'Edward [*sic*] Spenser for his fault may be duly tried and punished';[56] and he was a known part of the Leicester circle, the most prominent and coherent group of Protestant courtiers during the middle years of Elizabeth's reign, often highly critical of her policies, notably over the Dutch Wars and the Alençon marriage negotiations.[57] In Ireland, Spenser was connected with the circle of Robert Devereux, second earl of Essex, an enthusiast for Italianate republican thought which flourished in Ireland in the 1590s and who was executed after his failed *coup d'état* in 1601. In *A View*, Irenius urges the government to appoint a suitable Lord Lieutenant 'of some of the greatest personages in Englande' to oversee the actions of the Lord Deputy in Ireland itself, remarking somewhat cryptically, 'suche an one I Coulde name upon whom the ey of all Englande is fixed' (p. 228). In late 1596, when *A View*

---

[53] Paul McLane, *Spenser's 'Shepheardes Calender': A Study in Elizabethan Allegory* (Paris: University of Notre Dame Press, 1961), ch. 9; Patrick Collinson, *The Elizabethan Puritan Movement* (Oxford: Clarendon Press, 1967), 200–1.

[54] See Hadfield, *Literature, Politics and National Identity*, ch. 6; David Norbrook, *Poetry and Politics in the English Renaissance* (London: Routledge, 1984), ch. 5.

[55] See Muriel Bradbrook, ' "No Room at the Top": Spenser's Pursuit of Fame', in id., *The Artist and Society in Shakespeare's England: The Collected Papers of Muriel Bradbrook*, vol. i (Brighton: Harvester, 1982), 19–36; Rambuss, *Spenser's Secret Career*, 90–1.

[56] Maley, *Spenser Chronology*, 67–8. See also Richard A. McCabe, 'The Masks of Duessa: Spenser, Mary Queen of Scots and James VI', *ELR* 17 (1987), 224–42.

[57] See Eleanor Rosenberg, *Leicester, Patron of Letters* (New York: Columbia University Press, 1955), chs. 6, 7 and 9; Katherine Duncan-Jones, *Sir Philip Sidney: Courtier Poet* (New Haven: Yale University Press, 1991), ch. 12.

was probably written, the most likely candidate was the earl of Essex, who had just returned in triumph from his expedition to Cadiz.[58]

Spenser, it would seem, was no straightforward 'arse-kissing poet', as Karl Marx alleged.[59] The horrific description of famine in Ireland, leading to cannibalism, would seem to anticipate the bitterly satiric ventriloquism of the logical consequences of English complacency in Swift's *Modest Proposal*, where eating babies becomes the solution to poverty and overpopulation.[60] The stress upon the suffering of the rebel Irish clearly does serve *pour encourager les autres*, in the same way that the dismemberment of traitors on the scaffold and the placing of severed heads on town walls did.[61] But, given the author's own serious clashes with authority and his deliberately fashioned role as an Anglo-Irishman in opposition to the Crown in *Colin Clouts come home againe*, the description of the fate of the Irish at the hands of a brutal order enforcing its legitimacy becomes more problematic for the reader.[62] At this point, it is arguable that the text becomes genuinely dialogic, at one level, and only for a moment, uniting both the native Irish and the New English in Ireland as victims of the policies of the English Crown and deserving equal sympathy; a paradox, of course, given their diametrically opposed aims and positions within Ireland.

More plausible, perhaps, is a reading of Spenser's depiction of the native Irish as a displaced allegory, so that they serve either as a representation, in its most extreme form, of the sufferings and frustrations of the New English *vis-à-vis* central government, or as a representation of a society which, however lacking in other respects, possesses some desirable advantages over its more powerful neighbour. Irenius' description of the Irish bards is a case in point. The bards are shown to be more powerful than the patrons they praise:

---

[58] See *Variorum*, x. 428; Norbrook, *Poetry and Politics in the English Renaissance*, 143.

[59] Norbrook, *Poetry and Politics in the English Renaissance*, 311.

[60] See C. J. Rawson, 'A Reading of *A Modest Proposal*', in J. C. Hilson *et al.* (eds.), *Augustan Worlds: Essays in Honour of A. R. Humphreys* (Leicester: Leicester University Press, 1978), 29–50. Rawson's reading would imply that the distance between his version of Swift and mine of Spenser are not so far apart.

[61] Williams, *Tudor Regime*, ch. 11; John Bellamy, *The Tudor Law of Treason: An Introduction* (London: Routledge, 1979), ch. 5; Michel Foucault, *Discipline and Punish: The Birth of the Prison*, trans. Alan Sheridan (Harmondsworth: Penguin, 1977), prologue. In an Irish context see the description of the execution of Rory Oge O'Neill in Derricke, *Image of Ireland* (1581), woodcut 6 (see below, p. 159–60).

[62] See Jonathan Dollimore and Alan Sinfield, 'History and Ideology: The Instance of *Henry V*', in John Drakakis (ed.), *Alternative Shakespeares* (London: Methuen, 1985), 206–27, at 226–7.

Theare is amongst the Irishe a certen kinde of people Called Bardes which are to them in steade of Poets whose profession is to sett fourthe the praises and dispraises of menne in their Poems or Rymes, the which are hadd in soe highe regard and estimation amongest them that none dare displease them for feare to runne into reproch throughe theire offence, and to be made infamous in the mouthes of all men | ffor the verses are taken upp with a generall applause and usuall songe att all feastes and meetinges by certeine other persons whose proper function that is which also receive for the same great Rewardes and reputation besides. (p. 124)

Irenius emphasizes how the native Irish hold poetry in a high regard, echoing Sir Philip Sidney's complaint that the lack of interest shown in poetry in England can be demonstrated by the comparative enthusiasm shown 'In our neighbour country Ireland, where truly learning goeth very bare, yet are their poets held in a devout reverence'.[63] Whereas poets in England, like Spenser, were at the mercy of both the government at court and the whims of powerful patrons, in Ireland the boot was on the other foot: not only were poets revered and feared by all of society, but they performed a central function at the equivalent of English courtly displays, where lesser servants were employed simply to echo their words.

Nevertheless, Irenius is forced to condemn their central role in a bad society. Whereas the function of poetry should be to 'labour to better the manners of men and thoroughe the sweet bayte of theire numbers to steale into the yonge spirites a desire of honour and vertue', a statement which appears to echo Sidney's concerns in *An Apology for Poetry*, the Irish bards:

are for the moste parte of another minde and so farre from instructinge yonge men in morrall discipline that they themselves doe more deserue to be sharpelye discipled for they seldome use to Chose out themselues the doinges of good men for the argumentes of theire poems but whom soeuer they finde to be most Licentious of life moste bolde and lawles in his doinges moste dangerous and desperate in all partes of disobedience and rebellious disposicion him they set up and glorifye in theire Rymes him the praise to the people and to yonge men make an example to followe. (p. 125)[64]

Irish society inverts English society in two contradictory ways: first, in giving due reverence to poets and making them central to the social

[63]   *Apology for Poetry*, 97.
[64]   See ibid. 109–15. See also John Breen, 'Spenser's "Imaginative Groundplot": *A View of the Present State of Ireland*', *Sp. Stud.* 12 (forthcoming), on the generic form of *A View*, and its relation to the ideas of Sidney.

order (the good inversion); second, in abusing this power to urge men on to oppose, rather than accept, civilized values.

A *View* is, therefore, a fractured work which pulls the reader in multitudinous ways—something its author was probably all too painfully aware of, and a judgement shared by many of its commentators, not all for the same reasons.[65] Authority is said to reside in 'the powre of the prince', yet this authority is claimed on behalf of the prince by those who wish to administer Ireland as his representatives. Even when Irenius suggests that a Lord Lieutenant should be appointed, he wants such a figure to remain in England, thus effectively devolving power to the Deputy in Ireland rather than, as might seem to some readers, reinforcing an English control over events. A *View*, in terms of its form as well as its formal arguments, makes the case that the monarch must be represented because her power in England does not easily stretch to the shores of Ireland. She cannot represent herself and so needs to be represented, viceregally, a case the dialogue makes most forcefully.[66] In order to protect the core of the constitution, responsibility must be delegated to local officials or magistrates; to guarantee the authority of the centre, its power must be devolved to the margins. Given this model of social and political interaction, it is hardly surprising that a subversive 'view' sometimes comes into play, where the neglected figures who police the peripheries of society start to identify with the enemies beyond the borders (pale), against whom they are supposed to be protecting the society of which they form a crucial part and against whom their identity is supposedly constructed. English identity in Ireland could never be taken for granted: as Eudoxus exclaims, during the discussion of the desire of the Old English to intermarry and become Irish ('degeneration'), 'Lorde how quicklye dothe that country alter mens natures' (p. 210). Both speakers roundly condemn such change and stress that English and Irish should only be

---

[65] Brady, 'Spenser's Irish Crisis: Humanism and Experience', 36–8; Brady and Canny, 'Debate'; Bradshaw, 'Sword, Word and Strategy', 482, 497; id., 'Robe and Sword in the Conquest of Ireland', 154–6; Clark Hulse, Andrew D. Weiner, and Richard Strier, 'Spenser: Myth, Politics, Poetry', *SP* 85 (1988), 378–411; Baker, ' "Some Quirk, Some Subtle Evasion" '; McCabe, 'The Fate of Irena'.

[66] See Adrian Louis Montrose, 'The Elizabethan Subject and the Spenserian Text', in Patricia Parker and David Quint (eds.), *Literary Theory/Renaissance Texts* (Baltimore: Johns Hopkins University Press, 1986), 303–40, for a relevant analysis of *The Faerie Queene*. On the concept of 'viceroyalty', see Brady, 'Court, Castle and Country', in Brady and Gillespie (eds.), *Natives and Newcomers*, 22–49, at 41–9.

allowed to interact when English control has been established so that the Irish become English rather than vice versa (pp. 209–12).

Much of Spenser's political commentary on how societies function and attempts to suggest how the English may best rule Ireland can be regarded as common currency in sixteenth-century political theory. The notion that laws should be made to fit different peoples can be found in the writings of figures as diverse as Jean Bodin (1530–96), the French theorist of absolutism, the Florentine republican, Niccolò Machiavelli (1459–1527), as well as native English sources such as Thomas Starkey's (c.1495–1538) *Dialogue between Pole and Lupset* and Sir Thomas Smith's (1513–77) *De Republica Anglorum*, and Erasmus' vast array of political writings.[67] The danger of constitutional innovation is considered by all these figures, as well as Spenser.[68] All wrote of the dangers of rebellion, and Starkey was employed by Henry VIII to write a tract condemning the Pilgrimage of Grace (1536–7).[69]

Where answers given tend to differ is over the question of the precise form of the legitimate order or sovereignty. For Starkey and Erasmus, monarchy was the best form of government, being closest to and a reflection of God's rule over the universe; both were afraid of the prospect of tyranny, a parody of God's divine government. Erasmus suggested that, as princes could never attain the ideal of perfection, 'monarchy should be checked and diluted with a mixture of aristocracy and democracy'; Starkey argued that hereditary succession was necessary for stable government, although a strict adherence to the laws of reason would conclude that election was the best method of selecting a government (Irenius and Eudoxus condemn the election of chiefs in Ireland ('tanistry') as a 'daungerous Custome' which specifically

---

[67] Jean Bodin, *Les Six Livres de la République avec L'Apologie de R. Herpin* (Paris: Scientia Aalen, 1961, facsimile of 1583 edn.), trans. Ralph Knowles as *The Six Bookes of the Commonweale* (London, 1606), bk. 6. All subsequent references are to this translation. Machiavelli, *The Prince* trans. George Bull (Harmondsworth: Penguin, 1961), chs. 1–3, 9–11; id., *The Discourses*, 194–5, 247–8, 517–18 *et passim*; Starkey, *Dialogue Between Pole and Lupset* ed. Katherine M. Burton (London: Chatto & Windus, 1948), 106; Smith, *De Republica Anglorum* ed. L. Alston (Shannon: Irish Academic Press, 1972, rpt. of 1906), bk. 1, ch. 15.

[68] Bodin, *Six Bookes*, bk. 4, ch. 3; Starkey, *Dialogue*, ch. 4; Smith, *De Republica Anglorum*, bk. 1, ch. 5; Machiavelli, *The Prince*, ch. 5. See also Justus Lipsius (1547–1606), *Sixe Bookes of Politickes or Civil Doctrine*, trans. W. Jones (London, 1594), 62–3.

[69] Smith, *De Republica Anglorum*, bk. 2, ch. 2, bk. 3, ch. 4; Bodin, *Six Bookes, passim*; Thomas Starkey, *An Exhortation to the People, instuctynge theym to unitie and obedience* (London, 1540).

prevents the establishment of 'Civill gouerment', (p. 52).[70] To ensure that absolute power did not corrupt the king, he was entitled to his throne as king in Parliament and so was not above the dictates of the law (sense one of the law, as defined earlier), something also implicit in Thomas Smith's assessment of the current functioning of the English constitution earlier in Elizabeth's reign.[71]

However, Spenser's advocation of a ruthless policy in Ireland mirrors Jean Bodin's proposals for the establishment of an orderly constitution in France. Bodin had witnessed the effects of the rise of the Huguenots and the resulting civil war. The obsessive theme of his writings is the need to ensure that rebellion does not break out; his intellectual enterprise was formulated against a tradition of French constitutionalism.[72] It was to this end that he developed his theory of 'natural law' in *The Six Bookes of the Commonweale*, which argued that absolute monarchy was the mode of social organization sanctioned by God. Bodin took issue with Machiavelli's contention that a republic was the most stable form of government, alleging that despotism, in practice, was far more durable because subjects could be controlled more easily and were unable to resist as free men were.[73] The sovereign should be the sole law-maker and so beyond the law himself except for God's absolute injunctions such as the prohibition of murder. A prince's word was as sacred as a divine pronouncement which had to be obeyed, but he could break it if necessary to preserve the life of the state.[74] The legal principle most closely associated with Bodin is that of 'equity', the notion that mercy and justice can be balanced through the specific actions of the magistrate to override the codes of common and civil law.[75] It is the

[70] Erasmus, *Education of a Christian Prince*, 231; Starkey, *Dialogue*, ch. 4; Mayer, *Thomas Starkey*, chs. 4–5.

[71] Smith, *De Republica Anglorum*, bk. 2, chs. 1–3 *et passim*. Although not published until 1583, the work was written *c*.1565.

[72] J. H. Franklin, *Jean Bodin and the Rise of Absolutist Thought* (Cambridge: Cambridge University Press, 1973), chs. 1–2; id., 'Jean Bodin and the End of Medieval Constitutionalism', in H. Denzer (ed.), *Jean Bodin* (Munich: Beck, 1973), 151–66; Skinner, *Foundations of Modern Political Thought*, ii. 284–301. Bodin's influence on *A View* has been argued before by H. S. V. Jones: see *Spenser's Defense of Lord Grey*, Illinois Studies in Language and Literature, 5 (Urbana, 1919), 7–75; *A Spenser Handbook* (New York: F. S. Crofts & Co., 1930), ch. 30.

[73] Bodin, *Six Bookes*, bk. 2, chs. 2–3; Machiavelli, *Discourses*, bk. 1. For a reading of Machiavelli which would suggest that his political thought was actually quite close to that of Bodin, see Perry Anderson, *Lineages of the Absolutist State* (London: Verso, 1974), 32, 163–9.

[74] Bodin, *Six Bookes*, 92–3. See also Machiavelli, *The Prince*, ch. 18.

[75] Bodin, *Six Bookes*, bk. 3, ch. 4; Stuart E. Prall, 'The Development of Equity in Tudor England', *American Journal of Legal History*, 8 (1964), 1–19.

linchpin of the whole political system; a principle of excess, a supplement, which serves to protect and validate the natural law in preserving
the legitimate order (i.e. sense two of the law).[76] In a crucial sense,
Bodin's 'natural law' could be said to fold over itself, to redouble
backwards and stretch the concept of law towards an immanent rhetorical collapse. Bodin has legislated for the aporia noted above; the
manifestation of the law slides between the ordinances represented and
the power to represent them. Similarly, the investment of authority in
the magistrates as representatives of the sovereign serves both to
strengthen and diffuse that centralized power, opening up the possibility that it could be turned back against itself.

Spenser would probably have known of the works of Bodin, even
though he does not mention them in his writings. Spenser's friend and
mentor Gabriel Harvey observed that one could not enter a scholar's
room at Cambridge without seeing the works of Machiavelli or Bodin's
Six Bookes of the Commonweale open on the table.[77] It is more than
likely that Spenser's discussion of equity in *The Faerie Queene*, Book V,
owes much to Bodin's development of the concept.[78] Elizabeth is
allegorized as Mercilla in v. ix, swayed by Parliament to perform the just
and ethical act of having Duessa (Mary Queen of Scots) executed
against her own feelings of pity, which, in this instance, might be
considered wilful and false.[79] She lays aside considerations of abstract
rules and individual emotion in order to act in the way most suited to
preserving the constitutional foundations of the state:

> But she [Mercilla], whose Princely breast was touched nere
> With piteous ruth of her so wretched plight,
> Though plaine she saw by all, that she did heare,
> That she of death was guiltie found by right,
> Yet would not let iust vengeance on her light;
> But rather let in stead thereof to fall
> Few perling drops from her faire lampes of light;

---

[76] See Brook Thomas, 'Reflections on the Law and Literature Revival', *CI* 17 (1991),
510–39, at 529.

[77] *The Letter Book of Gabriel Harvey, 1573–80*, ed. E. J. L. Scott (London: Camden
Society, 1884), 79–80.

[78] See James E. Phillips, 'Renaissance Concepts of Justice and the Structure of *The
Faerie Queene*, Bk. V', *HLQ* 33 (1970), 103–20; Jones, *Spenser's Defense of Lord Grey*,
ch. 4.

[79] Douglas A. Northrop, 'Spenser's Defense of Elizabeth', *UTQ* 38 (1969), 277–94;
René Graziani, 'Elizabeth at Isis Court', *PMLA* 79 (1964), 376–89. See also John E. Neale,
Elizabeth I and her Parliaments, 2 vols. (London: Cape, 1957), vol. ii, pt. 2, chs. 1–2.

> The which she couering with her purple pall
> Would haue the passion hid, and up arose withall.

(v. ix. 50)[80]

Elizabeth as queen in Parliament affirms her authority in bowing to the logic of her represented subjects who desire to protect her from herself in failing to consider their interests. Elizabeth is shown feeling the need to disguise her inappropriate emotions; her public body has to be seen to control her private body.[81]

A similar principle seems to have been employed in a markedly different—but consistent—way in another context within *A View*. The invocation of the rights of conquest enables Spenser to justify an imperial, absolutist monarchical order, reminiscent of Bodin's conception of the French state, in English-ruled Ireland.[82] Irenius relies upon the myth of an original British conquest and submission of the Irish rulers to Gurguntius and, later, Arthur (see below, pp. 96–7). After the British invasion, the Saxons 'did whollye subdue it unto themselves' (p. 95), then Henry II 'utterlye vanquished and subdued' (p. 56) the Irish, before the Parliament of Henry VIII reaffirmed the English monarch's ancient rights when 'All the Irishe Lordes and principall men came in and beinge by faire meanes wroughte thereunto Acknowledged kinge *Henrye* for theire soueraigne Lorde' (p. 48). An original moment of supposedly voluntary submission, repeated on various occasions afterwards, is used to justify an 'absolute power of Principalitye' (p. 52) which can condemn as illegal anything which threatens its authority—including the Irish Parliament.[83]

Irenius' argument and construction of a locus of power would seem to have much in common with Bodin's—which is not to claim that they are *necessarily* derived from *The Six Bookes of the Commonweale*, simply that they both share a style of argument and a possible common root. Irenius' invocation of the rights of conquest could be read as the 'natural law' of equity writ large, the founding of a central authority sanctioned by God whose duty is to protect itself. Ireland in *A View* is the place

---

[80] Phillips, 'Renaissance Concepts of Justice', 115–20; see also the discussion in Colin Burrow, *Epic Romance: Homer to Milton* (Oxford: Clarendon Press, 1993), 132–9.

[81] Ernst H. Kantorowicz, *The King's Two Bodies: A Study in Medieval Political Theology* (Princeton: Princeton University Press, 1957), 171.

[82] See the discussion in Hans Pawlisch, *Sir John Davies and the Conquest of Ireland: A Study in Legal Imperialism* (Cambridge: Cambridge University Press, 1985), 9–11, 167–8 *et passim*.

[83] Ibid., chs. 1–3. See also Ch. 3 n. 82 below, and Salces, 'Politics, Literature and Colonization', 31.

where the usual functions of the law have to be forgotten and the experience of the magistrate, like Irenius, relied upon.[84] Just as Bodin argues
that the vicious state of nature when mankind preyed upon itself led
to the formation of communities and the surrender of individual liberty
for the greater good of civil society and overall security, so Irenius
points to the degeneration of the Irish when not under English rule:

> Trewe it is that thearby they bounde themselves to his [Henry VIII's] lawes and
> obedience, and in case it had bynne followed uppon them, (as it shoulde haue
> bene) and a gouernement thereauppon presentlye setled amongest them agre-
> able thereunto they shoulde haue byne reduced to *perpetuall Civilytie and
> Contayned in Continuall dewtye* . . . but beinge straighte left unto themselves
> and theire owne inordinate life and manners they eftsones forgote what before
> they weare taughte and soe sone as they weare out of sighte by themselves
> shoke of theire bridles and begane to Colte anewe more licentiouslye then
> before. (p. 49, my emphasis).

The Irish are represented as animals ('colts') who need to be tamed and
broken in, a common image.[85] The historical correlative of this analysis
is Irenius' argument that the English had the common law imposed upon
them by William the Conqueror, a harsh act performed for their own
good. The development of customary law cannot take place without the
establishment of the institutions which sanction it. Irenius claims that
'all Lawes are ordayned for the good of the Common weale and for
repressinge of licenciousnes and vice' and he employs the stock image of
the doctor/patient noted above: 'it falleth out in Lawes no otherwise
then it dothe in Phisicke, which was firste devised and is yeat dailye
mente and mynistred for the healthe of the patiente' (p. 46). He argues
that England had been a 'peaceable kingedome' under Edward the Con-
fessor and had agreed to accept William the Conqueror's rule and constitutional innovations because people felt that nothing could be worse
than the tyranny of Harold (Godwin) the usurper. However, 'the profe

---

[84] Bodin stresses the importance of magistrates to the functioning of 'equity' and the
law; *Six Bookes*, bks. 3–4. Calvin, another political theorist who places huge importance
on the role of magistrates, states that only magistrates are permitted to depose a tyrant; see
Jean Calvin, *Institutes of the Christian Religion*, trans. F. L. Battles, ed. J. T. McNeill,
2 vols. (London: SCM Press, 1961), ii. 1516–21. For a discussion of the two positions, see
Franklin, *Jean Bodin*, 94–7. On Spenser's relation to Calvinism, see Anthea Hume,
Edmund Spenser: Protestant Poet (Cambridge: Cambridge University Press, 1984), 61–4;
King, *Spenser's Poetry and the Reformation Tradition, passim*.

[85] See Derricke, *Image of Irelande*, 41; Patricia Coughlan, ' "Cheap and common ani-
mals": The English Anatomy of Ireland in the Seventeenth Century', in Thomas Healy and
Jonathan Sawday (eds.), *Literature and the English Civil War* (Cambridge: Cambridge
University Press, 1990), 205–23.

of the first bringinge in and establishinge of those Lawes . . . was to manye *full bitterlye made knowen*' (p. 47, my emphasis). Such suffering does not alter Irenius' opinion that laying the common law 'upon the necke of Englande' was a necessary and beneficial act. He suggests that the process will be worse in Ireland because the Irish are torn apart by internal conflict and know no civilized laws, but must not be avoided. Rhetorically, the counterpart is the harrowing description of the Munster famine where a state of nature threatens to undermine the natural law. A case can be made that the principle of equity, justice as exception and self-protection, is inscribed in the very rhetorical structure of *A View*'s most crucial set-pieces, analogies, and anecdotes, as well as being the logical basis for its formal arguments.

Spenser's conception of natural law both hides and reveals. In serving as the crucial device—or trope—which holds the text together, it also exists as the 'stitched seam', disguised yet visible, which enables the reader to pull it apart. In the former role, an attempt is made to end political discussion through the revelation of a principle which goes beyond what can be questioned and so abruptly halt legitimate debate; in the latter role, the (re)discovery of a rhetorical sleight of hand passed off as a limit to discourse pushes the text back into the public realm.

If *A View* would seem to validate an absolutist politics, it also comes dangerously close to supplanting the authority of the queen's title to Ireland in favour of her loyal English subjects in residence there.[86] In a sense, *A View* is caught between the politics of Bodin and the republican Machiavelli of *The Discourses* in a double movement simultaneously centripetal and centrifugal. Machiavelli is mentioned only once in *A View*, towards the end of the text, which in itself may signify that a lot of what went before owes much to his writings. Irenius uses Machiavelli as another authority to support his argument for devolved power in Ireland:

this I remember is worthelye observed by machiavell in his discourse uppon Livie wheare he Comendethe the manner of the Romaines gouernement in givinge *absolute power* to all theire Consulls and gouernours which if they abused | they shoulde afterwardes dearlie Answeare and the Contrarye thereof he reprehendethe in the states of Venice of florence and manye other principalities of Italye whoe used to limitt theire Chief officers so streightlye as that theareby some times they haue loste suche happie occacions as they coulde neuer come unto againe, the like wheareof who so hathe bene Conuersante in the government of Irelande hathe to often sene to theire great hurte (p. 229).

---

[86] See Baker, ' "Some Quirk, Some Subtle Evasion" ', for a related argument.

The passage recalls *The Discourses*, book II, section 33, which deals
with the need to devolve military power to individual generals, and, possibly, Machiavelli's praise of Cesare Borgia, the strange hero of *The
Prince*, for bestowing power on his general, Remirro de Orco, letting
him take the blame for the harsh rule imposed in Romagna, before having him put to death in the square.[87] On the one hand, Machiavelli
would seem to function like the other authorities (Classical and contemporary) cited in *A View* and this can be passed over as another piece
of supporting detail to help Irenius' argument that power needs to be
devolved to the magistrates and governors concerned. But, given the significance invested in so many authorities within the text, even ones mentioned no more than once (see below, Chapter 3, for further examples),
it is not safe to conclude that nothing can be read into a strategic citation
of Machiavelli. The reference perhaps serves two related functions:
first, Machiavelli's name lends weight to Irenius' conclusions that
devolved power is the only sensible defence of the central authority;
second, although Machiavelli is made to sound as though his political
theory coincides exactly with that of figures like Bodin, the deliberate
reference possibly signals an awareness of, if not involvement in, the
development of a series of alternative political ideas in Irish intellectual
society, ones which openly criticized the Queen and defended the rights
of subjects.[88]

Would this reference, in itself, have been enough to have explained
the non-appearnce of *A View* after it was entered into the register of the
Company of Stationers (the Stationers' Register) in 1598? It has been an
almost axiomatic assumption amongst recent scholars of the text that it
met with official disapproval, which was why it remained unpublished
until 1633, thirty-four years after Spenser's death. Many argue the work
was censored because its political rhetoric and analysis challenged the
assumptions of the authorities centred around the monarch (primarily,
the Privy Council).[89]

On 14 April 1598, the printer Matthew Lownes entered into the Stationers' Register 'a booke intituled A viewe of the present state of Ireland. Discoursed by way of a Dialogue betwene EUDOXUS and

---

[87] Machiavelli, *The Discourses*, 381–2; id., *The Prince*, 57–8; Edwin A. Greenlaw, 'The
Influence of Machiavelli on Spenser', *MP* 7 (1909), 187–202, at 198–9; *Variorum*, x, 429.

[88] See Jones, *Spenser's Defense of Lord Grey*, ch. 4; McCabe, 'The Fate of Irena',
109–11. Raab points out that Machiavelli was often used but rarely cited, and that his
work was cast a whole host of different ways: *English Face of Machiavelli*, 86.

[89] Jonathan Goldberg, *James I and the Politics of Literature: Jonson, Shakespeare,
Donne and their Contemporaries* (Baltimore: Johns Hopkins University Press, 1983), 9;

IRENIUS. uppon Condicion that hee gett further aucthoritie before yt be prynted'.[90] Although more than fifteen manuscripts remain extant, the work did not appear in print until Sir James Ware published it as one of his four *Ancient Irish Histories*, along with those of Campion, Hanmer, and Marleborough's brief continuation of the latter.[91] Ware commented in his preface that 'we may wish that in some pasages it had bin tempered with more moderation', blaming Spenser's harshness on '[t]he troubles and miseries of the time' and suggesting that 'if hee had lived to see these times, and the good effects which the last 30 yeares peace have produced in this land, both for obedience to the lawes, as also in traffique, husbandry, civility, and learning, he would have omitted those passages which may seeme to lay either any particular aspersion upon some families, or generall upon the Nation'.[92] Ware obligingly cut out references to Anglo-Irish magnates and some of Spenser's severest comments on native Irish and Old and New English inhabitants of Ireland in order to render the text less offensive and anachronistic.[93]

Such evidence would seem to confirm that it is a reasonable inference that *A View* was censored. Ware's use of the term 'Ancient' in the title of his anthology suggests a certain nervousness about the legitimacy of his project and a desire to neutralize any attempt to read the histories in terms of contemporary Irish history. Furthermore, given that Spenser's text is the only one of the four significantly altered, Ware's anxiety was presumably concerning *A View*, as the comments in the preface indicate.[94] The reader of the 1630s is invited to read *A View* purely as an antiquarian work, or as an example of an ancient (dead) historical tradition.[95]

Baker, ' "Some Quirk, Some Suvbtle Evasion" ', 151–2; Clark Hulse, 'Spenser and the Myth of Power', *SP* 85 (1988), 378–89, at 387; Brady, 'Spenser's Irish Crisis: Humanism and Experience', 25; Avery, 'Mapping the Irish Other', 264; Norbrook, *Poetry and Politics in the English Renaissance*, 143.

[90] *A Manuscript of the Stationers' Register, 1554–1640*, ed. Edward Arber, 5 vols. (London: privately printed, 1875–94), iii. 34. See also Brink, 'Constructing *A View*', 204–9, which reaches some conclusions similar to mine.

[91] Sir James Ware (ed.), *Ancient Irish Histories*, 2 vols. (Dublin, 1633), i. 1–293. For a list of manuscripts, see *Variorum*, x. 506–16.

[92] Ware, *Ancient Irish Histories*, i. 3.

[93] Ware's preface and a list of his excisions are conveniently reprinted in *Variorum*, x. 516–24, 530–2.

[94] Hanmer's *History of Ireland* is an antiquarian work which does not deal with Tudor policies in Ireland; Campion's *Two Bokes of the Histories of Irelande* contains one book which deals with antiquarian material, while the other, which does deal with the Tudor policies of the 1560s, contains none of the aggression of Spenser's comments.

[95] For some reflections on a related problem, see A. J. Polan, *Lenin and the End of Politics* (London: Methuen, 1984), ch. 1.

The entry in the Stationers' Register would also seem to provide further support for a conspiracy theory. Entries can be divided into roughly three types: those which grant licence to the printer who has submitted the work on the payment of a fee; those which demand that the printer needs to discover whether anyone else has rights in the work in question; and those which demand that the printer get further permission before the work can be published. The smallest category by far is the third, although a number of examples can be cited from the 1590s, and Jean Brink has estimated that 15 per cent of entries in the Stationers' Register between January and June 1598 are queried in some way.[96] However, it needs to be borne in mind that the purpose of entering books in the Stationers' Register was not primarily to have them checked by censors; rather, it was to register them as the property of the individual printer, in other words, an early form of copyright law.[97] The need for Matthew Lownes to get 'further aucthoritie' before he could publish A View does not necessarily mean that the text was put aside for state censors to examine further ; there might have been other explanations for its non-appearance. There is no clear evidence that the text was censored as survives in other cases like that of Samuel Harsnett's attempt to publish John Hayward's Henry IV, probably the most notorious case of Tudor censorship.[98]

Books did indeed sometimes fail to appear for other reasons.[99] It is not beyond the bounds of possibility that A View was not published simply because its author died before the text was ready for publication. Spenser died on 13 January 1599 and, given his close involvement with William Ponsonby in the publication of The Faerie Queene, as well as other works which appeared in his lifetime, there might not have been adequate time for the preparation of a carefully produced manuscript, especially given Spenser's attempts to oversee the production of his works (unusual by sixteenth-century standards) and his permanent residence in south-west Ireland.[100]

---

[96] Including the two previous entries in the Stationers' Register before A View (iii. 34), one of which was Henry Petowe's continuation of Christopher Marlowe's Hero and Leander, held up over a dispute between printers over rights in the work, and which appeared in print in the same year (1598): see Brink, 'Constructing A View', 208.

[97] John Feather, A History of British Publishing (London: Croom Helm, 1988), ch. 3.

[98] W. W. Greg, 'Samuel Harsnett and Hayward's Henry IV', in Collected Papers, ed. J. C. Maxwell (Oxford: Clarendon Press, 1966), 424–36.

[99] See W. W. Greg, 'Entrance in the Stationers' Register: Some Statistics', ibid. 341–8; id., Some Aspects and Problems of London Publishing between 1550 and 1650 (Oxford: Clarendon Press, 1956), passim.

[100] Michael Brennan, 'William Ponsonby: Elizabethan Stationer', Analytical and Enumerative Bibliography, 7 (1983), 91–110, at 96; id., 'William Ponsonby', Sp. Enc., 554–5.

A much more likely explanation is that *A View* failed to appear because of a serious dispute between the members of the Stationers' Company over the rights in Spenser's work. Matthew Lownes was involved in a series of conflicts with the much more powerful William Ponsonby over rights to publish the works of both Spenser and Sir Philip Sidney. Ponsonby had publicly stated his co-operation with Spenser in 'The Printer to the *Gentle Reader*' which prefaced the 1591 publication of Spenser's *Complaints*. In the same text he wrote of his attempt to trace the manuscripts of some of the poet's 'smale Poemes', which he had 'heard were disperst abroad in sundrie hands . . . some of them having bene diverslie imbeziled and purloyned from him [Spenser], since his departure over Sea'.[101] Ponsonby was understandably concerned that none of Spenser's—or Sidney's—texts should fall into unauthorized hands. In addition to being accepted as the official publisher of both Sidney and Spenser, Ponsonby was also an important figure within the Stationers' Company: in 1588 he had been elected to the livery of the company, and, more pertinently, in 1597–8, he was made an assistant and then a warden.[102]

Lownes's attempt to have *A View* published would appear to be an act of literary poaching. It is possible that one of the texts in circulation fell into Lownes's hands, with or without the author's permission, and he attempted to make money from it on the back of Spenser's burgeoning reputation. Ponsonby would presumably have been less than delighted at the prospect of another stationer laying claim to one of his major authors, especially given the fact that Lownes had already had an unauthorized text of Sidney's *Astrophil and Stella* published in 1597, a year ahead of Ponsonby's official edition. Spenser's *View* might well have been a victim of a powerful stationer's ire at an attempt to pirate an edition. Evidence would suggest that, by 1598, Ponsonby would certainly have possessed the power within the Stationers' Company to hinder Lownes's pursuit of a licence.

But this speculative hypothesis neither disproves the censorship of *A View* nor explains why Ponsonby himself never produced an edition. It is more than likely that the submission of the text for licensed publication would have raised a few official eyebrows anyway. An inspection of the records of the Stationers' Register should alert us to the fact that hardly anything dealing with Ireland was entered, let alone published,

---

[101] *Variorum*, iii. 33; Brennan, 'William Ponsonby: Elizabethan Stationer', 93, 99.

[102] Brennan, 'William Ponsonby: Elizabethan Stationer', 99–100. See also Brink, 'Constructing *A View*', 209.

during Elizabeth's reign. Nothing appeared in the 1560s; the records for most of the 1570s are lost; five texts were entered in the 1580s; three in the 1590s (including *A View*) and four in the period between 1600 and Elizabeth's death in 1603. Of these twelve entries, two are ballads, six are early newsbooks or broadsides (three of these celebrations of the victory at Kinsale in 1601), one a tract against rebellion, one a token of the citizens of London's support for the earl of Essex's expedition to Ireland in 1599, John Derricke's *The Image of Irelande* (1581), and *A View*.[103]

What is clear from this list is that Spenser's dialogue was the only analytic, exhortationary work on Ireland entered into the Stationers' Register during Elizabeth's reign. Although the soldier–poet Thomas Churchyard wrote numerous treatises which dealt in part with Ireland during this period which were entered into the register, it is noticeable that none of them contained the word 'Ireland' in the title.[104] Barnaby Rich, whose literary career spanned the reigns of both Elizabeth and James, wrote works dealing with Ireland throughout, but only in 1609 did he publish a work which mentioned 'Ireland' in the title.[105] After that point he became the only Jacobean author to use the word frequently in his book titles.[106]

It is possible that if *A View* was proscribed, it could have been censored for any number of reasons, possibly just for mentioning Ireland in its title, as we have no reason to assume that censors were any more assiduous and careful readers than they are now, or that the mechanisms of censorship worked in a more complex way. *A View* was submitted in 1598, a particularly sensitive year, when there seemed a real chance that Hugh O'Neill's rebellion would succeed. The sacking of the Munster Plantation later that year saw many unpublished tracts explaining the disaster (including another probably by Spenser), but these remain among the State Papers and none was entered into the Stationers' Register to be considered for publication (evidence which further suggests that Lownes's attempt to try and publish *A View* was highly unusual).[107]

---

[103] For full details see Appendix.

[104] See e.g. *A Generall Rehearsall of Warres* (1579); *A Scourge for Rebels* (1584).

[105] *A Short Survey of Ireland* (1609).

[106] After his *Short Survey*, Rich also wrote *A New Description of Ireland* (1610), *The Irish Hubbub* (1617), and *A New Irish Prognostication* (1624), among other works; previously he had written *Allarme to England* (1578) and *The Fruits of Long Experience* (1604), which discuss Irish affairs. In the whole of James's reign, I have counted only fourteen works in total which mention Ireland in the title, or are obviously dealing with Irish affairs, a rate of submission which only just outstrips that of Elizabeth's reign.

[107] See e.g., 'The Supplication of the blood of the English'; 'Paper on the Condition of Ireland endorsed by Sir Robert Cecil, "Observations" ' (1598) *CSPI* (1598–9), 443–5; 'A

The only tract published which compares to Spenser's *View* in the depth and breadth of its political analysis is Richard Beacon's *Solon his Follie* (1594). This work, by another official on the Munster Plantation, may have escaped official ire because it appeared at a less critical time than *A View* and was, to a certain extent, a disguised allegory; but, more likely, because it was published in Oxford rather than London. The Royal Charters which established the monopoly of printing for the Stationers' Company in 1557 and 1559 allowed the presses set up in Oxford and Cambridge to remain outside the jurisdiction of the company and free from its injunctions. While books published in the capital (supposedly all books) had to be licensed by the approved authorities (the law was changed in 1586 to make these the Archbishop of Canterbury and the Bishop of London, who were, of course, forced to delegate responsibility to secretaries and chaplains), those published in Oxford did not.[108] It is probably the case that *Solon his Follie* escaped censorship by default, having been published through the back door quite deliberately. The author or printer was certainly not at pains to advertise the contents of the work by placing the word 'Ireland' in the title.

What these rather unsatisfactory pieces of information prove is open to question. Perhaps some tentative conclusions can be drawn. It is quite possible that *A View* was censored, despite the lack of direct evidence, simply because it dealt with the problem of government in Ireland at a sensitive time. Its entry in the Stationers' Register can be regarded as odd and its publication would have been another departure from previous practice throughout Elizabeth's reign. It is possible that Spenser himself had nothing to do with the attempted publication of the work and that that had to do with a publisher's desire for profit rather than a more sophisticated intellectual motive. Certainly, there is little in common between the rigorous discussion of policy in *A View* and the collection of impressionistic prejudices and observations of the Irish gathered in the works of Barnaby Rich, John Derricke, and Thomas Churchyard.[109] *A View* would appear to have been written for manuscript circulation rather than publication, as the number of surviving manuscripts

Book on the State of Ireland, addressed to Robert, Earl of Essex by H. C.', *CSPI* (*1598–9*), 505–7; 'A Brief Declaration of the State wherein Ireland now standeth' (1599), *CSPI* (*1599–1600*), 365–70; Edmund Spenser, 'A Brief Note of Ireland', *Variorum*, x. 235–45.

[108] See Frederick Seaton Siebert, *Freedom of the Press in England, 1476–1776: The Rise of Government Censorship* (Urbana: University of Illinois Press, 1952), 61–2; Feather, *A History of British Publishing*, ch. 3; Greg, *Aspects and Problems*, ch. 1.

[109] For comments on these authors see Hadfield and McVeagh (eds.), *Strangers to that Land*, chs. 3–4.

suggests.[110] Its rhetoric was probably intended to persuade those in high places to adopt its political strategies, and not an attempt to impress a widespread audience, unlike most of the printed texts which discussed Ireland at this time.

Such conclusions are speculative and tentative; but they are much less dangerous and misleading than the straightforward assumption that *A View* was censored *specifically* because it was an especially transgressive text. Spenser's Irish politics appear to have always had the power to disturb and offend readers from the sixteenth to the late twentieth century, something tacitly acknowledged in the development of the dialogue, as Irenius' increasingly drastic proposals horrify Eudoxus' sense of political propriety.[111] Whether those in power sought to silence their author, or singled him out for special attention, is, however, by no means clear.

[110] See Christopher Hill, 'Censorship and English Literature', in *The Collected Essays of Christopher Hill*, i. *Writing and Revolution in Seventeenth-Century England* (Brighton; Harvester, 1985), 32–71; Harold Love, 'Scribal Publication in Seventeenth-Century England', *TCBS* 9 (1987), 130–54. I owe these references to Paul Hammond.

[111] For a relatively recent public exchange, see John Arden, 'Rug Headed Kerns and Irish Poets', *New Statesman*, 13 July 1979, pp. 56–7; Helen Watanabe-O'Kelly, 'Edmund Spenser and Ireland: A Defence', *PNR* 14 (1980), 16–19.

3

'Ripping up ancestries':
The Use of Myth in *A View of the*
Present State of Ireland

DURING the course of their discussion regarding the customs of Ireland and their baneful influence on its current political and social state, the conversation between Irenius and Eudoxus turns to the question of the origin of such practices. Irenius argues that such knowledge will be beneficial for their aim of determining a means of reforming contemporary Ireland, as well as interesting given the ancient origins of the Irish people, but that, unfortunately, the subject is too large for his current purposes and that he will limit his talk 'to tuche suche Customes of the Irishe as seme offensive and repugnante to the good government of that realme'. Instead, he suggests that 'maye be we maye at some other time of metinge take occacion to treate thearof more at lardge' (p. 82). Eudoxus concurs, and he ends the dialogue reminding Irenius of his words: 'I thanke youe *Iren*: for this your gentle paines withall not forgettinge now in the shuttinge up to put youe in minde of that which ye haue formerlye halfe promised that heareafter when we shall mete againe uppon the like good occacion ye will declare unto us those your observacions which ye have gathered of the Antiquities of Ireland' (pp. 230–1).

Sir James Ware, in his preface to the first published edition of *A View*, claimed that the non-appearance of this volume had simply been caused by Spenser's death.[1] It is equally possible that Spenser never intended to write the volume, but was teasing the comfortable humanist English reader of the tract who would have time to digest such knowledge at leisure, as opposed to the English reader resident in Ireland who would have had more pressing concerns. The fact that Eudoxus insists on

---

[1] Cited in *Variorum*, x. 430.

returning to Irenius' suggestion, as if that were the keynote of the text and, for him, the most fascinating part of that text, may well indicate a somewhat misplaced sense of concern. Irenius stresses that such knowledge has to be used to support an immediate political need, the safe foundation of the kingdom. *A View* does indeed contain a vast amount of antiquarian information which perhaps obviates the need for the further volume, an irony which would appear to be too studied to be accidental. What information there is, and the way it is used, serves a clear political purpose. Eudoxus, the English antiquarian and new student of Ireland may not realize that his thirst for ancient genealogies and customs has more relevance than is at first apparent to him. Although Eudoxus sometimes complains that Irenius wanders from the focus of his subject into antiquarian asides, the logic of Irenius' arguments and the careful connections he makes demonstrate that it is Irenius who grasps the true importance of the subject.

After Irenius' comments on the use of antiquities, the conversation does focus upon the ancient history of Ireland and the Irish in an attempt to chart the origins of their current customs, examining their links to the Spanish, Gauls, Africans, and Goths, as well as examining the history of the Scots, 'for Scotlande and Irelande are all one and the same' (p. 83).[2] Irenius makes the claim that, although little evidence remains, the Britons once inhabited Ireland, which they conquered and extensively colonized. The reason for the scanty remnants of such a significant historical event, according to Irenius, is that the subsequent invasions of Saxon and English involved the removal and/or absorption of the previous British settlers. However, he continues, some fragmentary etymological traces survive in Leinster: the clan of the Tooles being named from the 'olde Brittishe worde *Tol* that is an hillye Countrie', the Brins from a British word 'That is woddye', and the Cavanaghs from 'Caune' meaning 'stronge'. When a fugitive in this area seeks aid, he uses the old British word '*Cumeraigh*' or 'Cummericke' which means, unsurprisingly, 'help'. Of the British occupation there is also testimony from the Classical world: 'Irelande is by Diodorus *Siculus* and by *Strabo* Called Britannia And a parte of greate Britaine.'[3] As if this were not enough evidence, Irenius adds 'ffinallye it appearethe by good recorde yeat extante that kinge Arthur and before him Gurgunt had all that Ilande in

    [2] On the relationship between the Scots and the Irish in *A View* see Maley, 'The View from Scotland'.
    [3] See Rudolf Gottfried, 'Spenser as an Historian in Prose', *TWASAL* 30 (1937), 317–29, at 324.

his Allegiance and Subieccion', a British claim to Ireland which was
reinforced by subsequent Saxon invasions:

After all which the Saxons succedinge did whollye subdue it unto themselves for
first Egfide K: of the Northumbs did utterlye waste and subdue it As Appearethe
out of Bedas Complainte againste him And afterwardes kinge Edgar broughte it
under his obedience as appearethe by an ancient recorde in which is written that
he subdued all the Islands of the Northe even unto Norwaye and theire kinges
did bringe into his Subieccion. (p. 94–5)

Spenser is here basing his argument upon a host of precedents, as the
story enjoyed a common currency among English writers on Ireland, as
well as employing a style of evidence common within colonial propaganda.[4] Two types of authority are interrelated: a series of foreign remnants of a previous invasion enshrined in the language, and the existing
culture or the testimony of ancient authority. What perhaps seems most
curious is the reliance upon the Arthurian legends and the matter of
Britain, principally, as I shall demonstrate, through the use of Geoffrey
of Monmouth. In the letter to Raleigh which was appended to the first
edition of *The Faerie Queene* (1590), Spenser claimed that he had used
Arthur as his epic hero to represent 'magnificence' 'as most fitte for the
excellency of his person, being made famous by many mens former
workes, and also *furthest from the daunger of envy, and suspition of
present time*' (*FQ*, p. 737, my emphasis).[5] This seems an odd statement
to take at face value when Spenser is prepared to use the history of
Arthur in order to help justify an English right to rule Ireland. Perhaps
context is the key: if *The Faerie Queene* was aimed at a wider, British,
audience, then the legends serve a less specific purpose and Arthur, presumably, plays a less contentious role. *A View*, having been written for
a coterie manuscript audience rather than for print, could target material in a more pointed way and show the use that could be made of myth,
irrespective of its factual accuracy. The reason that the matter of Britain
might have seemed 'furthest from the daunger of envy, and suspition of
present time' was that serious historians were casting grave doubts upon
the authenticity of Arthur, despite the cult status which the legends

---

[4] See Anthony Pagden, 'The Principle of Attachment', in *European Encounters with
the New World: From Renaissance to Romanticism* (New Haven: Yale University Press,
1993), 17–49; Stephen Greenblatt, 'Kidnapping Language', in id., *Marvelous Possessions*,
86–118.
[5] For a recent discussion of the letter and its status within the text see Darryl J. Gless,
Interpretation and Theology in Spenser (Cambridge: Cambridge University Press, 1994),
48–9.

enjoyed through the labours of John Leland and his followers. It is usually assumed that, once the exiled Italian humanist, Polydore Vergil, had triumphed over his fervently nationalistic adversaries and led the way towards the establishment of the proper use of sources in historical investigation, the Arthurian legends dwindled in significance to no more than an origin myth which everybody knew to be false.[6] J. J. Scarisbrick, for example, has argued that 'early Tudor England did not produce a sudden renewal of Arthurianism . . . As the sixteenth century wore on, Geoffrey of Monmouth's patriotic fantasies received increasingly short shrift from reputable historians.'[7] However, this comforting narrative of increasingly thorough and careful scholarship ignores the fact that there was a form of history-writing in which the reliance upon myths of origin such as the matter of Britain and the Arthurian legends actually increased dramatically after the Reformation, namely, English histories and chronicles of Ireland.

One might argue that Spenser was able to refigure the same material, the matter of Britain, in markedly different ways in different narratives, depending on purpose and audience. Alternatively, the comments in the letter to Raleigh may be designed to mislead or challenge the reader, giving the impression that the poem has little to do with contemporary political issues when it is, in fact, saturated in them. The use of the figure of Arthur may actually indicate the importance of Ireland to *The Faerie Queene*. Arthur's supposed conquest of Ireland was a key aspect of English colonists' justification of their right to occupy that island, indicating that the ostensible hero of the narrative was not simply employed as a benign patriotic figure from the mythical heritage of the British Isles which the English adopted after the advent of the Tudors.[8] Arthur's role has generally baffled commentators; his appearance as a conquering prince rather than the doomed and aged tragic figure most frequently depicted in English versions of the legends may be explained by refer-

---

[6] T. D. Kendrick, *British Antiquity* (London: Methuen, 1950), chs. 3–6; F. J. Levy, *Tudor Historical Thought* (San Marino: Huntington Library Publications, 1967), ch. 2; Arthur B. Ferguson, *Clio Unbound: The Perception of the Social and Cultural Past in Renaissance England* (Durham, NC: Duke University Press, 1979), ch. 4; *Polydore Vergil's English History*, i. *Containing the first eight books*, ed. Sir Henry Ellis (London: Camden Society, 1846), 33–4, 121–2.

[7] *Henry VIII*, rev. edn. (London: Methuen, 1988), 271.

[8] For a recent overview which assumes this position, see Paul R. Rovang, *Refashioning 'Knights and Ladies Gentle Deeds': The Intertextuality of Spenser's* Faerie Queene *and Malory's* Morte D'Arthur (Madison: Fairleigh Dickinson University Press, 1996), ch. 4.

ence to the use of the matter of Britain in an Irish context, a myth
Spenser was clearly prepared to use elsewhere in his writings.[9]

When Arthur declares his 'loues and linage' to Una, the symbol of the
unified English church after the Reformation, he describes a strange
dream he had of a beautiful lady who laid down next to him one evening
when his frivolous knightly pursuits were over:

> Most goodly glee and louely blandishment
> She to me made, and bad me loue her deare,
> For dearely sure her loue was to me bent,
> As when iust time expired should appeare.
> But whether dreames delude, or true it were,
> Was neuer hart so rauisht with delight,
> Ne liuing man like words did euer heare,
> As she to me deliuered all that night;
> And at her parting said, She Queene of Faeries hight.

(I. ix. 14)

Arthur's relationship with Gloriana is far from straightforward.
Arthur's description of his defeat by Cupid in the previous stanza contains echoes of the Red Cross Knight's fall in the last canto when he surrenders to Duessa's charms (I. vii. 4–7); the appearance of the queen in
what may have been a dream would also seem to lead the reader back to
the attempted seduction of the Red Cross Knight by the false Una con-
jured up by Archimago as an 'ydle dream' (I. i. 46) in order to sever
the knight from his lady and the course of truth. The incident is
described in the letter to Raleigh, in terms of reference which further
emphasizes the Arthurian theme of the poem and its relevance to the
allegory of Elizabeth:

So much more profitable and gratious is doctrine by ensample, then by rule. So
haue I laboured to doe in the person of Arthure: whome I conceiue after his long
education by Timon, to whom he was by Merlin deliuered to be brought up, so
soone as he was borne of the Lady Igrayne, to haue seene in a dream or vision
the Faery Queen, with whose excellent beauty rauished, he awaking resolued to
seeke her out, and so being by Merlin armed, and by Timon thoroughly
instructed, he went to seeke her forth in Faerye land. In that Faery Queene

---

[9] See Hugh MacLachlan, 'Arthur, legend of', Sp. Enc., 64–6, and the perfunctory entry
by L. R. Galyon, 'Spenser, Edmund', in Norris J. Lacy (ed.), The Arthurian Encyclopedia
(Woodbridge: Boydell & Brewer, 1986), 521–2. On the transformation of Arthur from
Malory to Spenser, see John Pitcher, 'Tudor Literature, 1485–1603', in Pat Rogers (ed.),
The Oxford Illustrated History of English Literature (Oxford: Oxford University Press,
1987), 59–111, at 59–63.

I meane glory in my generall intention, but in my particular I conceive the most excellent and glorious person of our soueraigne the Queene, her kingdome in Faery land. (p. 737)

Spenser has been careful to make sure that readers of the poem would have recognized the importance of the Arthurian legends to the narrative of the poem, and, presumably, would have been surprised at the peripheral role they then play after Book I. In a sense, the epic role of Arthur the conqueror is neglected by Elizabeth who herself resembles the ineffectual, courtly Arthur of French romance, relying upon her knights to run her kingdoms.[10] Elizabeth/Gloriana leads Arthur on, but also holds him at bay: the dream of her may, in the end, be no more than a delusion. Arthur's role as conqueror of Ireland is not mentioned in *The Faerie Queene*; nevertheless it is clear that such legendary actions haunt the poem.

Even before Henry II's invasion of Ireland in the 1170s, Geoffrey of Monmouth's *Historia Regum Britanniae* (*History of the Kings of Britain*) (*c.*1138) described how Arthur expanded his empire after his marriage to Guinevere. Arthur, 'determined to subject [Ireland] to his authority', defeated King Gilmaurius's army which was 'naked and unarmed', and the remaining princes, 'thunderstruck by what had happened', surrendered to his authority: 'The whole of Ireland was thus conquered.'[11] Arthur continued his belligerence and conquered Iceland, Gotland and Orkney (whose kings surrender voluntarily), Norway, Denmark, and France (Gaul) (*History*, 222–8).

Geoffrey's purpose in writing the *History* is still a matter of fierce scholarly debate, as it was in the twelfth century, and it has even been suggested that the work is an elaborate hoax.[12] In the sixteenth century any such subtle nuance had been lost, and the *History*, whether taken seriously or dismissed as the bad history of an unhistorical age, was read

[10] See Roger Sherman Loomis (ed.), *Arthurian Literature in the Middle Ages* (Oxford: Clarendon Press, 1959); Rosemary Morris, *The Character of King Arthur in Medieval Literature* (Woodbridge: Boydell & Brewer, 1982), chs. 4–5.

[11] Geoffrey of Monmouth, *The History of the Kings of Britain*, trans. Lewis Thorpe (Harmondsworth: Penguin, 1966), 221–2. All subsequent references are to this edition.

[12] On Geoffrey as a historian see Valerie Flint, 'The *Historia Regum Britanniae* of Geoffrey of Monmouth: Parody and Purpose—A Suggestion', *Speculum*, 54 (1979), 447–68; Christopher Brooke, 'Geoffrey of Monmouth as a Historian', in Christopher Brooke and David Dumville (eds.), *The Church and the Welsh Border in the Central Middle Ages* (Woodbridge: Boydell & Brewer, 1986), 95–107; Lesley Johnson, 'Commemorating the Past: A Critical Study of the Shaping of British and Arthurian History in Geoffrey of Monmouth's *Historia Regum Britanniae*, Wace's *Roman De Brut* and the

as a chronicle.[13] Spenser himself made extensive use of the work in the British chronicles narrated in Books II and III of *The Faerie Queene* and appears not to situate them within an obviously ironic context (although they do appear to be critical of the queen's failure to secure the succession through the production of an heir, an impossibility in 1590 when the poem was published, as Elizabeth was 57).[14]

Geoffrey's work was often used by those keen to justify British imperial expansion, as it provided a seeming historical precedent, however dubious that might appear to be. One such thinker was John Dee, an influential figure keen to revive ideas of a British empire.[15] While many writers claimed England's right to territory in the Americas through John Cabot's voyage of 1497, Dee 'declared the Queen's title rested on discoveries first made by King Arthur, then Madoc'.[16] Following evidence from the Dutch geographer, Gerhard Mercator, Dee also laid claim to Norway, which was said to have been colonized by Arthur.[17] Hakluyt repeated this claim in his *Principal Navigations*, supplementing Dee's history with a full account of the voyage of Madoc (a Welsh prince) in 1170 to the West Indies.[18] Traces left by his followers authenticate their original presence: 'Therefore it is to be supposed that

Alliterative *Morte Arthure*' (Ph.D. thesis, King's College, London, 1990); John Gillingham, 'The Context and Purpose of Geoffrey of Monmouth's *Historia Regum Britanniae*', *Anglo-Norman Studies*, 13 (1990), 99–118; Francis Ingledew, 'The Book of Troy and the Genealogical Construction of History: The Case of Geoffrey of Monmouth's *Historia Regum Britanniae*', *Speculum*, 69 (1994), 665–704.

[13] See Kendrick, *British Antiquity*; Pocock, *Ancient Constitution and the Feudal Law*, 40, 96.

[14] See Carrie A. Harper, *The Sources of the British Chronicle in Spenser's* Faerie Queene (Philadelphia: John C. Winston, 1910); Charles Millican Bowie, *Spenser and the Table Round: A Study in the Contemporaneous Background for Spenser's Use of the Arthurian Legend* (Cambridge, Mass.: Harvard University Press, 1932); Jerry Leath Mills, 'Prudence, History and the Prince in *The Faerie Queene*, Book II', *HLQ* 41 (1977–8), 83–101; Hadfield, *Literature, Politics and National Identity*, 193–200.

[15] For details of Dee's life see Richard Deacon, *John Dee: Scientist, Geographer, Astrologer and Secret Agent to Elizabeth I* (London: Frederick Muller, 1968). Dee traced his own genealogy back to Roderick the Great, Prince of Wales, in order to confirm his own Britishness: see his *DNB* entry.

[16] On the former claim see John Parker, *Books to Build an Empire: A Bibliographical History of English Overseas Interests to 1620* (Amsterdam: New Israel, 1965), 105, 110, 138.

[17] E. G. R. Taylor, 'A letter dated 1577 from Mercator to John Dee', *Imago Mundi*, 12 (1956), 56–68.

[18] Hakluyt, *Principal Navigations*, i. 99–100. On the wide readership and massive influence of Hakluyt's collection see Wright, *Middle-Class Culture in Elizabethan England*, ch. 14; Richard Helgerson, *Forms of Nationhood: The Elizabethan Writing of England* (Chicago: Chicago University Press, 1992), ch. 4.

he and his people inhabited part of those countreys: for it appeareth by Francis Lopez de Gomara, that in Acuzamail and other places the people honoured the crosse. Whereby it may be gathered that Christians had been there before the coming of the Spanyards.'[19] The logic is analogous to that used by Irenius: an alien element within a given culture which resembles a contemporary linguistic or social phenomenon from another culture, and which cannot be explained within the terms of its own enclosed cultural history, necessarily implies the presence of that other culture at some past moment.[20]

Humphrey Gilbert, an active soldier and colonizer in Ireland and the Americas, also subscribed to Dee's view that the Tudors were restoring an ancient Arthurian empire rather than establishing a new one. He employed an identical argument to that used by Irenius to claim a British presence in Ireland: that etymological fragments of the colonizers' language remained. The animals on certain islands have 'sundry Welsh names', and a fruit called 'Gwynethes' corresponds to an original Welsh word. Gilbert failed to specify other examples, but he does cite the authority of David Ingram to testify that 'there are divers other Welsh wordes at this day in use'.[21] The chronicler of Ireland, Meredith Hanmer, who as archdeacon of Cork and Ross would almost certainly have known Spenser, repeated the story, which he seems to have copied faithfully from Hakluyt, locating the land in question as Mexico (as Gilbert did) and asserting the primacy of Madoc's claims to America over those of Columbus and Vespucci. Hanmer's work appeared alongside Spenser's in Ware's collection.[22]

Irenius' justification for the English right to Ireland and the logic used would seem to square exactly with other Tudor notions of the *restoration* of empire derived primarily from Geoffrey's *History*. The same text had been used 400 years earlier by Giraldus Cambrensis (Gerald of Wales), the main apologist for Henry II's invasion.[23] Gerald argued that the

---

[19] Hakluyt, *Principal Navigations*, v. 79–80.

[20] See Hogden, *Early Anthropology*, ch. 1.

[21] Humphrey Gilbert, 'A discourse of the necessities and commoditie of planting English colonies upon the north partes of America', in Hakluyt, *Principal Navigations*, vi. 42–78, at 58–9. On Gilbert see William Gilbert Gosling, *The Life of Sir Humphrey Gilbert: England's First Empire Builder* (Westport, Conn.: Greenwood Press, 1911).

[22] Meredith Hanmer, 'The Chronicle of Ireland', in Ware (ed.), *Ancient Irish Histories*, i. 221–3. On Hanmer see *DNB* entry; Maley, *Spenser Chronology*, 96.

[23] I shall persist in calling Giraldus, Gerald of Wales, despite Michael Richter's strictures that Gerald's hostility to the Welsh and lack of patriotic feeling mean that the name Giraldus de Barri should be used. The former name has the virtue of familiarity. See

English king had a fivefold right to the lordship of Ireland.[24] This could be divided up into the new and the old claims. The new claim consisted of three parts: first, the fact that Bayonne, the Basque city whence the Irish migrated, was now part of Henry II's possessions after his marriage to Eleanor of Aquitaine (Aquitaine held sovereignty over Gascony); second, the 'voluntary cession and fealty of the princes of Ireland (for every one is free to renounce his own rights)' to Henry II; and, third, the most immediately practical of the new claims, the papal bull *Laudabiliter*, quoted in full by Gerald (*Expugnatio*, bk. 2, ch. 6), conveniently granted by the English pope, Adrian IV, which gave Henry, at his own request, the title of Lord of Ireland, and 'the power of reforming the Irish people, who were then very ignorant of the rudiments of the faith, by ecclesiastical rules and discipline, according to the usages of the English church'.[25]

As late as the sixteenth and seventeenth centuries Gerald defined the tradition of English writing on Ireland, being the most widely read authority on Irish customs as well as Irish history. Commentators on both sides of the Irish Sea recognized his influence: Geoffrey Keating made it quite clear from the start of his *History of Ireland* whom his work was intended to combat: 'We shall set down here a few lines of the lies of the new foreigners who have written concerning Ireland, following Cambrensis; and shall make a beginning of refuting Cambrensis himself . . . because it is Cambrensis who is as the bull to the herd for them for writing the false history of Ireland, wherefore they have no choice of guide.'[26] John Hooker, who translated the *Expugnatio* and then continued the chronicle of Ireland up to the present of 1586, as part of the second edition of Holinshed's *Chronicles* (1587), a work Spenser undoubtedly knew, berated the failure of earlier historians of Ireland to record their debt to the Anglo-Welsh author:

Michael Richter, *Giraldus Cambrensis and the Growth of the Welsh Nation* (Aberystwyth: National Library of Wales, 1972), 3–4. See also Bartlett, *Gerald of Wales*, 185.

[24] Gerald, *Expugnatio Hibernica*, bk. 2, ch. 6; *History and Topography of Ireland*, ch. 92. Ironically, like so many Tudor historians, Gerald elsewhere ridicules Geoffrey's achievements as a historian: see Richter, *Giraldus Cambrensis*, 67, 75–6. See also Salces, 'Some Ideas on Spenser and the Irish Question', 108–9.

[25] On the *Laudabiliter* and its significance see F. X. Martin, 'Dairmait Mac Murchada and the coming of the Anglo Normans', in Art Cosgrove (ed.), *A New History of Ireland*, ii. *Medieval Ireland, 1169–1534* (Oxford: Clarendon Press, 1987), 57–60; Richter, *Medieval Ireland*, 129, 149, 161.

[26] *Foras Feasa ar Éirinn: The History of Ireland*, ed. and trans. David Comyn and P. S. Dinneen, 4 vols. (London: Early Irish Text Society, 1902–13), i. 153. On Keating see Brendan Bradshaw, 'Geoffrey Keating: Apologist of Irish Ireland', in Bradshaw *et al.* (eds.), *Representing Ireland*, 166–90.

In this they were much to be blamed, that all of them were beholding unto Giraldus, and not one of them would yield that courtesy either to publish his history,
or, using the same, to acknowledge it. For some misliking both method and
phrase, framed it in a more lofty style, and under that colour have attributed
unto themselves the honor and fruits of another man's doing.[27]

However, after the Reformation Gerald's authority on Irish affairs
clearly had its limits. The *Laudabiliter* could no longer be cited as an
authority, and neither could Henry II's ostensible motive for invading
Ireland: the desire to reform its wayward church and bring it into line
with the rest of European civilization. Hooker deliberately omitted
Gerald's lavish praise of Thomas Becket, substituting instead a sharp
criticism of his resistance to regal authority, which labelled him a trai-
tor. The reader is directed (p. 149) to John Foxe's *Acts and Monuments
of the Christian Church* for the true story of Becket's revolt against the
legitimate sovereign.[28] Most of Hooker's marginalia are simply sign-
posting for the reader but, against Gerald's lament that the civil government failed to give thanks to the church for its God-given victory in
Ireland and that it took away church lands, Hooker has exclaimed,
'Aha Giraldus! could you not see that curssed fault and abuse?' (bk. 2,
ch. 38). What is necessary and laudable in the *Expugnatio* threatens the
very foundations of translation in Holinshed's *Chronicles*, and so is
excised.[29] Hooker's citation of Foxe's *Acts and Monuments*, probably
the most widely read work of the English Reformation, signals an entry
into an interpretative world where the secular authorities are not to be
challenged, precisely what Becket's crime had been. The political and
intellectual world of *A View* is undoubtedly more complex, but starts
from the same premises (see ch. 2 above).[30] When Hooker adds a note
to agree with Gerald that the want of a thorough 'reformation'
amongst the English resulted in their failure to conquer the whole of
Ireland (bk. 2, ch. 26), it is quite clear that each writer has a different
goal in mind.

The point to be made is that pre- and post-Reformation English texts

---

[27] John Hooker, 'The Conquest of Ireland', in Holinshed, *Chronicles*, vi. 109. Subsequent references are given in parentheses in the text. On Hooker see *DNB* entry. For
Spenser's knowledge of Holinshed see *Variorum*, x. 266, 280, 354–8, 360–5, *et passim*.

[28] John Foxe, *Acts and Monuments of the Christian Church*, ed. S. R. Cattley and J.
Pratt, 8 vols. (London, 1837–41), ii. 196–256. See also David Knowles, *Thomas Becket*
(London: A.&C. Black, 1970), 2.

[29] See Gerald, *Expugnatio Hibernica*, bk. 2, chs. 24, 35, 39.

[30] J. F. Mozley, *John Foxe and his Book* (London: SPCK, 1940); A. G. Dickens, *The
English Reformation* (London: Collins, 1964), 416, *passim*; Wright, *Middle-Class Culture*, 333–4, *passim*.

on Ireland existed within different interpretative frameworks and with different conceptions of authority (however similar the actual practice might have been).[31] For Hooker there can be no question of the *Laudabiliter* having the authority to establish a political right, as it derives from a source explicitly denied such powers within his own text.[32] Spenser does not even mention the papal bull, choosing instead to emphasize the legitimate conquest of Henry II through the Anglo-Norman lord, Strongbow: 'for by the Conquest of Henrye the Seconde trewe it is that the Irishe weare utterlye vanquished and subdued so as no enemy was able to houlde up heade againste his power in which theare weaknes he broughte in his lawes and setled them as now they theare remayne' (*View*, pp. 55–6).

English historians were therefore left with a problem of legitimizing the reconquest of the whole of Ireland as the Tudors sought to reunite the British Isles and expand overseas. More often than not they turned to the British legends to supply an origin myth, Gerald's 'old' claim. Holinshed in his 'History of England' wrote that Arthur went to Ireland in 525, where he 'discomforted King [Gilmaurius] in batell, he constrained him to yield, and to acknowledge by dooing his fealtre to hold the realm of Ireland of him', the same story that Spenser used and derived from Geoffrey's *History*.[33] Meredith Hanmer also cites the same story and also uses the word, 'fealtre' (fealty, i.e. a vassal's acknowledgement of obligation to a lord).[34] The claim was well enough known for Geoffrey Keating to attempt to refute it at length, carefully noting, and then rejecting, all the English chronicles which mention Arthur's purported invasion. Keating admits the possibility that a 'close alliance' might have existed between Muircheartach, son of Earc, and Arthur, in that they agreed to aid each other in war; but 'it must not be thence inferred that either was tributary to the other'. Keating is at pains to dispel any notion of 'fealty'. Indeed, citing William of Newburgh, William Camden, and Gerald as authorities, he states that 'Ireland never lay under foreign domination'. Ireland was not only never conquered, but served as a haven for those seeking refuge from the advance of the

---

[31] See Gillingham, 'The English Invasion of Ireland'.

[32] It is worth noting that one modern commentator speculates that John of Salisbury, one of Henry II's emissaries to Pope Adrian IV and secretary to Archbishop Theobald, might have 'played the Arthurian card' to obtain authorization for Henry to enter Ireland on his own: Michael Dolley, *Anglo-Norman Ireland, c.1100–1318* (Dublin: Gill & Macmillan, 1972), 45.

[33] Holinshed, *Chronicles*, i. 576.   [34] 'Chronicle of Ireland', 101–2.

Roman empire.[35] Hans Pawlisch has noted that the belief in an imperial past dating back to Arthur had a direct strategic value for the Tudors, as it enabled 'jurists and polemicists' to deny any validity to papal counter-claims that Ireland only belonged to England via the *Laudabiliter*. When 'several independent Gaelic dynasts exploited the alleged theory of papal sovereignty over Ireland, either in deploying the forces of Catholic Europe in Ireland by offering an "Irish crown" to a foreign monarch, or in legitimising the independence of their own laws and institutions', English lawyers such as Sir John Davies or Sir Edward Coke were able to invoke the notion of an imperial authority dating back to Arthur in order to dismiss these assertions as legal errors, as well as argue that Gaelic customs they felt harmful to the Crown's ability to govern Ireland, such as gavelkind (land tenure which distributed land equally among the surviving sons) and tanistry (the selection of a chief by election rather than hereditary succession), should be swept away.[36] Whatever threatened Tudor sovereignty in Ireland could thus be classed as illegal, a circular argument.

There was also the matter of the other half of the 'old' claim to Ireland, mentioned by Irenius and, again, a commonplace among English chroniclers of Ireland.[37] This told the story of the Irish migration to Ireland during the reign of the British king, Gurguntius (Gurguit Barbtruc). In Geoffrey's *History* the story is relatively simple, deriving from Nennius' *Historia Brittonum* (c. ninth century).[38] According to Geoffrey, the British king encounters a group of Spanish exiles under the leadership of Partholoim, who do homage to Gurguntius and ask if they can inhabit any region of Britain. Gurguntius allows them to inhabit Ireland, 'which at that time was a completely uninhabited desert. He granted the island to them. They have increased and multiplied and they still hold the island today' (pp. 100–1). Not only were the Irish conquered by the British later, but they owe their geographical location and their subsequently developed identity as a people to a bargain they made with the British.

The story became more complicated in the sixteenth century, perhaps

---

[35] Keating, *History of Ireland*, i. 13–19. The controversy regarding Arthur's conquest of Ireland and the use of Geoffrey's *Historia* raged well into the 17th c.: see Peter Walsh, *A Prospect of the State of Ireland* (London, 1682), 396–401.

[36] Pawlisch, *Sir John Davies and the Conquest of Ireland*, 63.

[37] Campion, *Two Bokes of the Histories of Ireland*, bk. 1, ch. 9; Hanmer, 'Chronicle of Ireland', 26; Stanihurst, 'The Chronicle of Ireland', in Holinshed, *Chronicles*, vi. 77.

[38] Nennius, *British History and The Welsh Annals*, ed. and trans. John Morris (London: Phillimore, 1980), 20.

unsurprisingly, given its now central importance. In Edmund Campion's *Two Bokes of the Histories of Ireland* (*c*.1571), the Irish are descended from a Greek lord, Gathelus. They had all served under him when he was at the court of Amenophis, king of Egypt, following his marriage to the king's daughter, Scotia ('Whereof the Scottes are named'), and when the Pharaoh was drowned in the Red Sea, all left to settle in Spain, building the city Brigantia. Some of these Greeks then went off to inhabit Ireland, where they were honoured for their martial skills and 'cunnings in all languages', and under Gathelus' guidance the Irish tongue was 'greatly perfected and beautified' and the natives taught 'letters' and 'martial feates after his Greeks and Aegyptian manner'. The island was named after his wife, Scotia.[39] Later on, in the reign of Gurguntius, other descendants of Gathelus, understanding that the Western Isles were empty, sailed off to find them. They met Gurguntius returning from Denmark and begged him 'to direct and further them to some place of habitacion, proferringe to become his leige people and to hold the same of his and his heires for ever'. As the king was finding it difficult to subdue the Irish (presumably some of whom must have been the other descendants of Gathelus), he sent these Greeks/Spanish to do the job for him. Four now ruled the land until dissension broke out between them.[40]

Campion's elaborations and additions to Geoffrey enable him to posit a variety of 'colonial moments' which serve to reinforce each other.[41] He repeats a version of Gerald's 'new' claim by asserting that Bayonne had always been subject to Britain so that the Irish 'were subjects to the Crowne of Britayne before they set foote in Ireland'.[42] Hanmer and Stanihurst tell almost exactly the same version of the story, hardly surprisingly in Stanihurst's case as his chronicle is virtually copied from Campion's.[43] The story emphasizes a British claim to Ireland by conquest and by consent: both British military might, and a prior agreement whereby the Irish signed away their rights, establish a dominance over Ireland.

[39] Scotia is sometimes the mother of Gathelus, whose father was a Scythian: see J. P. Myers (ed.), *Elizabethan Ireland: A Selection of Writings by Elizabethan Writers on Ireland* (Hamden, Conn.: Archon, 1983), 32–3.

[40] Campion, *Two Bokes of the Histories of Ireland*, bk. 1, ch. 9.

[41] For further discussion of Campion's version of the story and its implications see Andrew Hadfield, 'Briton and Scythian: Tudor Representations of Irish Origins', *IHS* 112 (Nov. 1993), 390–408, at 396–7.

[42] *Two Bokes of the Histories of Ireland*, p. 81.

[43] Lennon, *Richard Stanihurst*, 38. For further details see Hadfield, 'Briton and Scythian', 397.

Spenser, on the other hand, while including stories of a British conquest of Ireland in *A View*, is keen to dismiss the stories of Spanish and Egyptian origins of the Irish as vain delusions, and devotes a considerable amount of space in his text to refuting them. Irenius corrects Eudoxus' opinion that all Irish chronicles 'are moste fabulous and forged' (p. 84), suggesting instead that 'some of them mighte saye truethe', because the Irish were one of the first nations to possess the skill of writing (p. 87). Nevertheless, Irenius attacks the story of Gathelus recorded in Irish chronicles, along with a host of other stories claiming Egyptian ancestry, as 'forged histories of theire owne Antiquitye which they deliuer to fooles and make them beleve them for trewe' (p. 89). Later on, Eudoxus is given one of his rare chances to contribute a substantial piece of information to the discussion when he ridicules Richard Stanihurst's tale of the supposed origin of the Irish battle-cry, 'Ferragh'. According to Stanihurst, this originates from the time when the Irish were in Egypt under the leadership of 'one *Scota* the daughter of *Pharo*', and used 'in all theire battells to Call uppon the name of *Pharo* cryinge *Ferragh Ferragh*'. Eudoxus uses Stanihurst's credulity to dismiss his judgement as a historian and humorously suggests an etymology of his own: 'But his *Scota* rather Comes of the greke *Scotos* that is darkenes which hathe not let him see the lighte of the truethe.' Irenius continues the joke: 'youe knowe not *Eudoxus* howe well mr *Stan*: Could see in the darke perhaps he hathe owles or Catts eyes but well I wote he seethe not well the verye lighte in matters of more weighte', and suggests a true origin for the cry in the fact that many Irishmen in the north are called 'Ferragh' (p. 104).[44]

The story has an important point in that the weight of the investigation carried out by Irenius and Eudoxus is shown to refute and displace the false history of the Irish. A true etymology is opposed to a false one and the frontiers of language are established whereby English truth stands opposed to Irish falsehood.[45] Irenius' assertion that the British colonized Ireland is based on precisely the same form of evidence as established the Spanish ancestry of the Irish. It is simply that one authority is believed, the other dismissed. However, the text would seem to undermine itself through the humorous banter between the two interlocutors. The fact that Eudoxus can invent a spurious etymology

---

[44] On Stanihurst see *Variorum*, x. 335.

[45] For a perceptive analysis of the etymologies used in *A View* see Anne Fogarty, 'The Colonisation of Language: Narrative Strategy in *A View of the Present State of Ireland* and *The Faerie Queene*, Book VI', in Coughlan (ed.), *Spenser and Ireland*, 75–108, esp. 84–5.

through using his Classical, humanist learning to ridicule Stanihurst, 'scotos' meaning 'dark', suggests that the whole enterprise, often regarded as a key strategy in humanist history-writing by historians of ideas, was seen by Spenser himself as a bit of a cheap trick, albeit useful for propaganda purposes, perhaps like the Arthurian legends.[46] Is it possible that the audience of *A View* is being treated like the foolish Irish who believe their own histories? Or is it more that they are being given a series of strategies whereby they can fool the public they wish to persuade, the joke being one shared among the audience of the text but not to be taken lightly by those on whom its arguments will be used, i.e. an English audience? Either way, the etymological root is established as an epistemological principle in Spenser's work, along with the perpetual fear that it might be undermined, not least by the use of the pun, the harbinger of uncertainty and insecurity.[47]

In a passage surviving in only one manuscript of the text in the Public Record Office, Irenius' attitude towards the British legends is developed.[48] It is, of course, possible that this is a passage interpolated by a scribe in the guise of Spenser but, whether authentic or not, it does serve to develop some of the points established above, and was included in Ware's edition of the text. Irenius affirms that Ireland was subject to both Arthur and Edgar, the Saxon king, and that the east coast was planted extensively by both Britons and Saxons, 'for it is usuallye in the Conquest of anye Countrye that manie of the Conquerours doe plant themselves in the lande of the Conquered' (p. 85). The argument for the presence of the Saxons is, again, etymological, based on the survival of the words: 'marrah', meaning 'horseman', and 'gemanus', meaning 'to ride'. The passage reiterates the attack on the story of Gathelus, suggesting that if it were true there would also be Spanish records of the migration (p. 82). In general it adds little to *A View* which is not there in other places, which might suggest that it is the work of another hand elaborating the text. It has sometimes occasioned comment because it contains a sceptical dismissal of the story of Brutus which may reflect the influence of Polydore Vergil. Irenius makes a telling comparison

---

[46] On humanist history and the search for the oldest, most authentic, source, see Elizabeth L. Eisenstein, *The Printing Press as an Agent of Change* (Cambridge: Cambridge University Press, 1979), ch. 3; Kendrick, *British Antiquity*, ch. 6; Levy, *Tudor Historical Thought*, ch. 2.

[47] See Jonathan Culler, 'The Call of the Phoneme: Introduction', id. (ed.), *On Puns: The Foundation of Letters* (Oxford: Blackwell, 1988), 1–16, at 2.

[48] Public Record Office, State Papers 63. 202, pt. 4, item 58. The passage is conveniently reprinted in *Variorum*, x. 85–6.

between English and Irish: 'But the *Irish* doe heerein no otherwise, then our vaine *Englishmen* doe in the Tale of *Brutus*, whom they devise to have first conquered and inhabited this Land, it being as impossible to proove, that there was ever any such *Brutus* of *England*, as it is, that there was any such *Gathelus* of *Spaine*' (p. 82).[49]

This passage, whether by Spenser or not, would seem to reinforce the suspicion that the use of the British legends to justify the English invasion of Ireland was either done in bad faith as propaganda or was an act of barely disguised hypocrisy. William Camden, in his geographical survey *Britannia* (Latin version, 1586; English translation, 1610), a major influence on *A View*, quotes the story of Gurguntius and the Spanish origins of the Irish derived from Irish chronicles, but declares, in the manner of Polydore Vergil, that an evaluation of the story's authenticity is beyond him: 'I shall neither meddle with the truth or falsity of these relations; antiquity must be allowed some liberty in such things.'[50] However, he does confirm that, just as the first inhabitants were British settlers (on linguistic evidence), so it is probable that northern Spaniards came, being close enough to travel across the sea and keen to leave their own land which was 'quite barren and unfit to live in'.[51] John Speed's *The Theatre of the Empire of Great Britain* (1611), a similar work in design and popularity (and clearly owing much to Camden), is less tactful and resembles Spenser's text in its attack on the stories of Pharaoh, Scotia, and Gurguntius (like Irenius, Speed suggests that the sole purpose of such tales is to make Ireland more famous); but it does affirm the

---

[49]   For a very different reading of this passage see Judith H. Anderson, 'The Antiquities of Fairyland and Ireland', *JEGP* 86 (1987), 199–214, at 202–3.

[50]   William Camden, *Brittania*, trans. Edmund Gibson (London, 1695), 966–8. On the legends of the genealogy of Brutus, Polydore Vergil comments: 'I have stedfastlie promised that I will neither affirme as trew, neither reproove as false, the judgement of one or other as concerning the originall of soe auncient a people, referring all things, as wee have don heretofore, to the consideration of the reader' (*Polydore Vergil's English History*, ed. Ellis, 31). Despite this disclaimer Vergil makes it clear that he has little time for such histories, believing that England, being so close to mainland Europe, must at some point have been colonized by Spaniards, French, Germans, or Italians, which approximates to Irenius' conception of the Irish (*View*, 84–5). He is similarly leading on the question of the authenticity of Arthur (*English History*, 121–2). As Denys Hay has noted, 'Vergil subjects both stories to a devastating historical analysis, although he politely concludes with a verdict of not proven' (*The Anglica History of Polydore Vergil*, ed. Denys Hay (London: Camden Society, 1950), p. xxiv). Camden's rhetorical manipulation of the reader is identical. On Camden's influence on *A View* see Frank F. Covington, Jr., 'Spenser's Use of Irish History in the *Veue of the Present State of Ireland*', *Texas Studies in English*, 4 (1924), 5–38; Smith, 'Spenser, Holinshed, and the *Leabhar Gabhala*', 398–9; R. D. Dunn, 'Camden, William', *Sp. Enc.* 131.

[51]   *Britannia*, 966–8.

emigration of Britons to Ireland.[52] Again the evidence is etymological: the Irish words for many lakes, mountains, and islands are often British ones. Speed cites Ptolemy as an authority to prove that Ireland was known as 'Little Britain' and was conquered before the reign of Henry II.[53]

Camden, in his desire to explain why he chose to include Ireland in the text of *Britannia*, cites the Classical authorities quoted by Spenser (undoubtedly via Camden), mentioned at the start of this chapter. He points to the similarities not only between language and names, but also makes the observation that 'the nature and manners of the people (as Tacitus says) differs not much from the Britaines'. All the ancients call it 'the British Island'; Strabo terms the inhabitants 'Britons', 'Diodorus Sicilius makes Irin a part of Britain', Festus Arienus writes of the two British islands and Ptolemy calls Ireland 'Britannia Parva'.[54] The immediate advantage of the use of such a British origin-story is apparent: if the two islands are merged, as indicated, under the very name of Britain, both can be regarded all the more easily as properties of the English monarch, who claimed to be a descendant of ancient line of British kings.[55] Such assumptions are present from Geoffrey onwards, and even historians as sceptical as Spenser and Camden follow this style of argument (how cynically is, of course, hard to tell).[56] The legend might also be said to help mask the problem of explaining a violent conquest: the word 'Britain' effectively exists outside history and without an origin itself, the name being simply reported back by the ancient geographers. The proper name, 'Britain' is used to bestow the property of Ireland upon the English Crown.[57]

---

[52] *The Theatre of the Empire of Great Britain* (London, 1625 edn.), 137. On the popularity of such geographical surveys see Wright, *Middle-Class Culture*, 315–19.

[53] Speed, *Theatre*, 137. Brittany was more usually referred to as 'Little Britain': see Denys Hay, 'The Use of the Term "Great Britain" in the Middle Ages', *Proceedings of the Society of Antiquaries of Scotland*, 89 (1955–6), 55–66.

[54] Camden, *Britannia*, 967.

[55] See Kendrick, *British Antiquity*, ch. 3; Levy, *Tudor Historical Thought*, 65–8; Millican, *Spenser and the Table Round*, ch. 2.

[56] On Camden's use of Irish sources see Rudolf B. Gottfried, 'The Early Development of the Section on Ireland in Camden's *Britannia*', *ELH* 10 (1943), 117–30. On Camden's reputation as an exemplary sceptical early modern historian, see Hugh Trevor-Roper, *Queen Elizabeth's First Historian: William Camden and the Beginnings of English 'Civil' History* (London: Cape, 1971); F. Smith Fussner, *The Historical Revolution: English Historical Writing and Thought, 1580–1640* (London: Routledge, 1962), ch. 3.

[57] For a discussion of the interrelationship between the 'proper name' and 'property' see Jacques Derrida, *Of Grammatology*, trans. G. C. Spivak (Baltimore: Johns Hopkins University Press, 1976), 106–18.

There is, however, another side to the use of myths of origin in *A View*. After Irenius has explained the dubious use of history by Irish historians, Eudoxus asks the obvious question: why are the Irish are so keen to perpetuate such myths about themselves? Irenius replies that it is 'Even of a verye desire of Newfanglenes and vanitye: for beinge, as they are nowe accounted the moste barbarous nacion in Christendome they to avoide that reproche woulde derive themselves from the Spaniardes whom they now see to bee a verye honourable people and nexte borderinge unto them' (p. 90). The Irish are trying to save themselves from the reputation of savagery, which other nations are so keen to impute to them, including Spenser himself (although, to some extent this misfires because the Spanish 'are nowe accounted the moste barbarous nacion in Christendome' (p. 90) on account of their mixed ancestry).[58] *A View* is at pains to stress that, although the Irish may be of mixed origin, the two races which define them are the Gauls and, more importantly, the Scythians, usually a byword for savagery, principally through the evidence of shared cultural practices.[59]

The two authorities cited by Spenser and Camden for the purpose of showing that the ancients perceived Ireland to be British, Strabo and Diodorus Sicilius, also supply ample evidence of the barbarian nature of the Irish. Both make the Scythian connection explicit. Diodorus Sicilius comments that 'the most savage people' among the Gauls dwell on the Scythian border and 'some, we are told eat human beings, even as the Britains do who dwell on Iris [Ireland]'.[60] Strabo, who, contrary to what Spenser alleges, appears to separate Britain and Ireland, is more extensive in his comparison:

Concerning this island [Ierne, Ireland] I have nothing certain to tell, except that its inhabitants are more savage than the Britons, since they are man-eaters as well as heavy eaters, and since, further, they count it an honourable thing, when their fathers die, to devour them, and openly to have intercourse, not only with other women, but also with their mothers and sisters; but I am saying this only with the understanding that I have no trustworthy eyewitnesses for it; and yet, as for the matter of man-eating, that is said to be a custom of the Scythians also,

[58] On anti-Spanish prejudice see Maltby, *Black Legend in England*. Given the English fear of the relationship between Ireland and Spain in the 1590s, Spenser's desire to denigrate the Spanish is easily explained: see J. J. Silke, 'The Irish Appeal of 1593 to Spain: Some Light on the Genesis of the Nine Years War', *Irish Ecclesiastical Record*, 5th ser., 92 (1959), 279–90, 362–70; *Ireland and Europe, 1559–1607* (Dundalk: Dundalgan, 1966).

[59] See Hogden, *Early Anthropology*, 97. The authority, more often than not, was Herodotus.

[60] *The Library of History*, ed. and trans. C. H. Oldfather *et al.*, 12 vols. (London: Heinemann, 1933–57), iii. 181.

and, in cases of necessity forced by seiges, the Celt, the Iberians, and several other peoples are said to have practised it.[61]

Strabo's 'observations' (again, as is almost inevitably the case with accounts of man-eating, there are no eye-witnesses) serve to define both the Irish and the Scythians as cannibals, a cultural practice which functions to label them as savage peoples.[62]

Not only do these texts abound with references to the savage nature of the Scythians, but so do the numerous other ancient and modern authorities (among whom are Herodotus, Tacitus, Buchanan, and Stanihurst) cited in A View.[63] Spenser's text attempts to demonstrate that the Irish are the modern descendants of the ancient Scythians and uses the same sort of comparative ethnology as his authorites to do so (as well as appealing to a historical narrative). Irenius tells Eudoxus that before they discuss the customs of the Irish they must 'Consider from whence they firste spronge' because that is where a large part of these customs 'which now remaine amongest them haue bene firste fetched'. Although the Irish stem from 'sundrie people of different Condicions and manners':

the Chiefest which haue first possessed and inhabited it I Suppose to be Scithians which at suche time as the Northern nacions ouerflowed all Christendome Came downe to the sea Coste wheare inquiringe for other Contries abroade and gettinge intelligence of this Countrye of Irelande fyndinge shippinge Conveniente passed over hither and Arived in the Northe parte thereof | whiche is now called Ulster which firste inhabitinge and afterwarde stretchinge themselves forthe into the lande as theire numbers increased. (pp. 82–3)

Later migrations bring the Spanish to the west, the Gauls to the south, and the Britons to the east (pp. 93–5), but it is the Scythians who have determined the nature of the Irish.[64] The argument is not simply one of

---

[61] Strabo, *Geography*, ed. and trans. H. L. Jones and R. S. Sterrett, 8 vols. (London: Heinemann, 1917–32), ii. 259–61.

[62] On the lack of eyewitness accounts of man-eating see Hulme, *Colonial Encounters*, 80–1.

[63] Herodotus, *The Histories*, trans. Aubrey de Selincourt and A. R. Burn (Harmondsworth: Penguin, 1972), 271–2, 289–95 *et passim*; Tacitus, *On Britain and Germany*, trans. H. Mattingly (Harmondsworth: Penguin, 1948), 135–9; Stanihurst, 'The Description of Ireland' and 'The Chronicle of Ireland', in Holinshed, *Chronicles*, vi. 6, 76, *passim*; George Buchanan, *The History of Scotland*, trans. James Aikman, 4 vols. (Glasgow, 1827), i. 154–5.

[64] Irenius also notes the strong connection between the Gauls and Britons, the latter being descended from the former (*A View*, 93), but nothing is made of this connection, presumably because it might serve to undermine the distinctions being made between English/British and Irish.

shared origin, but is based on the nature of the two societies. Irish culture, whatever additions have been made to it and whatever transformations it has undergone, is, at heart, still that of the ancient Scythians.

Irenius passes from the discussion of origins to the promised analysis of customs (given Irenius' logic, the two are interdependent): he begins with those inherited from the Scythians, as he plans 'to Counte theire Customes in the same order that [he] counted theire nacions' (p. 97). He manages to demonstrate to Eudoxus' satisfaction that 'bolling' (seasonal migration to follow cattle-herds), the wearing of huge cloaks called 'mantles' and excessive facial hair called a 'glib', various battle cries, the use of short, broad swords and other implements of war, loud lamentation at funerals, certain charms and superstitions, and solemn oaths sealed with the drinking of a bowl of blood, are inherited directly from Scythian society (pp. 97–112). All of these customs threaten the civilized order which the English wish to impose upon the Irish. Eudoxus asks why Irenius is so opposed to the wearing of mantles if they serve 'in steade of howsinge beddinge and Cloathinge' in a cold country. Irenius explains:

it is a fitt howsse for an outlawe a mete bedd for a Rebell and an Apte cloake for a thefe, ffirste the Outlawe beinge for his manye Crymes and villanies banished from the Townes and howses of honeste men and wanderinge in waste places far from daunger of lawe maketh his mantle his howsse . . . Likewise for a Rebell it is as serviceable, ffor in his warr that he makethe . . . it is his bedd yea and almoste all his houshoulde stuffe . . . when they are neare driven beinge wrapped aboute theire left arme in steade of a Targett for it is harde to Cutt thoroughe it with a sworde besides it is light to beare, lighte to throwe awaie, and beinge as they then Comonlye are naked it is to them all in all. (pp. 100–1)

As the last sentence states, without the mantle the Irish are completely naked, and the garment thus fashions their identity as a people. What Irenius argues is that the mantle enables its wearer to oppose ordered society more effectively, whether as a common lawbreaker or as a dangerous rebel against Crown forces. Coupled with the 'glib', both serve to disguise the wearer and avoid the adoption of a stable identity which can be recorded by the civil and military authorities who desire to impose a civilized order. The Scythian nature of Irish society makes it inimical to reform, so that the very identity of the individual Irish who come from such a 'primitive' society challenges civilized authority, a point which Irenius has to teach the more innocent Eudoxus, who cannot yet see the significance of seemingly benign social phenomena. Irenius has to explain to him the cultural semiotics of Irishness.[65]

[65] On the mantle in *A View* see Jones and Stallybrass, 'Dismantling Irena', 165–6.

Irenius mentions few specifically Gallic or Spanish customs of the Irish; hardly any remain as the regions these settlers inhabited were near the sea and hence culturally diluted and modified via contact with other nations: 'for the trade and enterdeale of seacost nacions one with another workethe more Civilitye and good fashions | then the inland dwellers' (p. 110) (one notes that here a mixture of races or customs is deemed desirable, when the point is to offset savagery). The only significant Gallic custom which the Irish have preserved is the ritual blood-drinking described by Irenius at the execution of Murrogh O'Brien: even so, it is transformed from the original consumption of enemies' blood to that of friends—in this instance, by the dead man's foster mother (p. 112).[66] In contrast, he runs out of space attempting to list all the Scythian traits, and stops when he feels his evidence has proved persuasive: 'Thus muche onelye for this time I hope shall suffise youe to thinke that the Irishe are auncientlye reduced from the *Scythyans*' (p. 109).

Perhaps the most important Classical work underlying *A View* is Lucian's *Toxaris*, a dialogue concerning the question of friendship. Both the disputants, the civilized Greek, Mnesippus, and the barbarian, Toxaris, believe that their own peoples are more loyal and friendly, towards others as well as to their own kind. Each tells five stories to prove his case. The outcome is a draw, as no umpire has been appointed, and both men depart swearing friendship with the other.[67] Lucian's dialogue is mentioned only once in *A View*, to show that the Scythians, like the Irish, make their common oaths by sword and fire, believing they possess 'speciall divine powers which should worke vengeaunce on periuours' (p. 108). In comparison, Diodorus warrants three mentions; Julius Caesar, Strabo, and Tacitus, two each.

The importance of *Toxaris* to Spenser may lie not so much in its anthropological material (for, after all, the other authorities supplied that just as well) as in its form as a dialogue (unique among works dealing with the Scythians), enabling special emphasis to be placed on 'the notion of the ethnically based opposition between two sets of values . . . and the manner of the interplay between the interlocutors, as rhetorical and fictional constructs'.[68] Like the matter of Britain, the

---

[66] For comment see Hadfield, 'The Naked and the Dead', 32–4.

[67] Lucian, *Toxaris, or Friendship*, in *The Works of Lucian*, ed. and trans. A. M. Harmon *et al.*, 8 vols. (London: Heinemann, 1913–67), v. 101–208.

[68] Coughlan, ' "Some secret scourge which shall by her come unto England": Ireland and Incivility in Spenser', in id. (ed.), *Spenser and Ireland*, 46–74, at 64; subsequent quotations are from pp. 64–70.

dialogue shadows the text of *A View* in a manner which is greater than the sum of the references to it. Patricia Coughlan, in her splendidly provocative reading of the relationship betwen the two texts, argues that Eudoxus takes the role of Mnesippus, and Irenius the role of Toxaris. Translated into Elizabethan terms, Eudoxus becomes the spokesman of the English administration, and Irenius the representative of the New English settlers: 'As Scythians are to Greeks and wild men are to the civil, so are the Irish to the English; but so too, in a sense, are the colonists and officials in the field to the distant metropolitan policy-makers.' Although this might seem to map out the roles of Irenius and Eudoxus a little too rigidly and make the text rather too evenly balanced between the arguments of the two speakers, the point is well made. Lucian's dialogue commences with a discussion of the cult of Orestes and Pylades, who were Greeks seized by the Scythians. Mnesippus tries to ridicule the Scythians' admiration for these men, but Toxaris defends his people's practices on two grounds. First, the bravery of their deeds—sailing through inhospitable lands surrounded by savage peoples, bearing their imprisonment with fortitude, and having enough wit to punish the king for his insolence—inspires admiration: 'Yet that is not what we see in Orestes and Pylades to treat them as heroes.' More important is their demonstration of comradeship: 'What especially impressed us in these men and gains our commendation is this: it seemed to us that as friends they, surely, had proved themselves the best in the world, and had established precedents for everyone else in regard to the way in which friends should share their fortunes.' The fact that they are not Scythian in origin 'is no hindrance to their having been accounted good men and their being cherished by the formost Scythian; for we do not enquire what country proper men come from, nor do we bear a grudge if men who are friendly have done noble deeds; we commend what they have accomplished and count them our own in virtue of their achievements'.[69]

What is clear from this summary of the opening of the dialogue is that *both* Mnesippus and Toxaris see themselves and their people in contradistinction to the savages. To be a barbarian in Lucian's text is most definitely not to be a savage, as Toxaris's comments regarding 'savage peoples' indicates. In Elizabethan usage the terms seem to be virtually interchangeable (certainly as regards the Irish); the reference in *A View* looks back nostalgically to an 'imagined community' in which the

---

[69] Lucian, *Toxaris*, 103–11.

civilized (Greeks/English) and the barbarian (Scythians/Irish) were able to tolerate each other's differences.[70] Beneath the hostile surface of the text, which emphatically asserts that peace cannot be achieved until the land has been purged of all its Scythian elements, is the suggestion of a unity which has been lost. The Scythian in Lucian's dialogue is not the creature of Diodorus Sicilius, Herodotus, or Strabo, but a relatively urbane being, perhaps slightly inferior to his civilized counterpart, but by no means intractable, irredeemable, or always in the wrong.[71] Irenius' 'rippinge up of Ancestries' (p. 95) (Eudoxus' phrase) shows us, albeit only fleetingly, that the root, the etymology, of 'Scythian' is Janus-faced, and can lead towards a reclamation of the barbarian as well as a repudiation of the savage. A similar point is made later in the narrative when Irenius laments the current state of Ireland and looks back to its name as an explanation: 'And this is the wretchednes of that fatall king-dome which I thinke thearefore was in olde time not Called amisse *Banno* or *sacra Insula* takinge *sacra* for accursed' (p. 145). This use of an etymology, yet again derived from Camden's *Britannia*, leaves an ambivalent message because both words, 'sacra' and 'banno', could be translated as 'holy', the more usual description of ancient Ireland and one which Spenser employed in 'Two Cantos of Mutabilitie' (VII. vi. 37, line 7), where Ireland is described as 'this holy-Island'.[72] In this case, the etymologies point both ways and it might seem as if a possible acknow-ledgement of a hybrid colonial scene has opened up where identities are fluid and certainties challenged.[73]

However to give credence to this delicate balancing-act is to take *A View* on its own terms and read it in too positive a light. Spenser's work may well lead towards a plan and a promise for peace in Ireland, as the characterization of Irena in *The Faerie Queene*, Book V, suggests, but it is a specifically English peace which excludes the native Irish.[74] If

---

[70] Barnaby Rich, for example, refers to the Irish as 'barbarous savages': *New Descrip-tion of Ireland*, ch. 5. See also Hooker, 'The Chronicle of Ireland', in Holinshed, *Chron-icles*, vi. 369.

[71] Lucian, *Toxaris*, 115, 119–21, 205–6. The tract concludes with a hope that their friendship will continue as they are bound together by 'this conversation . . . and the simi-larity of [their] ideals' (Mnesippus). The dialogue serves as a fictional narrative of their union. For a similar perspective see Jones and Stallybrass, 'Dismantling Irena', 159–60.

[72] For details see *Variorum*, x. 372.

[73] See Homi K. Bhabha, 'Of Mimicry and Man: The Ambivalence of Colonial Dis-course', in id., *The Location of Culture*, 66–84.

[74] For a reading which does take both *A View* and *The Faerie Queene* at face value see Sheila T. Cavanagh, ' "Such was Irena's Countenance": Ireland in Spenser's Prose and Poetry', *TSLL* 28 (1986), 24–50.

Irenius can be read as a Scythian, he is an Anglicized one, as Coughlan's comments suggest, and his proposals as to the means of pacifying Ireland are bloody in the extreme.[75] In effect, the civilized Englishman and the barbarian Anglo-Irishman unite to exclude any form of native Irish representation. Reclaiming the classical dialogue of civilized England and barbarian Ireland involves brutally suppressing the savage native.

What do Spenser's conflicting accounts of Ireland's/Irish origins tell us? The most obvious conclusion to draw is that, like most English writers under the Tudors and before, Spenser looked back to his own British origins and claimed that these validated a right to the possession of the Irish crown by virtue of an ancient conquest and colonization. Simultaneously, the savage, alien nature of the Irish inhabitants of Ireland was asserted. In other words, land and people were firmly separated, Irish land forming part of an ancient British unity and Irish people cast in the role of the intractable 'otherness' which must be removed, of voices which must be silenced, just as their chronicles must be refuted, if that unity is to be recovered. The two key words are 'Briton' and 'Scythian'. The history contained in these two words, their etymologies, and the parallel discovery that they lie behind the history of so many other words and social practices, serve to validate the notions of identity and difference upon which the political disourse of *A View* depends. Anne Fogarty has described the political function which such etymological speculation plays in her discussion of *A View*:

The etymology of a word is for Eudoxus the final frontier. Once this has been drawn up, meaning and signification, or in current terminology, signifier and signified, assume a clear and unequivocal identity, and the threat of uncertainty is removed ... Etymology becomes, then, one of [the] foremost weapons for marshalling and controlling the ambiguities of language. By laying bare the origins of words, they [Irenius and Eudoxus] uncover a nexus of meaning which seems to be preordained by a linguistic system greater than themselves.[76]

The word itself provides an authoritative history and history is made up of a series of words, so that recovering their meanings becomes the key to history itself. The problem is that, however hard one tries to establish a definite certainty through this process and recover an unequivocal root, language itself will betray its unstable and contrary nature and other possibilities will emerge, a process which not only seems to take

---

[75] Brady, 'Spenser's Irish Crisis: Humanism and Experience', 33–6.
[76] 'The Colonisation of Language', 84.

place in *A View*, but which appears to be acknowledged as an inescapable fact of the slipperiness of writing.[77]

The use of British material had a further function in that it helped to elide political and territorial distinctions which were not obvious even to Tudor rulers. As many commentators have pointed out, it was by no means clear to contemporary observers whether Ireland was a kingdom or a colony.[78] To some, moving to Ireland might have seemed like migrating to any other part of mainland Britain; to others, Ireland resembled one of the nastier parts of the New World.[79]

What has been lacking from answers to such questions is an awareness that the English monarch ruled over a 'multiple kingdom' which contained vastly different territories.[80] The formal title of Elizabeth was 'Queene of England, France and Ireland and Virginia', which implies that it is a dangerous enterprise to distinguish between Ireland and Virginia as Crown territory and colony *per se*.[81] Sir John Davies, for example, argued that English laws did not necessarily apply to Ireland, as each were separate kingdoms ruled by the same monarch (James I), which was no more than Poynings' Law (1494) had recognized, a law which remained in force for nearly three centuries.[82] Referring back to a nebulously conceived Britain enabled writers to assert an English claim to Ireland without being forced to define terms in the language of sophisticated political rhetoric. Myth has always proved a good substitute for analysis.[83]

---

[77] See Derek Attridge, 'Language as History/History as Language: Saussure and the Romance of Etymology', in id., *Peculiar Language: Literature as Difference from the Renaissance to James Joyce* (Ithaca, NY: Cornell University Press, 1988), 90–126.

[78] For a convenient overview see Karl Bottigheimer, 'Kingdom and Colony'.

[79] MacCarthy-Morrogh, *Munster Plantation*, 279–80; Canny, 'Protestants, Planters and Apartheid in Early Modern Ireland', 111–14; Payne, *Briefe Description of Ireland*; ed. Quinn, ' "A Discourse of Ireland" '.

[80] See Hiram Morgan, 'Mid-Atlantic Blues', *Irish Review*, 11 (Winter 1991–2), 50–5; Conrad Russell, 'The British Background to the Irish Rebellion of 1641', *Historical Research*, 61 (1988), 166–82; id., 'The British Problem and the English Civil War', *History*, 73 (1988), 395–415.

[81] See Brady, 'Court, Castle and Country'.

[82] Pawlisch, *Sir John Davies and the Conquest of Ireland*, 131. Davies was referring specifically to the use of the Customs practice of 'murage' in Bristol and Waterford. Poynings' Law decreed that the Irish Parliament could only meet with the permission of the English king and council, and was enacted to prevent the Irish Parliament giving official recognition to pretenders to the throne, such as Lambert Simnel in 1487. Its subsequent history often belied this intention: see R. Dudley Edwards and T. W. Moody, 'The History of Poynings' Law, Part One: 1494–1615', *IHS* 2 (1940–41), 415–24.

[83] Roland Barthes, 'Myth Today', in *Mythologies*, trans. Annette Lavers (London: Granada, 1973), 109–57.

Arguments based on etymologies like Camden's, Spenser's, and Hanmer's could be used to argue that Ireland was perceived as a British colony (a settlement of a group of people from one country in another), just as Brittany (Armorica) was.[84] Holinshed, relying on Geoffrey's *History*, states: 'Cadwallader [the last British king] . . . not onlie obteined the principalitie of Wales but also of Cornwall & Armorica now called Little Britain, which then was a colonie of the Britons, and under the kingdome of Wales.'[85] Equally, such logic could lead to the conclusion, one that Irenius does in fact reach, that Ireland was a 'parte of Great Britaine' (p. 95).[86]

The British/Arthurian legend of a royal title to Ireland was, as I have stated, by no means an invention of Tudor England, or even freshly discovered from ancient writers like Diodorus Sicilius and Strabo: the same material could be found in the histories of Ranulph Higden and William of Malmesbury, as well as those of Geoffrey and Gerald.[87] The same legend could also be culled from French and English literary works by writers such as Sir Thomas Malory, Wace, and Layamon, all probably familiar to Spenser, either directly or indirectly, as interpreters of the Arthurian cycle.[88]

The same can be said of the story of the supposed savage/Scythian origins of the Irish, which can be found in Higden, Henry of Huntingdon, Nennius, Geoffrey, and Gerald, but which was given more prominence in the sixteenthcentury as an explanation of Irish recalcitrance as the

[84] Geoffrey of Monmouth, *History*, 139–42, 149. On the problem of defining the term 'colony', which is often asssumed (erroneously) to be identical with the later historical phenomenon 'colonialism', see M. I. Finley, 'Colonies: An Attempt at a Typology', *TRHS*, 26 (1976), 167–88; Andrew Hadfield, 'The Spectre of Positivism?: Sixteenth-Century Irish Historiography', *Text and Context*, 3 (1988), 10–16. Richard Beacon uses the word in the same way (*Solon his Follie*, bk. 3, ch. 14), as does Spenser (*A View*, 179–80, 184, 209–12).

[85] Holinshed, *Chronicles*, i. 37. See also William Harrison, 'The Description of Britain', ibid. 201.

[86] For comment see Helena Shire, *A Preface to Spenser* (London: Longman, 1978), 51; Michael O'Connell, *Mirror and Veil: The Historical Dimension of Spenser's* Faerie Queene (Chapel Hill: University of North Carolina Press, 1977), 139; Norbrook, *Poetry and Politics in the English Renaissance*, 140.

[87] Ranulph Higden, *Polychronicon*, ed. Charles Babbington and J. R. Lumby, 9 vols. (London, 1865–86), vol. i, ch. 33; William of Malmesbury, *Gesta Regnum Anglorum* (c.1125), ed. J. A. Giles, trans. John Sharp (London, 1847), 443; Geoffrey of Monmouth, *History*, 197, 221–2; Gerald of Wales, *History and Topography of Ireland*, bk. 3, ch. 92; id., *Expugnatio Hibernica*, bk. 2, ch. 6.

[88] Sir Thomas Malory, *Le Morte D'Arthur*, ed. Janet Cowen, 2 vols. (Harmondsworth: Penguin, 1969), i. 22, 303, ii. 103; Wace, *Roman de Brut* (c.12th c.), in *Arthurian Chronicles*, trans. Eugene Mason (London: Everyman, 1962), 54–7; Layamon, *Brut* (c.12th–c.13th c.), ibid. 205–7.

English state sought to bend its new subjects to its will and establish an imperial hegemony within the British Isles.[89] More specifically, it could be argued that the Scythian origins of the Irish were likely to be emphasized in times of political crisis and by writers who despaired of assimilating them to an English form of government, or by those newcomers keen to convince the Crown administration that they had the best claim to govern Ireland ahead of their indigenous rivals, i.e. New English Elizabethan settlers desiring to replace an established Old English élite. Edmund Spenser qualifies on all three counts. A View was written in the 1590s at a time of desperate crisis for the Crown when it seemed as if English government in Ireland could be overthrown and replaced by a Spanish Catholic monarchy, a decade of vacillating policies in Ireland which culminated in the earl of Essex's disastrous campaign in 1599.[90] Its 'hardline' policies have frequently been analysed and a persuasive case has been made that it marks the dead end of a tradition of attempts to reform the Irish and the start of a series of English works advocating the extermination of the native Irish, as frustrated English officials removed their trust from the mechanisms of the state and placed them instead in a military solution.[91] Finally, Spenser's career in Ireland took the form of a variety of influential official positions followed by the possession of an estate on the Munster Plantation, Kilcolman, established through the confiscation of Irish lands after the Desmond Rebellion. This brought him into protracted legal conflict with the Old English aristocrat, Lord Maurice Roche, a telling instance of the conflict of the two colonial classes for the right to the land of Ireland. Lord Roche's son, David, came out in open rebellion during the Nine Years War, which was to lead to the destruction of the Plantation and Spenser's flight to London; so did John Barry, the brother of another of Spenser's neighbours in Munster (see above, pp. 19–21).[92]

---

[89] Higden, *Polychronicon*, vol. i, ch. 33; Henry of Huntingdon, *Historia Anglorum* (*c*.1129), ed. and trans. Thomas Forester (London, 1853), 10–11; Nennius, *British History*, 10, 21; Geoffrey of Monmouth *History*, 123–4; Gerald of Wales, *History and Topography of Ireland*, bk. 3, ch. 87, *passim*. On English policy see Philip Edwards, *Threshold of a Nation: A Study in English and Irish Drama* (Cambridge: Cambridge University Press, 1979), ch. 4; Brady, 'Court, Castle and Country'; Kearney, 'The Making of an English Empire'.

[90] See Hiram Morgan, *Tyrone's Rebellion: The Outbreak of the Nine Years War in Tudor Ireland* (Woodbridge, Suffolk: Royal Historical Society/Boydell Press, 1993); id., 'Hugh O'Neill and the Nine Years War in Tudor Ireland', *HJ* 36 (1993), 21–37; Ellis, *Tudor Ireland*, ch. 9. More generally see John Guy (ed.), *The Reign of Elizabeth I: Court and Culture in the Last Decade* (Cambridge: Cambridge University Press, 1995).

[91] See Brady, 'The Road to the *View*'; id., *The Chief Governors*, 300.

[92] Maley, *Spenser Chronology*, 74.

Spenser's dialogue can be seen to argue the classic colonial case, asserting the rights of the settlers to the land and making every effort to remove the natives; the former claim via the matter of Britain, the latter in stressing the alien origins and nature of the inhabitants who had forfeited all rights to their native land.[93] In this, *A View* can be seen to fit into familiar paradigms of English writing on Ireland, where scepticism at home went hand in hand with credulousness in Ireland, and where evidence which was scornfully dismissed in one context was eagerly seized upon in another. However, one has reason to doubt Spenser's gullibility and suspect that he was guilty of bad faith instead, as *A View* appears to signal quite clearly that the Arthurian legends are not to be trusted in some places and yet relies on them elsewhere.[94] This would support the contention that *A View* was probably not intended for publication but for a coterie audience of influential political figures, and thus emphasize its role as a piece of propaganda.[95]

A View would have formed part of the Machiavellian political culture of the New English in Ireland. In *The Prince* Machiavelli argued that, although it was vitally important that princes should be seen to keep their word, 'nevertheless contemporary experience shows that princes who have achieved great things have been those who have given their word lightly, *who have known how to trick men with cunning*, and who, in the end, have overcome those abiding by honest principles' (my emphasis).[96] The same would apply to the English in Ireland, although whether *A View* was designed to help the English fool the Irish, or other Englishmen, or help the New English dupe the English authorities, or simply advance the author's prestige, remains a matter of some conjecture.[97] Perhaps the point is rather that, once deception becomes enshrined as integral to the message of the text, the discovery of the truth itself becomes a problematic enterprise.[98]

[93] For another example of the same colonial logic see George Peckham, 'A True Report of the late discoveries . . . of the Newfound Lands', in Hakluyt, *Principal Navigations*, vi. 42–78, at 49–58. See also Pagden, *The Fall of Natural Man*, ch. 3; Greenblatt, *Marvelous Possessions*, ch. 3.

[94] For another accusation levelled at Spenser's 'bad faith', see Brady, 'Spenser's Irish Crisis: Humanism and Experience', 41.

[95] See Andrew Hadfield, 'Was Spenser's *View of the Present State of Ireland* Censored? A Review of the Evidence', *N&Q* 239 (Dec. 1994), 459–63, at 262–3.

[96] Machiavelli, *The Prince*, 99.

[97] David Baker argues that *A View* was censored because it exposed the instability of English policies in Ireland: ' "Some Quirk, Some Subtle Evasion" '.

[98] For a similar use of Machiavelli see Greenblatt, 'Invisible Bullets'.

4

Reading the Allegory of
The Faerie Queene

COMMENTATORS have long argued about the relationship between the politics of *A View* and the allegorical representation of them in *The Faerie Queene* and which truly expresses Spenser's opinions. Should both be read as historical documents, literary works, or different genres of writing entirely? If they do have different generic forms, then how do such forms demand to be read?[1] Clark Hulse has pointed to a clear distinction in the sixteenth century both between types of writing and male and female spheres of activity. Hulse suggests that a line was drawn between a language of political analysis, 'the natural speech of those . . . who saw reality as it was and kept their hands on the levers of power' and 'its polar opposite', poetry, which was 'impractical and sycophantic', which could be mapped onto the expected roles of the (significant) men and women:

An issue adjacent to the creation of a poetic sphere separate from the political is the reaffirmation in the sixteenth century of a sphere of female activity separate from formal politics (or, perhaps, the creation of a formal politics separate from women). While women were barred from offices and institutions (except where the chance of family lineage might make them queens or duchesses), they might participate in the 'feminized' politics of court intrigue and influence peddling.[2]

These spheres became less clear and distinct, as Hulse acknowledges, when 'the chance of lineage' produced a queen so that the language of

---

[1] For recent reflections on this problem, see Patterson, 'Egalitarian Giant'; John Breen, 'The Empirical Eye: Edmund Spenser's *A View of the Present State of Ireland*', *Irish Review*, 16 (Autumn/Winter 1994), 44–52.

[2] 'Spenser, Bacon, and the Myth of Power', in Heather Dubrow and Richard Strier (eds.), *The Historical Renaissance: New Essays on Tudor and Stuart Literature and Culture* (Chicago: Chicago University Press, 1988), 315–46, at 316, 341. See also Pierre Saint-Amand, 'Terrorizing Marie Antoinette', *CI* 20 (1994), 379–400.

politics and the language of poetry became intertwined and genres inextricably mixed.[3]

The Faerie Queene is indisputably an allegorical work which contains a vast series of representations of political and historical events. But it demands to be read within a cultural context where its status is uncertain and insecure. Spenser's attempt to participate in a political sphere, the writing of *A View*, would seem to have provided him with a much smaller—albeit, possibly, more influential—audience than the writing of his epic poem dedicated to the queen, so that the latter reached a significantly wider public sphere as a printed text, even though it could be defined as a less straightforwardly public (masculine) statement. Spenser's defence of his erstwhile patron, Lord Grey, in *A View* would seem to point to a certain sense of frustration in terms of the gendered genres he was forced to work with. Eudoxus, referring to what he feels was Grey's premature recall after complaints at court of his excessive use of force, comments:

I remember that in the late goverment of that good Lo. Grey when after longe travaill and manye perilous assayes he had broughte things allmoste to this passe that ye speake of ['the soone finishinge of the warr'], that it was even made readie for reformacion and *mighte have bene* broughte to *what her maiestie woulde*, like Complainte was made againste him that he was a blodye man and regarded not the lief of her subiectes no more then dogges. (p. 159, my emphasis)

The past conditional tense illustrates that Grey, as representative of the sovereign, knew her desires and needs better than she knew them herself. Had she followed the dictates of the masculine political culture, rather than the feminized politics of courtly gossip, Ireland could have been saved. Grey's legitimate expression of the powers of the state represented by the queen has been undermined and slandered by the illegitimate powers of a whispering campaign—which *A View* seeks to set right—so that the queen has effectively been turned against herself. Eudoxus continues, somewhat bitterly, 'He noble Lord eftsones was blamed the | The wretched people pittied and new Councells plotted in which it was Concluded that a generall pardone shoulde be sente ouer to all that woulde accepte of it . . . all that hope of good which was even at the dore put backe and Cleane frustrate' (p. 160).

The key word here is 'pity', echoed by Irenius in his further comments on the unfortunate episode: 'the more the pittye for I maye not forgett so

<hr>

[3] Arthur F. Marotti, ' "Love is Not Love": Elizabethan Sonnet Sequences and the Social Order', *ELH* 49 (1982), 396–428.

memorable a thinge' (p. 160). Spenser's narration of the episode can easily be read as a contrast between the brutal but sensible masculine policy
of Grey, which makes enemies only of those who fail to see the political
logic of his strategy; and the deluded feminine pity of the queen who pardons the suffering people, not realizing that her mistaken gesture of
peace will lead only to greater violence. Grey represents the masculine
public body of Elizabeth, who herself represents the private female body
which needs to be kept subordinate, a case Elizabeth allegedly made in
her famous speech at Tilbury: 'I know I have the body of a weak and feeble woman, but I have the heart and stomach of a king.'[4] In Ireland,
Spenser claims, the wrong body rules and Irenius' 'pity' is for a lost
(masculine) political ideal.

The Faerie Queene is similarly caught between these two interrelated
but opposing poles of representational and political possibilities, which
to a large extent accounts for its hybrid, generically elaborate, and con-
fusing form. The poem is dedicated to a queen whom it represents, but,
according to the letter to Raleigh, aims 'to fashion a gentleman or noble
person in vertuous and gentle discipline' (p. 737). The poem owes a great
deal to Italian romance, traditionally a feminized genre, but equally to
the masculine world of the epic, as the letter also indicates: 'I haue followed all the antique Poets historicall, first Homere . . . then Virgil . . .
after him Ariosto . . . and lately Tasso.' The letter appears quite deliberately to balance the heroic world of the Classical against the Italianate.[5]
Similarly, the letter balances the descriptions of the two (supposedly)
most important figures, Arthur and the Faerie Queene herself, the one
standing for 'magnificence in particular, which vertue for that (according to Aristotle and the rest) it is the perfection of all the rest', the other,
'glory in my general intention', as well as Elizabeth.[6] The poem is
presented as both a national epic and a romance, the mediating figure
being the queen, who stands as both 'a most royall Queene or Empresse'

---

[4] Cited in J. E. Neale, *Queen Elizabeth* (London: Cape, 1934), 298. See also Helen
Hackett, *Virgin Mother, Maiden Queen: Elizabeth I and the Cult of the Virgin Mary* (Basingstoke: Macmillan, 1995), 56–60.

[5] On Spenser's debt to Classical ideals, particularly Virgil, see O'Connell, *Mirror and
Veil*; Helgerson, *Self-Crowned Laureates*, ch. 2. On Italian romance, see Graham Hough,
A Preface to The Faerie Queene (London: Duckworth, 1962); Paul J. Alpers, *The Poetry of*
The Faerie Queene (Princeton: Princeton University Press, 1967), ch. 1; A. Bartlett Gia-
matti, *Play of Double Senses: Spenser's* Faerie Queene (Englewood Cliffs, NJ: Prentice-
Hall, 1975), chs. 2–3; Linda Gregerson, *The Reformation of the Subject: Spenser, Milton
and the English Protestant Epic* (Cambridge: Cambridge University Press, 1995), ch. 1.

[6] Aristotle, *The Nichomachean Ethics*, trans. David Ross (Oxford: Oxford University Press, 1980), 85–9.

as well as 'a most vertuous and beautifull Lady' (p. 737).[7] The majority of the dedicatory sonnets are addressed to men, important figures in terms of both Anglo-Irish and English politics—Sir William Cecil, Lord Burghley, the Lord Treasurer and principal adviser to the queen; Edward de Vere, earl of Oxford, Lord Chamberlain; Thomas Butler, earl of Ormond and Ossory, Lord Treasurer of Ireland; Henry Percy, earl of Northumberland—as well as Spenser's patrons, mentors, and friends—Sir Walter Raleigh, Lord Grey, Robert Devereux, second earl of Essex, Sir John Norris, Lord President of Munster. However, the last three are dedicated to women: Mary Sidney, countess of Pembroke, and Lady Elizabeth Carey, both poets and patrons of poets, with the final sonnet addressed to 'all the gratious and beautifull Ladies in the Court', demonstrating that a poem intended to 'fashion a gentleman', was also designed for a female audience.[8]

Therefore the poem sets out a series of opposing gendered markers for the reader before the text is even read, signalling its experimental nature. The narrative itself, with its self-consciously archaic English style and lexicon, original and hybrid verse form, seemingly balancing French 'rhyme royal' and Italian 'ottava rima', and timeless fictional world which contains historical, contemporary, mythical, and literary figures from a range of cultures (English, Classical, and European), further unsettles the reader and confronts him or her with a self-consciously experimental poem which clearly aims to go beyond previously accepted generic boundaries.[9] It could be argued that *The Faerie Queene* aims to challenge the separation which Hulse has noted, one that marginalizes poetry as a feminine game, while at the same time feminizing the epic by incorporating romance. This would seem to be the logic behind the ending to the first edition of the poem published in 1590. The last of the three books deals with a female heroine, Britomart, the Knight of Chastity, who is able to go beyond and qualify the virtues of the first two knights; she supersedes the virtue of the Red Cross Knight because she is a British heroine, not an English one, and is therefore able to unify rather than divide the British Isles and not just one of

---

[7] David Lee Miller, *The Poem's Two Bodies: The Poetics of the 1590* Faerie Queene (Princeton: Princeton University Press, 1988).

[8] Black, '*The Faerie Queene*, commendatory verses and dedicatory sonnets'. See also Maureen Quilligan, *Milton's Spenser*, ch. 4.

[9] See Paul J. Alpers, *The Poetry of* The Faerie Queene (London: Duckworth, 1967), ch. 2; William Blissett, 'stanza, Spenserian', *Sp. Enc.* 671–3; Andrew Hadfield (ed.), *Spenser* (London: Longman, 1996), introduction, 3–4; Isabel E. Rathborne, *The Meaning of Spenser's Fairyland* (New York: Cornell University Press, 1937).

its constituent nations; she supersedes the achievements of Guyon, the Knight of Temperance, because she has to deal with the dictates of the body and not simply attempt to control unwanted desires and urges.[10] Nevertheless, Britomart is presented as a warrior woman dressed in a suit of armour, whose characteristics owe as much to the men she is frequently mistaken for as to specifically female virtues.[11] In the first canto the narrator describes her as 'full of amiable grace, | And *manly* terrour mixed therewithall, | That as the one stird up affections bace, | So th'other did mens rash desires apall' (III. i. 46, my emphasis). The passage is, yet again, neatly and deliberately balanced between the sexes; Britomart's feminine side attracts men, which is, here, a problem; yet her masculine qualities repel such unwanted advances. The irony of this particular incident is that it is not a man but a woman, the lustful Malecasta, who is attracted to Britomart, thus providing the reader with a contrast between the continent, 'masculinized' heroine and the incontinent woman, trapped by her 'feeble sexe' (III. i. 54).[12] Nevertheless, when Britomart reveals her sex to Malecasta and the latter bursts into tears, the warrior woman feels nothing but sympathy for her would-be seducer, even though, as the narrator states, Malecasta's weeping is feigned rather than genuine and only deludes Britomart because of her inexperience in affairs of the heart: 'the chaste damzell, that had neuer priefe | Of such malengine and fine forgerie, | Did easily beleeue her strong extremitie' (III. i. 53). The bond between the two women may be based on a false equation of their respective experiences on one level; but, on another, it is genuine and the narrator hastens to excuse the Knight of Chastity's error:

> Full easie was for her to haue beliefe,
> Who by self-feeling of her feeble sexe,
> And by long triall of the inward griefe,
> Wherewith imperious loue her hart did vexe,
> Could iudge what paines do louing harts perplexe.
> Who meanes no guile, be guiled soonest shall,
> And to faire semblaunce doth light faith annexe;

---

[10] See Hadfield, 'From English to British Literature'; Isabel G. McCaffrey, *Spenser's Allegory: The Anatomy of Imagination* (Princeton: Princeton University Press, 1976), 237–9; A. Leigh DeNeef, *Spenser and the Motives of Metaphor* (Durham, NC: Duke University Press, 1982), 115.

[11] See, Simon Shepherd, *Amazons and Warrior Women: Varieties of Feminism in Seventeenth Century Drama* (Brighton: Harvester, 1981), ch. 1.

[12] For further comment see David Mikics, *The Limits of Moralising: Pathos and Subjectivity in Spenser and Milton* (Lewisburg: Bucknell University Press, 1994), 94–8.

The bird, that knowes not the false fowlers call,
Into his hidden net full easily doth fall.

(III. i. 54)

There is a crucial ambiguity in these lines: on the one hand, the metaphor of the trapped birds refers to Britomart who has been manipulated by Malecasta; on the other, the traditional use of such imagery was to describe women abused by men, in other words a common experience of women as victims, so that the vehicle and logic of the metaphor would appear to be firmly at odds.[13] One also needs to read this incident in the light of a stanza which precedes it, addressed to 'Ladies' in general, an address which echoes the title of the last dedicatory sonnet:

Faire Ladies, that to loue captiued arre,
And chaste desires do nourish in your mind,
Let not her [Malecasta's] fault your sweet affections marre,
Ne blot the bounty of all womankind;
'Mongst thousands good one wanton Dame to find:
Emongst the Roses grow some wicked weeds;
For this was not to loue, but lust inclind;
For loue does alwayes bring forth bounteous deeds,
And in each gentle hart desire of honour breeds.

(III. i. 49)

Malecasta's behauiour and use of the *ars amores* is said to function only as a negative example for other women, singling her out as one among many. However, the portrayal of Malecasta as an exception which proves the rule also raises the question as to why Britomart is so easily taken in by her, and why Spenser's narrator apparently chooses to separate the two women's experiences via a metaphor which actually draws them together. The reading established by the narrator serves to raise a series of problems as it draws attention to the representation of women within the text, specifically demanding that the reader, whether male or female, decide what actually constitutes the boundaries of typical female behaviour. The problem raised by the whole incident, which sets out the lines along which the Book of Chastity will develop,

---

[13] Spenser may have in mind Chaucer's use of a similar metaphor to describe Criseyde trapped by Troilus via Pandarus: *Troilus and Criseyde*, III. 171, 177. On Spenser's use of Chaucer, see John A. Burrow, 'Chaucer, Geoffrey', *Sp. Enc.* 144–8; Alice S. Miskimin, *The Renaissance Chaucer* (New Haven: Yale University Press, 1975), ch. 9; Georgia Ronan Crampton, *The Condition of Creatures: Suffering and Action in Chaucer and Spenser* (New Haven: Yale University Press, 1974), *passim*.

is whether Britomart herself, rather than Malecasta, is the exceptional woman, able to act in a man's world only by transforming herself into a man. One commonly held line of defence of female rulers was that they were chosen by God to rule and so had to be separated from the rest of their sex and made masculine, a Calvinist-inspired argument made, for example, by Bishop Aylmer, and an issue clearly relevant to the representation of gender and power in the poem. The second edition of *The Faerie Queene* (1596) contains the counter-example of Radigund, the false female ruler whom Britomart defeats and kills in v. vii, perhaps further emphasizing the point that few women could be called or trusted to rule.[14]

The first edition ended, significantly enough, with the union of Scudamore and Amoret, whose passionate embrace promises to break down the distinction between the sexes. Again, the narrator addresses the reader to direct his or her attention to the significance of the verses: 'Had ye them seene, ye would haue surely thought, | That they had beene that faire *Hermaphrodite*' (III. xii. 46; 1590 edn.). Commentators have frequently seen this as an image of perfect sexual union of married lovers and refer to Genesis 2: 24, where it is stated that man 'shal cleave to his wife, and they shalbe one flesh'.[15] But the closure of the edition is not quite so clear-cut as this unreservedly positive reading would imply. In the same—the penultimate—stanza, Britomart is left watching jealously: 'That *Britomart* halfe envying their blesse, | Was much empassiond in her gentle sprite, | And to her selfe oft wisht like happinesse, | In vaine she wisht, that fate n'ould let her yet possesse.' It is notable that Britomart only *half* envies their happiness, as befits her nature: like the couple, hermaphrodite; the final line with its conditional tense, reminds the reader that it is possible that Britomart's union with Artegall will not occur, either in the poem itself (and the extant fragment does not represent the consummation of their union) or in terms of her representation of Elizabeth, who will not follow Britomart's example and get

[14] For a full discussion of these issues, see Pamela Joseph Benson, *The Invention of the Renaissance Woman: The Challenge of Female Independence in the Literature and Thought of Italy and England* (Philadelphia: Pennsylvania University Press, 1993). See also Clare Carroll, 'The Construction of Gender and the Cultural and Political Other in *The Faerie Queene* V and *A View of the Present State of Ireland*: The Critics, the Context, and the Case of Radigund', *Criticism*, 32 (1990), 163–91.

[15] Cited in *FQ*, p. 421. See also C. S. Lewis, *Spenser's Images of Life*, ed. Alastair Fowler (Cambridge: Cambridge University Press, 1967), 38; Thomas P. Roche, Jr., *The Kindly Flame: A Study of* The Faerie Queene, *III and IV* (Princeton: Princeton University Press, 1964), 134–6; Donald Cheney, 'Spenser's Hermaphrodite and the 1590 *Faerie Queene*', *PMLA* 87 (1972), 192–200; Watkins, *Specter of Dido*, 171–2.

married (clearly the case in 1590 with Elizabeth well past childbearing age).[16] The ending of the first edition would appear to confront the reader with two opposed images of the hermaphrodite, setting the union of the lovers against the voyeuristic and unsatisfied Britomart.[17]

What such an analysis, which barely scratches the surface of Spenser's complex sexual politics, demonstrates is that both the generic identity (form) of The Faerie Queene and the modes of gender identity represented within it (content) are problematic.[18] The poem seeks to explore various types of political authority and the concomitant possibilities for (male) subjects which exist under the aegis of a female ruler, while at the same time attempting to control and limit the influence of women's invasion of male space and the transformation of male spheres of activity. In these ways, The Faerie Queene is a work of excitement and fear, replete with new ideas and experiments, but anxious about their future.

In her recent work on allegory, Deborah L. Madsen has pointed out that no work can ever be a 'pure' allegory and separate itself from alternative ways of reading:

In order to be manifest as an identifiable trait, the dominant genre must suppress all heterogeneous traits within the text, each of which is a potential generic mark. So all genres are inescapably mixed ... All allegorical narratives and contiguous forms—the sermon, typological history, spiritual autobiography, morality drama—participate in the genre while remaining generically mixed.[19]

Certainly such an analysis applies to a genre which marks itself out as 'mixed' in terms of its textual signals to the reader; not quite Fielding's 'comic Epic-Poem in Prose',[20] but 'coloured with an historicall fiction',

---

[16] See Hadfield, Literature, Politics and National Identity, 190–201; Hackett, Virgin Mother, Maiden Queen, 191–7.

[17] For further reflections on this episode and a more positive reading of Spenser's use of the hermaphrodite, see Lauren Silberman, Transforming Desire: Erotic Knowledge in Books III and IV of The Faerie Queene (Berkeley: University of California Press, 1995), ch. 3.

[18] Hence the widely different readings of Spenser as a 'proto-feminist' and misogynist. For the former reading, see Benson, Invention of Renaissance Woman and Silberman, Transforming Desire; for the latter, Shepherd, Spenser, ch. 2 and Sheila T. Cavanagh, Wanton Eyes and Chaste Desires: Female Sexuality in The Faerie Queene (Bloomington: Indiana University Press, 1994). As Cavanagh notes, 'we have only just begun to explore the configurations of sexuality and desire in the epic' (p. 172).

[19] Rereading Allegory: A Narrative Approach to Genre (Basingstoke: Macmillan, 1995), 26.

[20] Henry Fielding, Joseph Andrews and Shamela, ed. Douglas Brooks-Davies (Oxford: Oxford University Press, 1970), 4.

following 'all the antique Poets historicall' (*FQ*, p. 737). Madsen also describes how allegories function:

In all allegories, the status of the narrative as an interpretation raises the *question of the narrative's hermeneutic validity*. For allegory is twofold: it is simultaneously an interpretation and a metacritical statement that regulates interpretation. So in allegory two kinds of truth are confounded: truth as the meaning of the narrative and truth as the interpretation of a prior text.[21] (my emphasis)

In other words, allegory tells the reader what he or she already knows and attempts to tell a new story, so that the allegorical narrative becomes a battle for control between the person making sense of that narrative, whether author or reader, and the material allegorized, the pretext for the narrative in the first place.

A. C. Hamilton has stated that 'What is chiefly needed to understand the allegory [of *The Faerie Queene*] fully is to understand all the words', a formulation which raises as many questions as it answers. Hamilton explains how he reads the words in the poem:

Through his art of language, Spenser seeks to purify words by restoring them to their true, original meanings. When Adam fell, he lost that natural language in which words contain and reveal the realities they name . . . By his language of allegory he recreates that natural language in which the word and its reality again merge. Like Adam, he gives names to his creatures which express their natures.[22]

Hamilton reads *The Faerie Queene* in terms of Madsen's second function of the allegorical aporia, 'truth as the interpretation of a prior text', subsuming other possibilities under this hermeneutic umbrella (Spenser's intention and the reader's understanding of the text are conveniently conflated). The poem becomes a 'classic text', a readerly discourse which leads the reader towards the disclosure of a transcendental signified of the proper name. If we gloss 'transcendental signified' as 'fallen language', then Roland Barthes' description of the way in which the narrative of Balzac's *Sarrasine* works serves as an explanation as to how readers like Hamilton perceive the allegory of Spenser's poem:

The connotative signified is literally an *index*: what it points to is the name, the truth as name; it is both the temptation to name and the impotence to name . . .

[21] *Rereading Allegory*, 95. See also Nick Davies, 'Narrative Composition and Spatial Memory', in Hawthorn (ed.), *Narrative*, 23–40.
[22] *FQ*, pp. 17–18. See also A. C. Hamilton, 'Our New Poet: Spenser's "well of English undefyld" ', in Judith M. Kennedy and James P. Reither (eds.), *A Theatre for Spenserians* (Manchester: Manchester University Press, 1973), 101–23.

with its designating, silent movement, a pointing finger always accompanies the classic text: the truth is long desired and avoided, kept in a kind of pregnancy for its full term, a pregnancy whose end, both liberating and catastrophic, will bring about the utter end of the discourse.[23]

Hamilton's desire to reproduce the one-to-one relationship of words and things is a product of a faith in the metaphoric nature of allegory as a chain of one-to-one correspondences between the literal signified resulting from the signifier in the text and the second-order signified of the allegorical level.[24] This faith in allegory as a vehicle for the production of 'truth' seeks to impose an absolute control over the text and bring to light a system of differences which is, in effect, a metalanguage made up of names which are 'already read'.[25] These names will signal, as Barthes noted, 'the utter end of discourse', because discourse has to be articulated through narrative, which requires movement resulting from difference and the desire to change: 'narrative, by its nature, always contains the seeds of its own subversion.'[26] Hamilton's reading of *The Faerie Queene*, is an attempt to complete a work, which is described as 'endlesse' (IV. xii. 1), to make the narrative stop so that the static plenitude of meaning can be revealed.[27]

Hamilton's search for origins is a mode of reading the poem as if it were an allegorical text of the same order as Augustine's *City of God*, a key patristic work which helped establish the writing and reading of allegory within a subsequent Christian tradition.[28] Augustine's aim was to draw distinct lines between the earthly City of Men and the heavenly City of God, so that the good of the latter could be separated from the

---

[23] Roland Barthes, *S/Z: An Essay*, trans. Richard Miller (New York: Hill & Wang, 1974), 62. See also Derrida, *Of Grammatology*, 110–12. Barthes' narratological categories have been applied to *The Faerie Queene*, Book IV, in Jonathan Goldberg, *Endlesse Worke: Spenser and the Structures of Discourse* (Baltimore: Johns Hopkins University Press, 1981).

[24] A mode of reading Barthes himself rejected when he came to reconsider his early work: see *Mythologies*, 9.

[25] Barthes, *S/Z*, 20.

[26] Patrick O'Neill, *Fictions of Discourse: Reading Narrative Theory* (Toronto: University of Toronto Press, 1994), 3. See also Tzvetan Todorov, *Genres in Discourse*, trans. Catherine Porter (Cambridge: Cambridge University Press, 1990), 28.

[27] Barthes, *S/Z*, 88–90. Similar assumptions have been a staple feature of much interpretation of Spenser's allegory: see T. K. Dunseath, *Spenser's Allegory of Justice in Book V of* The Faerie Queene (Princeton: Princeton University Press, 1968), 235; A. C. Hamilton, *Allegory in* The Faerie Queene (Oxford: Clarendon Press, 1961); Paul Alpers, 'How to Read *The Faerie Queene*', EC 18 (1968), 429–43. A less static reading of Spenser's allegory is to be found in McCaffrey, *Spenser's Allegory*, pt. 1.

[28] Harold L. Weatherby, *Mirrors of Celestial Grace: Patristic Theology in Spenser's Allegory* (Toronto: University of Toronto Press, 1994), 55; McCaffrey, *Spenser's Allegory*, 352; Gordon Teskey, 'allegory', *Sp. Enc.* 16–22.

evil of the former, before the two antitheses were put back together and
man could perceive the path back to the promised heaven. Augustine
argued that man could not ever hope to hear the truth of the speech of
God, which is 'beyond our describing . . . on a higher plane; it precedes
his action as the changeless reason of the action itself; and his speaking
has no sound, no transitory noise; it has a power that persists for eternity
and operates in time'.[29] We can only understand this perfect speech
indirectly and comprehend the City of God as 'a kind of shadow and
prophetic image . . . which served rather to point towards it than
to reproduce it on earth at the time when it was due to be displayed'
(p. 597). The City of God is inhabited by saints in heaven, 'although it
produces citizens here below, and in their persons the City is on pilgrimage until the time of its kingdom comes' (p. 596). Similarly, we must
understand that in the Scriptures, 'One part of the earthly city has been
made into an image of the Heavenly City, *by symbolising something
other than itself* . . . Thus we find in the earthly city a double significance:
in one respect it displays its own presence, and in the other it serves by its
presence to signify the Heavenly City' (pp. 597–8, my emphasis). The
symbol serves as a doubling of significance within the narrative, so that
it stands as a sign in its own right yet also has a supplementary meaning;
it is this additional meaning, according to Augustine, which orders the
narrative. He justifies the exclusion 'of righteous men who worshipped
God' from the biblical narrative of the times between the sons of Noah
and Abraham on the grounds that, if they were all mentioned, 'the narrative would become tedious, and would be more notable for historical
accuracy than for prophetic foresight' (p. 652). Hence we are asked to
believe that the events narrated in the Scriptures are not only historical,
but go beyond such a straightforward level of understanding, having a
'symbolic meaning', which is 'a prophetic picture of the church' (p. 648).
Such events as occur on earth are 'directed from heaven', being 'the
actions of men, but the operation of God' (p. 701).

For Augustine, Scripture is the key authority which legitimizes the narrative: the translators of the Vulgate and the seventy scholars who com-
plied the original version of the Bible are said to speak with God's voice
(pp. 652–3). Although the evidence is far from extensive, the early readers
of *The Faerie Queene* would appear to have conceived of the poem in an

[29] *Concerning the City of God against the Pagans*, trans. Henry Bettenson (Harmondsworth: Penguin, 1972), 659–60. Subsequent references are given in the text in parentheses. Cf. Derrida, *Of Grammatology*, 15–17; Ernst Robert Curtius, *European Literature
and the Latin Middle Ages*, trans. Willard Trask (London: Routledge, 1953), 310–11.

analogous manner, extracting the most obviously historical details from the narrative in order to read the work as a prophetic history of England past, present, and future. The first reader of *The Faerie Queene*, John Dixon, saw the poem as 'a celebration of religious and national history ... an English Protestant heroic poem'.[30] He annotated his copy of the first edition with a series of straightforward correspondences. The Red Cross Knight is identified as the earl of Leicester beside the line 'Right faithfull true he was in deede and word' (I. i. 2); in the following stanza Gloriana is glossed as 'Elizabeth', and in the next, Una as 'truth' (p. 2). Beside the lines, 'For well I wote, thou springst from ancient race | Of *Saxon* kings, that haue with mightie hand' (I. x. 65), addressed by Contemplation to The Red Cross Knight, Dixon has written, 'Arthur raigned ouer the britons: 26: yeares, and began his raigne the yeare of our Lord: 517: he was a magnificent prince, and a myghtie Conquerer' (p. 8), as well as suggesting that the figure of Arthur also refers to the earl of Cumberland, a prominent Elizabethan naval hero (an identification which is unique to Dixon). This illustrates that Dixon read the allegory in Augustinian terms, selecting the relevant historical details and fitting them into a wider typological narrative so that the allegory works at more than one level; here, a dual historical schema (Dixon heavily annotates the Briton chronicles in II. x. demonstrating his belief in the historical reality of Arthur, providing evidence that the poem was read in terms of its British material (pp. 12–14)). The headnote to I. xii, 'Faire Una to the Redcrosse knight | betrouthed is with ioy: | Though false Duessa it to barre | her false sleights doe imploy', receives the note, 'a fiction of Queene Eliz: the maintainer of the gospell of Christe, to be by god himselfe betrouthed unto Christe, though by k:p. [King Philip] and rc: [Roman Catholics] for 6: yeares it was debared' (p. 9), showing that Dixon was capable of reading the text as an allegory where historical events fitted into a wider symbolic pattern of Christian eschatology.[31] Dixon's readings are flexible and involve being able to read the surface narrative in divergent ways: after Archimago manages to separate Una and the Red Cross Knight, Dixon glosses her 'wandring in woods and forrests' (I. ii. 9) as 'daughter and heir to a persian kinge, but is rightly to be understood the daughter of Israel or the true Church, which was led by the wylldernese 140 yeares', an inter-

---

[30] *The First Commentary on* The Faerie Queene, ed. Graham Hough (privately printed, 1964), 18. Subsequent references are given in parentheses in the text.

[31] See Florence Sandler, '*The Faerie Queene*: An Elizabethan Apocalypse', in C. A. Patrides and Joseph Wittreich (eds.), *The Apocalypse in English Renaissance Thought and Literature* (Manchester: Manchester University Press, 1984), 148–74, at 165–6.

pretation which clearly does not square perfectly with that of Una as Elizabeth. These allegorical meanings are combined in a prophetic mode when he comments on Duessa as a usurper of righteous values (I. ii. 22–3): 'Antichriste taketh one hir nam of Truth, fained to be the daughter of a persian kynge: but truth is only to be ment. to our Soueraigne Eliz. Christe and his gospell' (p. 4). The progress of biblical history and the rise of the English Protestant nation are seen to converge.[32]

The Faerie Queene demands to be read as an intervention into Elizabethan political thought and clearly points out ways of reading past, present, and future.[33] However, there is an opposite force of meaning operating within the text, one which denies the stability of allegory: the poem does not close with a symbol pointing towards a transcendental meaning or even an Augustinian shadow of a prior text. The poem may well begin with the figure of Una, but she can only be defined tautologically, perhaps echoing God's answer to Moses' question concerning the name and nature of the deity: 'I AM THAT I AM' (Exod. 3: 14). Una is 'Who in her selfe-resemblance well beseene, | Did seeme such, as she was, a goodly maiden Queene' (I. xii. 8), a deliberate contrast to Duessa's disguised nature.[34] Duessa, unlike Una, provides her own description of herself to Night in the course of appealing to him to help the Saracens defeat the Red Cross Knight: 'I that do seeme not I, Duessa am, | (Quoth she) how euer now in garments gilt, | And gorgeous gold arayd I to thee came; | Duessa I, the daughter of Deceipt and Shame' (I. v. 26). The contrast might seem fundamentally straightforward, albeit problematic. However, one should refer back to the first description we have of Una at the start of the book, riding next to the Red Cross Knight:

> A louely Ladie rode him faire beside,
> Upon a lowly Asse more white then snow,
> Yet she much whiter, but the same did hide
> Under a vele, that wimpled was full low,

---

[32] See William Haller, Foxe's Book of Martyrs and the Elect Nation (London: Cape, 1963). Further evidence of similar readings of The Faerie Queene are provided in Alastair Fowler, 'Oxford and London Marginalia to The Faerie Queene', N&Q 206 (1961), 416–19; Walter Oakeshott, 'Carew Raleigh's Copy of Spenser', The Library, 5th ser., 26 (1971), 1–21; Alastair Fowler and Michael Leslie, 'Drummond's Copy of The Faerie Queene', TLS, 17 July 1981, pp. 821–2.; John Manning, 'Notes and Marginalia in Bishop Percy's Copy of Spenser's Works (1611)', N&Q 229 (1984), 225–7.

[33] See O'Connell, Mirror and Veil; Angus Fletcher, The Prophetic Moment: An Essay on Spenser (Chicago: University of Chicago Press, 1971); Hadfield, Literature, Politics and National Identity, ch. 6.

[34] Roland M. Smith argues that both names have Irish origins; 'Una and Duessa', PMLA 50 (1935), 917–19.

> And ouer all a blacke stole she did throw,
> As one that inly mournd: so was she sad,
> And heauie sat upon her palfrey slow:
> Seemed in heart some hidden care she had,
> And by her in a line a milke white lamb she lad.

(I. i. 4)

The description seems to be a positive endorsement of Una's holiness; her wearing of a veil places her as a familiar representation of truth, hidden to fallen man (as Augustine recognized); the lamb marks her out as Christlike and innocent; the ass suggests humility as well as providing a further parallel with Christ; her simple white attire contrasts the purity of the reformed church to the gaudy show of the Catholic church represented by Duessa's gilt and gold garments, which disguise her true nature; her sombre appearance and quiet grief also contrast her to the 'faire disport and courting dalliaunce' and lavish crowns and jewels worn by Duessa when she is first seen (I. ii. 13–14).[35] But, the point is that, in the fallen world, even truth has to be hidden—as Augustine indeed recognized—opening up the fear that truth will never be revealed, however scrupulous the seeker. Una is disguised and hidden when we first see her, which links her to Duessa, however keen one may be to separate them. There are uncomfortable echoes of the description of Una in the stanza which introduces us to Archimago, the equivocating magician whose aim is to separate Una and the Red Cross Knight:

> Sober he seemde, and very sagely sad,
> And to the ground his eyes were lowly bent,
> Simple in shew, and voyde of malice bad,
> And all the way he prayed, as he went,
> And often knockt his brest, as one that did repent.

(I. i. 29)

Like Una, Archimago is solemn in demeanour and the same word, 'sad', is used. Both are simple in appearance. The narrator draws our attention to his impressionistic knowledge of each through the use of 'seemed' and the relative pronoun, 'as'. Of course, one might argue that Archimago, who turns out to be an obviously Catholic figure once Una and the knight have entered his hermitage ('He told of Saintes and

---

[35] See Douglas Brooks-Davies, Spenser's Faerie Queene: *A Critical Commentary on Books I and II* (Manchester: Manchester University Press, 1977), 14–16; id., 'Una', *Sp. Enc.*, 704–5; James Nohrnberg, *The Analogy of* The Faerie Queene (Princeton: Princeton University Press, 1976), 97, 128, *et passim.*

Popes, and euermore | He strowd an *Aue-Mary* after and before' (1. i. 35),
is there to test both the characters within the poem and, by implication,
the reader, who is supposed to be fashioned into a gentleman via the
narrative. However, the fear is that there will simply be no way out
of the labyrinthine structures of language, which demand that 'truth'
has to be represented in order to exist, and so can only appear as a self-
referential tautology. The difficulty in separating the first descriptions
of Una and Archimago becomes more apparent if one returns and
rereads the former in the light of the latter. One could easily make a case
that Una is a false figure because she only appears to mourn and seems
to have a hidden care in her heart. The wimple she wears could be taken
to mark her out as a nun, the very antithesis of a Protestant stress on
active life in the world and the importance of marriage.[36]

James Norhnberg has perceptively demonstrated that Una and the
Red Cross Knight depend on each other in order to make 'truth' appear
and that, in separation, their unity is lost: 'Without Una, Redcross's
dedication can be neither wholly one, nor wholly true . . . And without
the single-minded Redcrosse, Una herself cannot be wholly true, for
truth is not itself when it is unknown and unappreciated, nor when it is
adulterated and vulgarized.'[37] But this does not resolve the problem of
the narrative: truth has to appear as a metaphorical hermaphrodite, a
comparison which undermines the pure teleological thrust of the concept in the first place. As Barthes has noted, 'to read is to struggle to
name . . . even while the discourse is leading us toward other possibilities, toward other related signifieds', the nature of narrative moves
sideways rather than forwards because 'reading is absorbed in a kind of
metonymic skid, each synonym adding to its neighbour some new trait,
some new departure'.[38]

What I have outlined is a commonplace of post-structuralist criticism.[39] Many critics have already commented on the problematic nature

---

[36] See Patrick Collinson, *The Birthpangs of Protestant England: Religious and Cultural Change in the Sixteenth and Seventeenth Centuries* (London: Macmillan, 1988),
ch. 3.

[37] *Analogy of* The Faerie Queene, 281. Roland Smith notes that in November 1579 Sir
William Pelham proclaimed that all horsemen in the queen's service in Ireland should
wear two red crosses. Pelham presented the sword of state to Lord Grey when he took up
the post of Deputy in September 1580 so that Spenser would undoubtedly have known of
Pelham's proclamation, and, Smith argues, the representation of the Red Cross Knight is
given a further Irish dimension: 'Origines Arthurianae: The Two Crosses of Spenser's Red
Cross Knight', *JEGP* 54 (1955), 670–83, at 672–7.

[38] *S/Z*, 92.

[39] The most brilliant exposition of this principle is Jacques Derrida, 'White Mythology: Metaphor in the Text of Philosophy', in id., *Margins of Philosophy*, trans. Alan Bass

of the later books, especially Book VI, which appear to question the very possibility of allegorical narrative (see below, Ch. 6): but it would appear that this problem is acknowledged by Spenser from the start of his enterprise. If so, the poem is conceived as a battle for the possession of a fundamental concept, 'truth', which its author recognizes may not even exist, an admission which irrevocably undermines the designs the work has of fashioning the reader; instead, the act of reading serves to fashion the existence of the poem.[40] At the end of the second canto, Fradubio, who has been turned into a tree by Duessa, explains the 'truth' of his situation to the Red Cross Knight. Duessa, recognizing the story ('And knew well all was true', II. iii. 44), pretends to faint until she is lifted up by the knight. The narrator comments with studied ambiguity: 'with trembling cheare | Her up he tooke, too simple and too trew' (45). Not only is it not clear who has a 'trembling cheare', but it is an open question whether the figure who is 'too simple and too trew' is Duessa or the knight.[41] The words either represent the knight as too innocent and gullible to discover the truth (i.e. he is a bad reader), or they apply to Duessa with bitter irony, suggesting that she has gone beyond mere 'truth' and constancy, and returned to deception. Whichever way they are read, however, they illustrate that even the word 'truth' can be misleading (untrue) and possess supplementary, excessive meanings beyond its proper signification, which serve to falsify it.

This battle between the two poles of allegorical significance and interpretation in The Faerie Queene cannot be read as an abstract, formalist dispute.[42] Rather, I would argue, the problem is intimately related to both Spenser's wider and his more specific concerns. Stephen Greenblatt, writing against those who would delimit the Irish context to Book V, has argued that the question of Ireland 'pervades the poem'.[43] In a sense this is the case, but only if the converse is also stated. The

---

(Brighton: Harvester, 1982), 207–71. See also Jonathan Culler, 'The Turns of Metaphor', in The Pursuit of Signs: Semiotics, Literature, Deconstruction (London: Routledge, 1981), 188–209; Paul De Man, 'The Rhetoric of Temporality', in id., Blindness and Insight: Essays in the Rhetoric of Contemporary Criticism, 2nd. edn. (London: Routledge, 1986), 187–228.

[40] See Goldberg, 'Pretexts' in id., Endlesse Worke; id., Voice Terminal Echo: Postmodernism and English Renaissance Texts (London: Methuen, 1986), 13.

[41] As acknowledged in FQ, p. 54.

[42] On this problem see Paul De Man, 'The Dead-End of Formalist Criticism', in id., Blindness and Insight, 229–45; Edward Said, 'Roads Taken and Not Taken in Contemporary Criticism', in id., The World, the Text and the Critic (London: Faber & Faber, 1983), 140–57.

[43] Renaissance Self-Fashioning, 186.

figure of Ireland serves as a vehicle for expressing the ideological anxieties of Spenser's understanding of Elizabethan culture, so that such fears pervade the representation of Ireland. Like the union of Una and the Red Cross Knight, or Amoret and Scudamore, the two will not function if separated and the question of which came first will turn out to be a futile search for lost origins.

Although A. S. P. Woodhouse's influential distinction between the order of grace represented in the first book of *The Faerie Queene* and the natural world of secular ethics announced in the second as setting the tenor for the rest of the poem has been shown to be full of pitfalls, that book is still often read as if it were endorsing a self-sufficiency which is subsequently shown to be challenged in the later stages of the poem.[44] A concomitant reading is that Spenser started out with great confidence to write a public epic, but gradually became more disillusioned with the queen as he languished in Ireland until he started to become more openly critical of her in the last two completed books, so that, if one excepts the continuity which Book IV shares with Book III (probably due to the two surviving from an earlier form of the poem), there is a huge gulf between the praise of Book I and the hostility of Books V and VI.[45] However, it should be remembered that Spenser had already been in Ireland for (at least) ten years when he published the first edition of *The Faerie Queene*, and a year later, according to the preface, he wrote *Colin Clouts come home againe*, a bitter poem of colonial exile. It would be strange if his Irish experience had not modified his sense of identity, especially given his willingness to articulate (fashion) this in his poetry elsewhere, and remembering that *The Faerie Queene* is a poem which foregrounds the question of personal and national identity in the very logic of its narrative.[46] Unlike the works of the Mirror for Princes tradition, *The Faerie Queene* serves as a mirror of authority for the reader, rather than being a straightforward reflection which assumes that the two—reader and prince/governor—are synonymous.[47]

[44] A. S. P. Woodhouse, 'Nature and Grace in *The Faerie Queene*', *ELH* 16 (1949), 194–228. See Hume, *Edmund Spenser*, ch. 4 for criticism in terms of Elizabethan theology. See also Norbrook, *Poetry and Politics in the English Renaissance*, ch. 5; O'Connell, *Mirror and Veil*, introduction; Richard Mallette, 'The Protestant Art of Preaching in Book One of *The Faerie Queene*', *Sp. Stud.* 7 (1987), 3–25.

[45] Thomas H. Cain, *Praise in* The Faerie Queene (Lincoln, Nebr.: University of Nebraska Press, 1978). On the probable composition of the poem, see J. W. Bennett, *The Evolution of* The Faerie Queene (Chicago: Chicago University Press, 1942).

[46] See Montrose, 'Elizabethan Subject and the Spenserian Text'; Gregerson, *Reformation of the Subject*, introduction.

[47] Donald Cheney, *Spenser's Image of Nature: Wild Man and Shepherd in* The Faerie Queene (New Haven: Yale University Press, 1966), 149. For a recent reassessment of the

Book I has usually been straightforwardly decoded by commentators from the seventeenth century to the present day without reference to Ireland.[48] To summarize: Una (truth) is separated from the Red Cross Knight, later revealed to be the patron saint of England, St George, by the wiles of the Catholic magician, Archimago; the primitive, pure Church of England has been corrupted by Catholic duplicity. There then follow a series of adventures which reach a climax when the knight, weakened by his battle with the giant, Orgoglio, is tempted to commit suicide by the figure of Despair. Rescued by Una and Arthur, the knight is re-educated in the House of Holiness, so that he is able to fight and kill the satanic dragon who has imprisoned Una's parents (allegorically, Adam and Eve). The two lovers are reunited and betrothed.[49] The book ends with the knight promising to return to marry Una, after having served the Faerie Queene for six years, a number which corresponds both to the days of creation and the length of the reign of Mary and Philip.[50] It appears that the reader is directed forward to the triumphs of Elizabeth's reign, as England throws off its religious shackles and the influence of the Antichrist (though the non-consummation of Una and the Red Cross Knight's marriage implies that this freedom is tempered).

But within the book there is a troubling episode, when Una is rescued from the Saracen Knight, Sansloy, by a troop of fauns and satyrs who have been dancing in the wood (I. vi). This 'rude, misshapen, monstrous rablement' (8), take her to the wood-god, Sylvanus, and proceed to worship her as a deity who exceeds their current religious knowledge and forms of representation. Therefore, she throws their notion of the sacred into crisis and inaugurates a whole new series of religious practices.[51] While 'The woodborne people fall before her flat, | And worship her as

tradition, see John L. Watts, *Henry VI and the Politics of Kingship* (Cambridge: Cambridge University Press, 1996), ch. 2.

[48] See e.g. the comments of George de Malynes and John Hughes, cited in Cummings (ed.), *Spenser: The Critical Heritage*, 115, 263–4; *First Commentary*, ed. Hough; Virgil K. Whittaker, 'The Theological Structure of *The Faerie Queene*, I', *ELH* 19 (1952), 151–64; O'Connell, *Mirror and Veil*, ch. 2; Elizabeth Heale, The Faerie Queene: *A Reader's Guide* (Cambridge: Cambridge University Press, 1984), ch. 1; King, *Spenser's Poetry and the Reformation Tradition*, ch. 5.

[49] See Hume, *Edmund Spenser* ch. 5.

[50] Hough, *First Commentary*, 10; O'Connell, *Mirror and Veil*, 61.

[51] The literature on idolatry and iconoclasm after the Reformation is vast. Most commentaries on Spenser concentrate on Guyon's destruction of Acrasia's bower. Useful in terms of this episode are Alan Sinfield, *Faultlines: Cultural Materialism and the Politics of Dissident Reading* (Oxford: Clarendon Press, 1992), 193–7; Ernest B. Gilman, *Iconoclasm and Poetry in the English Reformation: Down Went Dagon* (Chicago: Chicago University Press, 1986), ch. 3; Greenblatt, *Renaissance Self-Fashioning*, 188–91; Kenneth Gross,

Goddesse of the wood' (I. vi. 16), Sylvanus tries to figure her in terms of his previous conception of beauty. Sometimes he sees her as Venus ('But Venus never had so sober mood'), sometimes as Diana ('But misseth bow, and shaftes, and buskins to her knee'); but eventually he comes to see in her a reminder of his dead love, Cyparisse, who pined away after Sylvanus had accidentally shot his beloved hind (I. vi. 17).[52] The female wood-nymphs 'Flocke all about to see her louely face: | But when they vewed haue her heavenly grace, | They enuie her in their malitious mind, | And fly away for feare of fowle disgrace'. The male satyrs, in contrast, reject their womenfolk and gaze at Una, seeing everything that is beautiful as a part of her (I. vi. 18); eventually, they transform her into an idol, and when she refuses their dubious honour, they worship her ass, possibly recalling the exiled Israelites' idolatry in Exodus 32. Una becomes rather distressed at all this unwelcome attention and tries to teach them more wholesome doctrine, but they remain transfixed with visual images:

> During which time her gentle wit she plyes,
> To teach them truth, which worshipt her in vaine,
> And made her th'Image of Idolatryes;
> But when their bootlesse zeale she did restraine
> From her own worship, they her Asse would worship fayn.
>
> (I. vi. 19)

Eventually, when the satyrs leave her alone, Una is rescued by Sir Satyrane.

Usually the satyrs have been interpreted as representatives of a form of 'natural' animistic religion; ignorant, primitive Christians; or, even, the Jews, Egyptians, Greeks, and Romans.[53] The incident has been considered within the context of the narrative of the book as an expression of Spenser's religious thought, as if such questions could be isolated and dealt with separately, as well as illustrating the problem of selecting in advance exactly what the significant details of the narrative are and relegating other details to secondary significance.[54] But the satyrs are referred

---

Spenserian Poetics: Idolatry, Iconoclasm, and Magic (Ithaca, NY: Cornell University Press, 1985).

[52] On Cyparisse, see Ovid, *Metamorphoses*, trans. Mary M. Innes (Harmondsworth: Penguin, 1955), 228.

[53] See Richard D. Jordan, 'satyrs', *Sp. Enc.*, 628; Nohrnberg, *Analogy of* The Faerie Queene, 218–22; Frank Kermode, *Shakespeare, Spenser, Donne: Renaissance Essays* (London: Routledge, 1971), 48–9; Norbrook, *Poetry and Politics in the English Renaissance*, 123.

[54] Cf. also the ways in which the Irish setting of 'Two Cantos of Mutabilitie' has been read as merely incidental.

to as 'The saluage nation' (I. vi. 11), a description which links them to the series of representations of savages and savagery which occurs throughout Books IV, V, and VI of the poem, as well as to the satyrs with whom Hellenore decides to spend her life (III. x. 44–52). This would suggest that the question of the identity of the satyrs ought not to be read simply in terms of the religious allegory of Book I, but also as part of the wider themes and debates running throughout the whole narrative of the unfinished poem. The representation of the satyrs early on within the narrative, in a book which allegorizes the legend of holiness, provocatively forces the reader to recognize that theological distinctions cannot be made without reference to questions of social being, exactly the same point made by Irenius in *A View* when he argues that religion can only be taught in 'quiett times' after the rule of the godly has been established.

One of the most striking aspects of the reactions of members of the 'saluage nation' to Una is the diversity of their responses and their attempt to understand Una in terms of their own experience of sacred images, a division noted in Una's fear of 'commit[ing] | Her single person to their barbarous truth' (I. vi. 12). She represents the fundamental indivisibility of a monolithic conception of religious 'truth', which their reactions split up into a variety of representations.

The story raises important questions concerning the nature of 'truth' within the narrative, and not simply in terms of the need for Una to be represented and so having to exist within the duplicity of an impure, fallen language. Una herself, as the betrothed of the Red Cross Knight, is a specifically English representation of the 'truth' within a particular national language, English, so that she also exists within a series of differential signs and cannot stand outside a system already in use. She may well alter that system, but that is to undermine the stability of allegory and move the reader into new levels of understanding, the 'metonymic skid' Barthes described, as much as a move onwards to the 'already read' of allegorical conclusion. Readers of *The Faerie Queene* cannot securely assume that their understanding of their own religious representations and images avoids the misreadings, confusions, and contradictions of the 'saluage nation's' inability to read something beyond its particular system of representation (significantly described in great detail by Spenser). The separation of Una and the Red Cross Knight can be read as a glaring example of dramatic irony, where the reader knows far more than the characters acting out the story; however, such an encounter also serves to problematize this textual relationship, putting the over-confident reader back to the same level of awareness as the hapless knight and the 'saluage nation'.[55] The Red Cross Knight is able to defeat a dragon called 'Error' easily enough, but fails to see that in killing her he has actually made life more rather than less difficult. As she finally expires, 'Her vomit full of bookes and papers was' (i. i. 20), illustrating that the unified symbol has given way to the hazardous labyrinth of a multitude of erroneous narratives.[56] Sorting out which one to read and how, then, to read it will be the future problem. In the same way, the satyrs' various interpretations of Una's significance demonstrate the problems which will beset even the most thoughtful and careful readers, putting the readers of the English text on the same level as the savages, not separating them out as antitheses as might at first appear, a problematic link which looks forward to the representation of Serena abducted by the cannibals.

The encounter between Una and the satyrs may not appear to possess great significance within the narrative of Book I, but it assumes importance within the developing project of *The Faerie Queene*. The existence of the 'saluage nation' within the boundaries of a book which has been assumed to be both self-contained and self-sufficiently English is troubling and paves the way for the series of qualifications and changing definitions which take place in the later books. 'Sa(l)vage' stands as a foundational pun within the poem, simultaneously expressing the hope of salvation and the fear of disintegration, a linguistic trope which works in the same paradoxical mode as the two poles of allegorical interpretation function within the extended narrative. While Spenser's work deals with the act of transformation (fashioning the reader)—salvaging what has been lost—such a pun also points in the opposite direction, articulating the horror that what has to be transformed might well be precisely that which resists transformation. For Spenser, Ireland does more than problematize the relationship between English religion and the politics of a wider world; it also exists as the site of potential chaos where Englishness and its attendant certainties (truths) are turned against themselves in an orgy of violence, never to be redeemed. In a sense, Ireland inhabited the English Spenser used, turning ('troping') the literal into the pun that goes beyond the author's intention, threatening to collapse clear and distinct ideas and make the language of politics become the rhetoric of apocalyptic destruction.[57]

---

[55] See Mikics, *Limits of Moralising*, ch. 1, for a recent reflection on this question.

[56] See Brooks-Davies, *Spenser's* Faerie Queene, 22. More generally, see John M. Steadman, 'Error', *Sp. Enc.*, 252–3.

[57] For an overview of the impact of Irish English on Spenser's language, see Maley, 'Spenser's Irish English'.

One should also note that *A View* opens with Eudoxus asking what courses can be taken for 'reducinge that salvage nacion to better gouerment and Cyvilitye' (p. 43), illustrating the continuity of such puns between poetry and prose.

Book I shows that the Reformation will not survive if it is conceived of as merely English, as the Faerie Queene rules over Ireland too, a fact registered in the representation of her lands in the poem ('her kingdome in Faery land'). Duessa is stripped and banished to 'the wastfull wildernesse' (i. viii. 50), but she returns again to try and disrupt the betrothal of the Red Cross Knight and Una at the end of the book, and their marriage is delayed with Una 'left to mourne' (i. xii. 41). The Reformation is left unfinished because the Red Cross Knight has to destroy the monstrous beast as he has promised the Faerie Queene. In the second edition of the poem the forces which threaten the reformed English nation are quite clearly associated with Ireland. Not only do wastelands become more recognizably Irish in the representation of Malengin's rocky hideout (v. ix. 4) and the description of Ireland after Diana/Cynthia has left her curse on the island (vii. vi. 55), but the figure who is left naked and vulnerable in the face of hostile Irish opposition is herself, a representation of Elizabeth (see below, Ch. 6). The significance of Book I becomes clearer in retrospect: the Red Cross Knight's struggles will all be in vain if it is not recognized that England is not the 'sceptred isle' of John of Gaunt's imagination.[58] Ireland will transform England into a land of chaos like itself, rather than England civilizing Ireland.

Hints of this danger occur elsewhere in the first edition of *The Faerie Queene*. In the penultimate episode of Book III, Malbecco's wife, Hellenore ('This second *Hellene*', iii. x. 13), is seduced by Paridell, descendant of Paris, thus repeating the disastrous union which led to the foundation of Britain via Brutus, material which, like the Arthurian legends, was most readily available in Geoffrey of Monmouth's *History*.[59] At supper in Malbecco's castle before the seduction takes place, Paridell tells stories of his ancestry, principally in order to impress Hellenore, but, at Britomart's insistence, he narrates the foundation of Britain by Brutus, his defeat of the previous inhabitants, the Giants 'That fed on liuing flesh, and druncke mens vitall blood' (iii. ix. 49), and the establishment of the New Troy, Troynouant (51). During the night he abducts Hellenore, before abandoning her in the wood. Her fate is an almost exact repetition of Una's experiences in Book I canto vi:

[58] Shakespeare, *Richard II*, ii. i. 40.   [59] *History*, pt. i.

The gentle Lady, loose at randon left,
The greene-wood long did walke, and wander wide
At wilde aduenture, like a forlorne weft,
Till on a day the *Satyres* her espide
Straying alone withouten groome or guide;
Her up they tooke, and with them home her led,
With them as housewife euer to abide,
To milk their gotes, and make them cheese and bred,
And euery one as commune good her handeled.

(III. x. 36)

Hellenore quickly becomes 'their May-lady' (III. x. 44), having sex with all the satyrs in turn, in a dramatic modification of Una's treatment as a goddess to be worshipped ('housewife' ('hussy') could, of course, signal a wanton woman in Elizabethan English), as well as a demonstration of how close different languages of love could be.[60] As a result of his failure to persuade his wife to return—as well as the loss of his buried treasure—Malbecco is transformed into 'an aery Spright' (III. x. 57) and retreats to live in a cave on a 'craggy cliff' where he ceases to be human and becomes a manifestation of jealousy (60).

The episode clearly has a number of references and resonances within the allegorical plot of the poem.[61] What is important to note in terms of the argument here is the double movement of the matter of Britain towards either resolution and unity through Britomart or towards chaos and disorder through Paridell and Hellenore.[62] Hellenore's encounter with Paridell leads to her being crowned as the queen of the satyrs: 'She proud of that new honour, which they red, | And of their louely fellowship full glade, | Daunst liuely, and her face did with a Lawrell shade' (44). Yet the truth is that she is less their queen than their concubine (or 'quean'), another common contemporary pun.[63] They rule her rather than vice versa, so that the legacy of the fall of Troy and the establishment of Britain is a grotesque inversion of proper order. It is hard not to read these satyrs as Irish within the developing significance of the poem; satyrs only appear twice in *The Faerie Queene* (both in the

[60] E. A. M. Colman, *The Dramatic Use of Bawdy in Shakespeare* (London: Longman, 1974), 199.

[61] See Harry Berger, Jr., 'The Discarding of Malbecco: Conspicuous Allusion and Cultural Exhaustion in *The Faerie Queene* III. ix–x', in id., *Revisionary Play: Studies in the Spenserian Dynamics* (Berkeley: University of California Press, 1988), 154–71, for one interpretation of the wider significance of the episode.

[62] For further comment see Hadfield, *Literature, Politics and National Identity*, 193–200.

[63] Colman, *Dramatic Use of Bawdy in Shakespeare*, 211.

first edition) and each time they provide a challenge to the forms of established authority (the English Reformation settlement, the foundation of Britain) as well as straightforward allegorical interpretation, exactly the function Ireland and the Irish play within the narrative. The first time the satyrs are troublesome but benign; the second, they overcome and absorb the identity of Hellenore who becomes the sort of 'queen' they desire. Hellenore is not obviously a type of Elizabeth, but she serves as a prefiguration of Faunus' attempt to see Diana without her clothes, a warning that failure to deal sternly with recalcitrant elements will lead to their returning—like Duessa—as well as of spectacular degeneration for those not always on their guard, or for whom civilization is only a form of restraint. Hellenore is someone Elizabeth could (metaphorically) become if she refuses to support the New English and simply tries to placate the Irish and the 'degenerate' Old English.[64] Malbecco's retreat into the wilderness and transformation into a figure of jealousy links him to those beyond the boundaries of civilization—like the stripped Duessa, Malengin, the salvage nation—who wait, ready to haunt those unlucky enough to encounter them; once again, a problem associated with life in Ireland.[65]

The lust of the satyrs signals a loss of control, a dominance of the dictates of the body over those of the rational head. The same can be said of the original inhabitants of Britain, the giants, who eat 'liuing flesh' and drink men's blood.[66] Whether or not they are cannibals depends on whether or not they possess human status. Either way, they resemble the savages of the Old World described by Herodotus, the savages recently discovered in the New World, and the Irish described in contemporary accounts, notably A View, with its description of Murrogh O'Brien's death and the behaviour of his foster mother.[67] If civilized values are not carefully and properly established in Britain and Ireland, the poem warns, there could be a return to such savageness, a victory of the values

[64] Hellenore is described as 'incontinent' (III. ix. 1) which recalls the description of Malacasta in the first canto of Book III. Such an echo may well signal the importance of Britomart's sympathy for Malacasta's plight.

[65] Malbecco is clearly to blame for his own fate, and his reluctance to offer hospitality to Paridall, Satyrane, and Britomart can be read—amongst other things—as a rejection of values crucial to the maintenance of a civilized military society in a hostile land (i.e. Ireland). On the duties of hosts to travelling guests see Felicity Heal, *Hospitality in Early Modern England* (Oxford: Clarendon Press, 1990), ch. 5.

[66] On the significance of the British giants in *The Faerie Queene*, see Suzanne Lindgren Wofford, 'Spenser's Giants', in Mihoko Suzuki (ed.), *Critical Essays on Edmund Spenser* (New York: G. K. Hall & Co., 1996), 199–220, at 203.

[67] See Hadfield, 'The Naked and the Dead', 32–7.

of the 'wild' Irish. Often only military might separates the two states of humanity, a lesson *The Faerie Queene* and *A View* repeat almost endlessly.

The shadowy presence of Ireland and the Irish, haunting the narrative as a threat to allegorical stability and order, is more fully established in the second edition of the poem. There is a series of careful echoes and links, demanding that incidents be read in the light of earlier events. Book IV sees the first real appearance of Artegall, who until now has only appeared at second hand, described by the Red Cross Knight to Britomart (III. ii. 8–10), and who, significantly, is searching for him because she believes that he 'hath unto me donne | Late foule dishonour and reprochfull spight' (III. ii. 8); Artegall appears later in that canto in Merlin's magic mirror as her future husband (24). He arrives, as an unknown warrior, on the third day of the tournament that Satyrane has held with the Knights of Maidenhead for Florimell, in 'saluage weed, | With woody mosse bedight, and all his steed | With oaken leaues attrapt, that seemed fit | For saluage wight' (IV. iv. 39). The repetition of 'saluage' serves to emphasize his affiliation and identity at this stage. Satyrane was the knight who had rescued Una from the 'saluage nation' (I. vi), and had himself been brought up in the forest, 'noursled up in life and manners wilde, | Emongst wild beasts and woods, from lawes of men exilde' (I. vi. 23). The son of a human mother, Thaymis ('passion') and a satyr father, Therion ('wild beast'), himself described as a 'saluage sire', Satyrane forms a link between the virtues and vices of nature and nurture, being represented as 'a wild man of the woods'.[68] Artegall defeats all the Knights of Maidenhead, including Satyrane, triumphing in violent and bloody fashion, 'Hewing, and slashing shields, and hel- mets bright, | And beating downe, what euer nigh him came, | That euery one gan shun his dreadfull sight, | No lesse then death it selfe, in daunger- ous affright' (IV. iv. 41), until he is defeated in turn by his future wife (44).

There is a whole series of careful studies and deliberate echoes between the descriptions of the two knights and the two episodes: while Satyrane rescues the female representation of truth from the salvage nation, Arte- gall, a salvage knight, takes the honours at the tournament of another sal- vage knight before a woman defeats him; Satyrane starts to listen to Una teaching the satyrs, which curbs his savage excesses, 'Thenceforth he kept her goodly company, | And learnd her discipline of faith and veritie' (I. vi. 31), the same fate which befalls Artegall; both have been brought up

---

[68] Cheney, *Spenser's Image of Nature*, 106. More generally, see Richard Bernheimer, *Wild Men in the Middle Ages* (Cambridge, Mass.: Harvard University Press, 1952).

by the wild beasts with whom they are frequently compared (I. vi. 21–7; v. i. 5–8); both dress and live like wild men of the woods.

Artegall's shield boasts a motto, '*saluagesse sans finesse*', straightforwardly translatable as 'wildness without refinement or ornament', but which the narrator explains shows 'secret wit' (IV. iv. 39).[69] It is unclear exactly what this 'secret wit' can be, unless it is the potential recuperation of savagery as a crucial component of the civilized, a theme which develops more extensively in Book V. The combat at the tournament is Janus-faced within the narrative of the poem. On the one hand the episode looks back to Satyrane's rescue of Una from the satyrs and shows that Artegall possesses virtues which go beyond those possessed by the previous salvage knight Satyrane, as well as indicating that the theme of the 'savage/salvage' will assume an important role within the second edition of the poem, and forcing the attentive reader to return to the first books and reread them in the light of later developments.[70] On the other, it looks forward to Artegall's resumption of the role of the Knight of Justice in the subsequent book, making the connection between justice and the need for savagery if the ideal is to be implemented. Artegall's frantic style of fighting, which makes his opponents see him as the figure of Death, shows that he still has a long way to go before he can become a figure adequate to fulfil his titular role. In Book V it is Artegall's lieutenant, Talus, the iron man, who is represented as the 'sower of death'.

Britomart's early perception of Artegall as a knight who has performed a 'foule dishonour and reprochfull spight' 'to beguile | A simple mayd, and worke so haynous tort, | In shame of knighthood' (III. ii. 12), represents him as a potential rapist, presumably a symptom of her fear of her developing sexuality, which is described at length in this canto.[71] A related incident occurs at the start of canto vii, when Amoret, the future bride of Scudamore (Spenser rewrote the ending of Book III for the second edition so that Amoret and Scudamore remain separated for the rest of the poem),[72] wanders out 'through the wood, for pleasure, or

---

[69] *FQ*, p. 457.

[70] See Ronald A. Horton, 'Satyrane', *Sp. Enc.* 628. On this general process of qualifying the titular virtue of one knight by the next, see Alpers, *Poetry of* The Faerie Queene, pt. 3.

[71] Silberman, *Transforming Desire*, 20–6; Cavanagh, *Wanton Eyes and Chaste Desires*, 139–44. The truth of Britomart's early image of Artegall is never established; Paridell represents the type of knight Britomart imagines Artegall to be before she first meets him in IV. iv.

[72] See Thomas P. Roche, Jr., 'Amoret', *Sp. Enc.*, 29–30.

for need' (IV. vii. 4), the narrator leaving the purpose of or motive for her journey unspecified. She is attacked by a 'wilde and saluage man' (5). Britomart, who has accompanied her into the 'saluage forrests' (2) after the tournament for the prize of the girdle of Florimell, has fallen asleep.

The 'saluage man' is given a long description which merits quotation in full as it serves the important function of qualifying the representations of the salvages encountered so far:

> It was to weet a wilde and saluage man,
> Yet was no man, but onely like in shape,
> And eke in stature higher by a span,
> All ouergrowne with haire, that could awhape
> An hardy hart, and his wide mouth did gape
> With huge great teeth, like to a tusked Bore:
> For he liu'd all on rauin and on rape
> Of men and beasts; and fed on fleshly gore,
> The signe whereof yet stain'd his bloudy lips afore.
>
> His neather lip was not like man nor beast,
> But like a wide deepe poke, downe hanging low,
> In which he wont the relickes of his feast,
> And cruell spoyle, which he had spard, to stow:
> And ouer it his huge great nose did grow,
> Full dreadfully empurpled all with bloud;
> And downe both sides two wide long eares did glow,
> And raught downe to his waste, when up he stood,
> More great then th'eares of Elephants by *Indus* flood.
>
> (IV. vii. 5–6)

His abduction of Amoret involves him carrying her off to his cave, where Amoret learns from another captive, Aemylia, that the salvage man first rapes then eats his female victims (12). Eventually, he is slain by Belphoebe with her bow and arrow, who liberates the women. The phallic woman has saved her sisters from the tyranny of the male.[73]

This encounter has usually been read as a psychomachia, as Amoret, the daughter of Chrysogone, conceived asexually by sunbeams, born without causing her mother pain, and then adopted by Venus as a substitute for Cupid, who brings her up in the Garden of Adonis (III. vi), has to come to terms with the more base manifestations of love before

---

[73] Silberman, *Transforming Desire*, 120–2. My use of the term 'phallic woman' has only a tangential relationship to the concept of the 'phallic mother' as articulated by Jane Gallop; see her *The Daughter's Seduction* (Ithaca, NY: Cornell University Press, 1982). See also James H. Kavanagh, *Emily Brontë* (Oxford: Blackwell, 1985), ch. 2.

she can be united with her lover, Scudamore.[74] The salvage man's appearance clearly resembles an erect penis, with its engorged purple nose and drooping ears.[75] In the absence of the sleeping Britomart, for whom the incident serves—as it does for Amoret—as a prophetic dream of desire and fear, Belphoebe has to kill the salvage man because she is 'the only person for whom Lust is not a possible Temptation'.[76] Given that in the letter to Raleigh Spenser explicitly states that he 'shadows' the queen as 'a most vertuous and beautifull Lady . . . Belphoebe' (FQ, p. 737), the episode is double-edged, praising the figure of the queen as immune to the temptations which others have to suffer, but also excluding her from the narrative of the advance and control of sexuality, so that she becomes isolated and aloof.[77]

Such readings, are, of course, valid on one level; but the significance of the figure of the salvage man is much wider. The fact that he is fed by 'the milke of Woluves and Tygres' (IV. vii. 7), refers the reader back to the two salvage knights; Artegall, who is described as fighting 'like a lyon in his bloodie game' (IV. iv. 41) and later as having been forced by Astrea, the Goddess of Justice, who reared him, 'to make experience | Upon wyld beasts, which she in woods did find' (V. i. 7), until they come to 'feare his awfull sight' (8); Satyrane, who fights a whole series of wild beasts in order to increase his power, namely, the panther, boar, antelope, and leopard, as well as the tiger and the wolf (I. vi. 26). The oak staff he carries (IV. vii. 7) links him to Orgoglio (I. vii. 10), and the 'yvie greene' which is the only garment covering him, resembles that covering Sylvanus and serves as a symbol of lust (I. vi. 14).[78] The comparison of the salvage man's ears to those of the Indian elephant provides an exotic context— as in the much analysed stanza which compares the romance of fairyland to the discovery of empire at the start of Book II (proem, ii)[79]—implicitly

---

[74] Silberman, *Transforming Desire*, 117–20; Rosemary Freeman, *The Faerie Queene: A Companion for Readers* (London: Chatto & Windus, 1970), 237–9; Roche, *Kindly Flame*, 136–7. On the Garden of Adonis, see Berger, 'Spenser's Garden of Adonis: Force and Form in the Renaissance Imagination', in id., *Revisionary Play*, 131–53.

[75] As noted in *FQ*, p. 474.

[76] Roche, *Kindly Flame*, 137.

[77] Given that, later in the canto, there is a clear allegory of Raleigh's banishment for falling prey to the temptation of lust via his hidden marriage to Elizabeth Throckmorton, the criticism of Elizabeth's cult of virginity is cutting. See James P. Bednarz, 'Ralegh in Spenser's Historical Allegory', *Sp. Stud.* 4 (1983), 49–70, at 61–5; Walter Oakeshott, *The Queen and the Poet* (London: Faber & Faber, 1960), 93–8.

[78] See *FQ*, p. 474.

[79] Greenblatt, *Renaissance Self-Fashioning*, 190–1; A. Bartlett Giamatti, 'Primitivism and the Process of Civility in Spenser's *Faerie Queene*', in Chiappelli (ed.), *First Images of America*, 71–82, at 71–2.

equating the representations of savages within the poem to those recently observed in the accounts of Elizabethan voyages of discovery, so that sexuality and sexual politics have to be considered in terms of wider questions of identity and a discourse of savagery/civility.[80] The salvage man's lack of restraint and bestial sexual appetite resemble numerous accounts of savage peoples by travellers who, almost as a matter of routine, claimed that primitive peoples were slaves to the dictates of bodily lust and unable to control their base desires. His behaviour also recalls that of the satyrs at the end of Book III, so providing a narrative link to a representation of the Irish, in addition to their part in the general representation of savagery and savage peoples. William Strachey observed that it was a practice amongst the women of Virginia, with their husbands' consent, to 'embrace the acquaintance of any stranger for nothing, and it is accounted no offence. And incredible it is with what heat both sexes of them are given over to those intemperances; and the men to preposterous Venus, for they are full of their own country disease, the pox, very young.'[81] Francis Petty's account of Thomas Candish's voyage to the South Seas (1586–8), describes a 'strange kinde of order among' the people of the island of Capul, whereby 'every man and man-child among them hath a nayle of Tynne thrust quite through the head of his privie part, being split in the lower end and rivetted . . . This custome was granted at the request of the women of the countrey, who finding their men to be given to the fowle sinne of Sodomie, desired some remedie against that mischiefe, and obteined this before named of the magistrates'.[82] In neither instance is the savage body given over to lust able to regulate itself: in the first case, this leads to the depopulation of Virginia, as the 'tired body cannot have those sexual helps . . . to hold up those immoderate desires . . . [which] make it generally unfit to the office of increase'; in the second, the excessive lust of men results in 'unnatural' homosexual practices and the handing over of control to the women.[83]

Even more obviously, 'the wilde and saluage man' is a cannibal who devours his victims after raping them, as Aemylia testifies, showing that

[80] See, in addition to the voluminous writings concerning the representation of the Americas, Elred D. Jones, *The Elizabethan Image of Africa* (Charlottesville: University of Virginia Press, 1971), 7. *Variorum*, iv. 236–7, provides examples of large-eared wild men in contemporary travel literature.

[81] Cited in Porter, *The Inconstant Savage*, 329.

[82] 'The admirable and prosperous voyage of the Worshipfull Master Thomas Candish . . . into the South sea', in Hakluyt, *Principal Navigations*, viii. 206–55, at 242.

[83] See also ibid. iii. 173, 187, vi. 282, viii. 11–12, *passim*; *First Three English Books on America*, ed. Arber, 17, 237, *passim*.

his appetite is not simply sexual. He resembles a common representation of the aggressive, naked savage, who inverts and opposes European civilization as a manifestation of a bad, atavistic nature which has to be superseded in terms of mankind's progress (a clear recollection of the giants who inhabited Britain before the Britons).[84] Such a figure again looks both ways, qualifying our image of the benign savage, representing a less hostile, more innocent, natural man who can be educated into the ways of the civilized, as was the case with the salvage nation, Satyrane—although both had obvious limits—and, most importantly, Artegall. Within the narrative of the poem, it appears that the cannibal, rapist savage is a creature who has to be absorbed rather than discarded or destroyed, so that he stands for a bodily, sexual appetite which must be regulated, rather like the experience at the Castle of Busirane.[85] In the same way, the bestial desires of the cannibal were often described as a stage of civilization's past: what Europeans once had been, contemporary primitive peoples now were. The artist, Theodore De Bry, in his retouchings of and additions to the New World drawings of Jacques Le Moyne de Morgues and John White, decided to place the figures of five 'Pictes which in the Olde tyme dyd habite one part of the great Bretainne . . . to show how the Inhabitants . . . haue bin in times past as sauuage as those of Virginia'.[86] It is noticeable that the narrator of *The Faerie Queene* avoids stating where this savage comes from, or whether he actually is human at all (like the giants), thus inviting the reader to make such connections and speculate beyond the confines of the text's narrative drive. However, and most ominously, this incident also looks forward to the abduction of Serena by (yet another) 'saluage nation'.

Book IV reaches a climax in canto xi, with the lavish description of the marriage of the Thames and the Medway, the two principal rivers of

---

[84] See *First Three English Books on America*, ed. Arber, 180; Hakluyt, *Principal Navigations*, v. 272, vii. 20; Sheehan, *Savagism and Civility*, ch. 3; Hulme, *Colonial Encounters*, chs. 1–2.

[85] See Thomas Hyde, 'Busirane', *Sp. Enc.* 123–5; Harry Berger, Jr., 'Busirane and the War between the Sexes: An Interpretation of *The Faerie Queene* III. xi–xii', in id., *Revisionary Play*, 172–94. Contrast the reading of Silberman, *Transforming Desire*, 58–67.

[86] Paul Hulton, 'Images of the New World: Jacques Le Moyne de Morgues and John White', in Andrews *et al.* (eds.), *The Westward Enterprise*, 195–214, at 211. On the historical assumptions made, see Arthur B. Ferguson, 'Circumstances and the Sense of History in Tudor England: The Coming of the Historical Revolution', *Medieval and Renaissance Studies*, 3 (1967), 170–205, at 193–6. For more general reflections on the problems of anthropology, see Claude Lévi-Strauss, 'The Concept of Archaism in Anthropology' and 'Race and History', in id., *Structural Anthropology*, trans. Claire Jacobson, Brooke Grundfest-Schoepf, and Monique Layton, 2 vols. (Harmondsworth: Penguin, 1977), i. 101–19, ii. 323–62.

southern England which serve the capital, London. The celebratory procession of gods, many of whom have founded nations, dynasties, and rivers, takes place in Proteus' hall under the ocean, just after Marinell has been healed. The union occurs at a seemingly inappropriate moment in the narrative and may well be a remnant of an earlier project dealing with the English rivers which has been incorporated into *The Faerie Queene*, discussed in a letter to Harvey in 1580 and provisionally entitled *Epithalamion Thamesis*, which was either never completed or is no longer extant.[87] The marriage of the rivers appears to allude to Elizabeth's marriage to England and is, in Alastair Fowler's words, 'a festival piece, celebrating a visionary England—and Ireland—united in friendly alliance, and married to a sovereign whose policy promises a strong and prosperous peace'.[88] In fact, after starting out on a global scale, the geographical focus of the procession gradually narrows inwards towards the British Isles. The Orinoco inspires memories of the Amazons in the narrator, who heaps praise upon these women for keeping a kingdom for so long from male explorers, and chastizes men for failing 'in the conquest of gold'. The British are exhorted to conquer the land and find the gold: 'But this to you, O Britons, most pertaines, | To whom the right hereof it selfe hath sold; | The which for sparing litle cost or paines, | Loose so immortall glory, and so endlesse gaines' (IV. xi. 22). The image of the rivers flowing into each other is not shifting and formless, but a principle of generation and harmony, a *discordia concors*. The names shape the elements and the elements fill out the names, so that form and content are dialectically united in meaning.[89] The rivers all bring elements of their histories with them, and, although some rivers transport sad memories, ultimately the image appears to be one of unity and harmony. The stanzas describing the English countryside appear to be celebrating the pastoral idyll of easy life denied the New English In Ireland in *Colin Clouts come home againe*. To select a verse almost at random:

> Then came the Rother, decked all with woods
> Like a wood God, and flowing fast to Rhy:
> And Sture, that parteth with his pleasant floods
> The Easterne Saxons from the Southerne ny,

[87] See Bennett, *Evolution of* The Faerie Queene, 156; W. H. Herendeen, 'rivers', *Sp. Enc.*, 606–9, at 608.

[88] *Spenser and the Numbers of Time* (London: Routledge, 1964), 174–5. On Elizabeth's marriage to England see Shire, *Preface to Spenser*, 40; Hackett, *Virgin Mother, Maiden Queen*, 56–60, 223–4, 229–30.

[89] Giamatti, *Play of Double Senses*, 130–2; Roche, *Kindly Flame*, 181.

> And Clare, and Harwitch both doth beautify:
> Him follow'd Yar, soft washing Norwitch wall,
> And with him brought a present ioyfully
> Of his owne fish unto their festiuall,
> Whose like none else could shew, the which they Ruffins call.

(IV. xi. 33)

The plethora of detail inspires imaginative joy in the excited narrator:

> All which not if an hundred tongues to tell,
> And hundred mouthes, and voice of brasse I had,
> And endlesse memorie, that mote excell,
> In order as they came, could I recount them well.

(IV. xi. 9)

In other ways, however, the episode portrays a much darker picture of a fragile harmony which is unlikely to last. Proteus has been tamed, but his presiding over 'the renewal of life and beauty' in his hall serves as a pointed contrast to his previous role, when he had actually seemed more of a deity of the underworld in his undersea dungeon, where he held Florimell captive (perhaps recalling Hades' kidnapping of Persephone).[90] Proteus was also the god of mutability, giving rise to the proverb 'more shapes than Proteus', implying that at the moment the allegory can be controlled and fashioned by the author and reader, but that at a future point this may no longer be the case and that the forces of chaos, Proteus among them, will triumph instead.[91] In this way, the marriage looks forward to the debate between Mutability and Jove (see Ch. 6 below).

The Irish rivers are amongst the wedding-guests, but only on the condition that much of the history they carry with them is hidden from view:

> Ne thence the Irishe Riuers absent were,
> Sith no lesse famous then the rest they bee,
> And ioyne in neighbourhood of kingdome nere . . .
> Though I them all according their degree,
> Cannot recount, nor tell their hidden race,
> Nor read the saluage cuntreis, thorough which they pace.

(IV. xi. 40)

---

[90] Norhnberg, *The Analogy of* The Faerie Queene, 576–7, 580.
[91] Tilley, 596. See also Giamatti, *Play of Double Senses*, 115–50; Norhnberg, *The Analogy of* The Faerie Queene, 568–98; Edgar Wind, *Pagan Mysteries in the Renaissance* (New Haven: Yale University Press, 1958), ch. 13; Supriya Chaudhuri, 'Proteus', *Sp. Enc.*, 560–1.

Although stories are attached to the Irish rivers, including the myth of the nymph, Rheusa, who was raped by the giant, Blomius, and, as a result, gave birth to 'three faire sons' who run as three rivers down from the Slieve Bloom mountains, details of the 'saluage cuntreis' remain absent, apart from one. The river Oure is described as 'balefull . . . late staind with English blood' (44), a clear reminder of the history which has been excluded from the nuptials. The 'saluage nation' is tactfully omitted from the guest list, so that the marriage does not have to be exogamous. Festive celebration appears to depend upon an ability *not* to be able to read the history of the 'saluage cuntreis' and a pretence that such hostility will disappear if it is ignored, a message at odds with all that has gone before. But, a clear threat hangs over the appearance of unity as the 'saluage cuntreis' undoubtedly contain creatures such as the 'saluage man' who threatened to rape Amoret only a few cantos earlier. The fate of both the allegorical meaning of the poem and the unification of Elizabeth's realms, symbolized by yet another hermaphroditic union (the Thames serves as the bridegroom and the Medway as the bride, but such gender divisions are self-evidently arbitrary), are challenged by the ghostly presence of Ireland, a presence which becomes more sinister and dangerous in the last three books.

5

The Spoiling of Princes:
Artegall Thwarted, Calidore Confused

IF Book IV would appear to provide clues that the second edition of *The Faerie Queene* was becoming increasingly and more obviously concerned with Ireland, there has been a general agreement among critics that the allegory of justice in Book V is directly—though not exclusively—centred around Spenser's Irish experience.[1] Artegall's quest for justice begins and ends in Ireland; in between, there are numerous key representations of the Irish at significant points, constantly reminding the reader that discussions of concepts such as justice cannot be considered in an abstract manner, a lesson Irenius had to teach Eudoxus in *A View*. The pastoral setting of Book VI is related to an Irish landscape via the expansion of the role of the Blatant Beast, who first emerges in Book V, once again demanding that the series of representations of savages who appear throughout the book are related to English perceptions of the Irish.[2]

Book V opens with a description of the decay of the world from the Golden Age to the current age of stone, the standard narrative of the corruption of nature from its Edenic origins.[3] The myth was often used—most famously in Montaigne's essay 'Of the Cannibals'—as a counter-narrative to the story of endless progress, from primitivism to civilization, and supplied Europe with the figure of the 'savage critic'

---

[1] See, e.g. Lewis, *Allegory of Love*, 349; Jones, *Spenser Handbook*, 263; William Nelson, *The Poetry of Edmund Spenser: A Study* (New York: Columbia University Press, 1963), 274; Peter Bayley, *Edmund Spenser: Prince of Poets* (London: Hutchinson, 1971), 138; Healy, *New Latitudes*, 94–8.

[2] A point which appears to have escaped Thomas Dunseath in *Spenser's Allegory of Justice in Book V of* The Faerie Queene, one of the rare book-length studies of the book.

[3] The usual source is Ovid: see *Metamorphoses*, 31–3; see also Isabel Rivers, *Classical and Christian Ideas in English Renaissance Poetry* (London: Allen & Unwin, 1979), ch. 1; A. Bartlett Giamatti, *The Earthly Paradise and the Renaissance Epic* (Princeton: Princeton University Press, 1966).

who was clear-sighted enough to analyse the greed and corruption of the supposedly superior Old World.[4] In invoking such associations, Artegall is set aside as a heroic savage, like Lord Grey in *A View*, who needs to be distinguished from the savages of bad nature, assuming that such a process is possible, because this is precisely what Book V articulates as problematic.[5] Indeed, the narrator points out the difficulties of the terms he is obliged to use and the purpose they are supposed to serve in an aggressive disclaimer of responsibility for his words:

> Let none then blame me, if in discipline
> Of vertue and of ciuill uses lore,
> I doe not forme them to the common line
> Of present dayes, which are corrupted sore,
> But to the antique use, which was of yore,
> When good was onely for it selfe desyred,
> And all men sought their owne, and none no more;
> When Iustice was not for most meed outhyred,
> But simple Truth did rayne, and was of all admyred.

> (v. proem, 3)

Even the very words that the poet is obliged to use to make his case are not secure, and the terrible fear, one implicit in the project of *The Faerie Queene*, is that the good and the bad cannot be told apart. Artegall may be a good savage, but to many readers he will seem a bad one, his actions cruel and indefensible, a judgement nearly all critics of the poem have had no compunction about making.[6] Such straightforward condemnation is complicated if it can be seen that Spenser identified the problem and actually sought to goad the reader into condemning the knight. However, a counter-argument might suggest that the poet as well as the reader fell into a series of traps and had to recognize the hypocrisy of wanting omelettes without breaking eggs, a charge *The Faerie Queene* levels at Elizabeth.[7] The stanza cited above effectively acknowledges

---

[4] Anthony Pagden, 'The Savage Critics', 32–45; Hogden, *Early Anthropology*, ch. 5.

[5] On the historical relationship between Spenser and Grey, see Raymond Jenkins, 'Spenser with Lord Grey in Ireland', *PMLA* 52 (1937), 338–53.

[6] See Michael O'Connell, '*The Faerie Queene*, Book V', *Sp. Enc.*, 280–3. As well as that of Lewis, a vital reading is that of W. B. Yeats, 'Edmund Spenser', in id., *Essays and Introductions* 356–83, at 361.

[7] Spenser has had his defenders over the years; see Edwin A. Greenlaw, 'Spenser and British Imperialism', *MP* 9 (1911–12), 347–70, at 364–5; Watanabe-O'Kelly, 'Edmund Spenser and Ireland'; Cavanagh, ' "Such was Irena's Countenance" '; id., ' "That Savage Land": Ireland in Spenser's Legend of Justice', in David Lee Miller and Alexander Dunlop (eds.), *Approaches to Teaching Spenser's* Faerie Queene (New York: MLA, 1994), 143–52; Fowler, 'Spenser and War', 159–60.

that 'ciuill uses' of the notion of justice have become inextricably mixed with their implied opposites, savage uses, suggesting that the savagery of Artegall and the quite opposite savagery of Ireland may not be as far apart as they should be.[8] The threat Ireland poses to Englishness is that the two nations may end up being variations on the same theme.

The description of justice in the age of Saturn serves as an ironically inverted mirror image of justice in the age of iron:

> For during *Saturnes* ancient raigne it's sayd,
> That all the world with goodnesse did abound:
> All loued vertue, no man was affrayd
> Of force, ne fraud in wight was to be found:
> No warre was knowne, no dreadfull trompets sound,
> Peace uniuersall rayn'd mongst men and beasts,
> And all things freely grew out of the ground:
> Iustice sate high ador'd with solemne feasts,
> And to all people did diuide her dred beheasts.

(v, proem, 9)

This stanza predicts exactly what the reader will actually find in the course of the book: it is saturated with problems which can only be solved by the use of force and fraud, starting with Artegall's brutal punishment of Murena and Pollente, and the Egalitarian Giant;[9] war and its effects is a major theme, particularly in the later cantos describing Henry IV in France and English involvement in the Netherlands and Ireland; the abundant fertility described in line 7, alluding to the luxuriant growth which precluded the need for work in the Golden Age, contrasts with the representation of Talus as the sower of death, and sits uneasily with the recommendations in *A View* that Ireland be starved into submission and its natural food supplies destroyed; justice is not adored by everyone and the question of its equal distribution is challenged by the gaint's scales in the second canto.[10] Spenser's description of the age of Saturn follows Ovid's carefully, although the concept of justice is seen to be a key element of the Golden Age, rather than a later development

---

[8] Dunseath, *Spenser's Allegory of Justice*, 21, 50–1.

[9] Jane Aptekar, *Icons of Justice: Iconography and Thematic Imagery in Book V of The Faerie Queene* (New York: Columbia University Press, 1969), ch. 2; Patterson, 'Egalitarian Giant'.

[10] On 'distributive justice', see Aristotle, *Nichomachean Ethics*, 112–14. For more general discussions of justice in the book, see Phillips, 'Renaissance Concepts of Justice'; Joel B. Altman, 'justice and equity', *Sp. Enc.* 413–15. Michael O'Connell links the Giant to the Titans ('Giant with the scales', *Sp. Enc.* 331–2), so that he can be related to the myth of Jove and the Titans which haunts Book V.

to cope with the degeneration of the world.[11] This change highlights how useless an ideal conception of justice is, because justice can only function when forced to deal with practical problems of injustice; an ideal justice is, self-evidently, an unreadable fiction. In the dark world of the poem, made up of a patchwork of fictional and historical time which includes the present, the danger of inversion is paramount: 'For that which men then did vertue call, | Is now cald vice; and that which vice was hight, | Is now hight vertue, and so us'd of all' (proem, 4).[12] Not only is there an obvious problem in terms of usage, but also one of general application, a festering doubt which unsettles the reader of the poem, who clearly cannot be certain that he or she has secured a right reading.

The elaborate praise given to Elizabeth in the last two stanzas of the proem may, therefore, be read as an implicit criticism of her implementation of justice. The narrator describes her as 'Dread Souerayne Goddesse, that doest highest sit | In seate of iudgement, in th'Almighties stead' (11). The lines portray Elizabeth as a deity, but, equally, suggest that she is aloof, cut off from her people, and that she represents a version of justice which refers only to a series of abstract principles of no use in the real world. The description of her sitting in 'th'Almighties stead', further suggests that she is a usurper of the true (i.e. less exalted and more false) principles of justice, effectively a demand that she and her advisers take heed of the unpleasant lessons Spenser is about to teach them in his poem.

A reading of the poem as a critical tract becomes more explicit at the start of the first canto. This opens with a description of Artegall's upbringing by Astrea, the Goddess of Justice. She teaches him to separate right from wrong, training him by example of wild beasts in the forest as is appropriate for a 'salvage knight'. However, Astrea eventually finds it no longer possible to remain on earth:

> Now when the world with sinne gan to abound,
> *Astrea* loathing lenger here to space
> Mongst wicked men, in whom no truth she found,
> Return'd to heuen, whence she deriu'd her race;
> Where she hath now an euerlasting place
>
> (v. i. 11)

---

[11] Ovid, *Metamorphoses*, 31–2; *FQ*, p. 528.
[12] Rathborne, *The Meaning of Spenser's Fairyland*; Michael J. Murrin, 'fairyland', *Sp. Enc.*, 296–8.

Astrea is significantly absent from the narrative of the book, unable to tolerate the devious and messy world where sorting the good from the bad is a fiendishly difficult task. Astrea deems herself too pure to perform the actions which will implement justice; instead, she delegates responsibility to a male deputy, a viceregal figure, akin to the Lord Lieutenant or Deputy of Ireland, a position of enormous power but also uncertain responsibility, signalled here by the seeming absence of the monarch/goddess who, nevertheless, in a different guise, recalls him to her court at the end of the book before his task is finished.

The frequent representation of Elizabeth as Astrea is too well established to merit special attention here.[13] What is important to note is that Astrea is shown to be more keen to distance herself from problems than to sort them out herself, letting others do her dirty work for her, while she ascends to heaven, an image which sheds light on the representation of Elizabeth at the end of the poem (see below pp. 189–90), and forces the reader to reconsider their understanding of the earlier passage. Before she leaves, Astrea hands Artegall Chrysaor, the sword which Jove used to defeat the Titans, 'that whylome rebelled | Gainst highest heauen' (9). Once again, the ironies abound in this action which, taken at face value, appears to defend the established order of the Elizabethan state. Jove himself was a usurper who overthrew his father Saturn, consigning him 'to the darkness of Tartarus', and so inaugurating the age of silver, the first stage in the decay of the world, significant for the onset of winter in the previously harmonious seasons.[14] Far from making secure a timeless dynasty, Astrea's gift functions as a symbol of violent change and usurpation, precisely what she herself wished to avoid.[15] Chrysaor serves both to mystify the ruling order and expose its myth. Artegall is also left a more sinister gift, Talus, 'An yron man', Astrea's groom, 'Immoueable, resistlesse, without end. | Who in his hand an yron flale did hould, | With

[13] See, Frances A. Yates, *Astrea: The Imperial Theme in the Sixteenth Century* (London: Routledge, 1975); Roy Strong, *The Cult of Elizabeth: Elizabethan Portraiture and Pagentry* (London: Thames & Hudson, 1977), 47–55; Marie Axton, *The Queen's Two Bodies: Drama and the Elizabethan Succession* (London: Royal Historical Society, 1977), 76–7, 131–3; Philippa Berry, *Of Chastity and Power: Elizabethan Literature and the Unmarried Queen* (London: Routledge, 1989), 39–41, *passim*; Hackett, *Virgin Mother, Maiden Queen*, 31–2, 109.

[14] Ovid, *Metamorphoses*, 32.

[15] See Kathleen Williams, *Spenser's* Faerie Queene: *The World of Glass* (London: Routledge, 1966), 155–7. On Spenser's use of the myth of Saturn, Jove, and the Titans, see Aptekar, *Icons of Justice*, ch. 1; Fowler, *Spenser and the Numbers of Time*, ch. 12; Maurice Evans, *Spenser's Anatomy of Heroism* (Cambridge: Cambridge University Press, 1970), 38–9.

which he thresht out falshood, and did truth unfould' (v. i. 12). Talus is a figure who reflects the age of iron and acts as a fearsome counterpart to Artegall; the one will preside over the spread of justice, the other will provide the brute force to support such an authority, a separation carefully made by Irenius in *A View* in his elaboration of the two senses of the law as the possibility of order and a series of ordinances. Talus' iron flail depicts him as the sower of death, the harvest of the iron age.[16] The literary allegory enables Spenser to separate what had to be intimately connected in his prose tract, so that Artegall is distanced from the brutality of Talus' actions.[17]

The specific quest which Artegall has to complete is the standard romance narrative motif of the knight having to rescue a damsel in distress. A 'cruell Tyrant' (v. i. 13), Grantorto, has laid a false claim to the land which should rightfully belong to Irena. She appeals to the Faerie Queene, 'that mightie Emperesse, | Whose glorie is to aide all suppliants pore, | And of weake Princes to be Patronesse' (4). Grantorto 'kept the crowne in which she should succeed' (13), separating legitimate authority from the land, a situation which mirrors not only the battle between Jove and the Titans, but also that between Saturn and Jove, the first preserving the status quo, the latter inaugurating a revolution. If a solution to such complicated and confusing struggles is to be found, it must be through a reassertion of the rights of conquest. Elizabeth must look back to her Arthurian past and make use of Artegall, the equal of Arthur, in order to reconquer the ancient British empire.

Irena is an image of Elizabeth's sovereignty over Ireland, the bodily manifestation of her legal right to rule a separate kingdom justified by her imperial power and now threatened by the marauding usurper, Grantorto, whose claim is illegitimate.[18] Elizabeth's sovereignty derives from her prior right as the British monarch, a right of conquest (as Irenius argued in *A View*), so that Grantorto's claim is tyrannous 'because he is attempting to wrest the sovereignty from the hands of its rightful possessor'.[19] Irena's name directs us to consider her as a symbol of Ireland, but also derives from the Eirene, the Greek goddess of peace.[20] Artegall's quest is to discover the true peace which justice will bring.

Irena stands as one of the many manifestations of Gloriana; the letter

---

[16] Aptekar, *Icons of Justice*, 49–51; *FQ*, p. 532.

[17] McCabe, 'The Fate of Irena', 122–3.

[18] On the concept of the 'multiple kingdom' applied to Ireland in this period, see above, Ch. 3. n. 80.

[19] Northrop, 'Spenser's Defense of Elizabeth', 280. See also Norbrook, *Poetry and Politics in English Renaissance Literature*, 142.

[20] Northrop, 'Spenser's Defense of Elizabeth', 289; *FQ*, p. 530.

to Raleigh declares that the Faerie Queene herself could be doubly shadowed as 'glory in my generall intention' and as Elizabeth, who herself was represented as two bodies, the one 'a most royall Queene or Empresse, the other of a most vertuous and beautifull Lady', represented by Belphoebe and fashioned after Raleigh's own figuration of Elizabeth as Cynthia (Diana) (*FQ*, p. 757). Given that both Diana and Cynthia appear in the poem (Diana in the central section of the second edition, when she takes Belphoebe from Chrysogone (III. vi), and Cynthia in the 'Two Cantos of Mutabilitie'), clear comparisons are made between Britomart and Elizabeth. Given too, that Una, as the symbol of the English church who marries St George, can also be regarded as a type of the queen, it can be seen that the representations of Elizabeth are multiple, going beyond the figures signalled in the letter. After Henry VIII's declaration, on 18 June 1541 in the Irish Parliament, that he was king of Ireland, the English monarch claimed rights to Ireland, so Irena must stand as a figure of Elizabeth.[21] Given that Artegall has been assigned the quest to rescue Ireland by Astrea (Elizabeth) this means that two figures exist which should claim the Arthurian legacy of the British right to rule Ireland, one a representative of the queen, the other a representation of the queen. Significantly, it is the former, the Arthurian knight, who has the power and means to implement the rule of the latter and whose rejection leads to the chaos of the later books, just as Elizabeth's rejection of Grey's policies, described at length in *A View*, was responsible for the failure of orderly rule of Ireland in that text, and for the chronic insecurity of the New English.

As Louis Montrose has pointed out, *The Faerie Queene* 'by representing the queen in a text, ineluctably reconstitutes the queen as a textual product'. The conventional humility topos, with Spenser's narrator referring to his own inability to 'produce an adequate reflection of the glorious royal image', is, in effect, 'the methodological process of fragmentation and refraction by which the text appropriates that image, imposing upon it its own specificity'.[22] The bodies of the queen reflected in the variety of female figures scattered throughout the narrative constitute the manifestations of Gloriana, who only appears fleetingly to Arthur (I. ix. 13–17).[23] Arthur is unsure if what he saw was real: 'But

---

[21] Ellis, *Tudor Ireland*, 5.

[22] 'Elizabethan Subject and Spenserian Text', 322, 324–5. See also Elizabeth J. Bellamy, 'The Vocative and the Vocational: The Unreadability of Elizabeth in *The Faerie Queene*', *ELH* 54 (1987), 1–30.

[23] For analysis, see Sheila Cavanagh, ' "Beauties Chace": Arthur and Women in *The Faerie Queene*', in Christopher Baswell and William Sharpe (eds.), *The Passing of Arthur: Loss and Renewal in the Arthurian Tradition* (New York: Garland, 1988), 207–20.

whether dreames delude, or true it were, | Was neuer hart so rauisht with delight' (14). The queen's presence is shown to be a ghostly one at two removes from reality, a fiction within a fiction. Arthur's comment, 'So faire a creature yet saw neuer sunny day' (13), appears, if taken at face value, to be hyperbolic praise of the sovereign; equally, it could be taken to mean either that such a creature does not really exist, or that she hides herself away in the dark. The only clue to suggest that Arthur has not been dreaming is the imprint of her body, the 'pressed gras, where she had lyen' (15), an effect of the queen's body, not the body itself.

Irena is a similarly ghostly figure: rescuing her is the quest of the Knight of Justice, yet she disappears from the narrative—like Astrea and Gloriana—after three stanzas in the first canto and only reappears in the last canto, where Artegall meets her 'at the saluage Ilands syde' (v. xi. 39)—thus linking the representation of Irena to the catalogue of savages appearing throughout the poem, a theme developed further in Book VI. There is a pointed contrast between the weeping and helpless Irena and the vigorously armed tyrant, who appears dressed like an Irish foot-soldier, armed in a coat of mail and with a 'huge Poleaxe', 'With which he wont to fight, to iustifie his wrong'.[24] Irena is led out to be executed by Grantorto, in 'squalid garments, fit for such a day, | And with dull countenance, and with dolefull spright'. When she sees her champion, she cheers up significantly:

> Like as a tender Rose in open plaine,
> That with untimely drought nigh withered was,
> And hung the head, soone as few drops of raine
> Thereon distill, and deaw her daintie face,
> Gins to looke up, and with fresh wonted grace
> Dispreds the glorie of her leaues gay;
> Such was *Irenas* countenance, such her case,
> When *Artegall* she saw in that array,
> There wayting for the Tyrant, till it was farre day.

>   (v. xii. 13)

Irena is represented as absolutely dependent upon Artegall for her salvation. He duly defeats Grantorto, using Chrysaor, and re-establishes Irena to her rightful rule. Her grateful subjects grant her an enthusiastic welcome on her return to sovereignty when Artegall finally kills the tyrannical giant:

---

[24] *FQ*, p. 615; Kenneth Borris, *Spenser's Poetics of Prophecy in* The Faerie Queene, V, English Literary Studies, Monograph Series 52, (Victoria, BC: University of Victoria, Canada, 1991), 67–8.

Which when the people round about him saw,
They shouted all for ioy of his successe,
Glad to be quit from that proud Tyrants awe,
Which with strong powre did them long time oppresse;
And running all with greedie ioyfulnesse
To faire *Irena*, at her feet did fall,
And her adored with due humblenesse,
As their true Leige and Princesse naturall;
And eke her champions glorie sounded ouer all.

(v. xii. 24)

With the kingdom restored to peace, Artegall and Talus set about reforming 'the ragged commonweale'; the former plans 'true Iustice how to deale', the latter is sent to root out any opposition, 'that usd to rob and steale, | Or did rebell gainst lawfull gouernment' (26). However, before the land can be properly reformed and restored to civilization, Artegall is called back to the Faerie Court, 'that of necessity | His course of Iustice he was forst to stay | And *Talus* to reuoke from the right way, | In which he was that Realme for to redresse'(27). Although Gloriana is not explicitly blamed, the narrator is clear that Artegall's recall is not only a mistake—and a decision neither Artegall nor Irena desire ('So hauing freed *Irena* from distresse, | He tooke his leaue of her, there left in heauinesse')—but also one made for discreditable motives: 'But enuies cloud still dimmeth vertues ray' (27). Gloriana may not have made such a decision herself, unprompted, but it is clear that, as God's representative of justice on earth, she is guilty of, at best, culpable political naïvety and neglect of her Irish subjects; at worst, a tyranny as dangerous and cruel as Grantorto's.

The allegory is a clear defence of Lord Grey's deputyship in Ireland, as has long been recognized.[25] It is also a stern criticism of the monarch for her feeble attempts to deal with the question of Ireland, a clear message that Irena cannot rule without the legacy of Arthur in the form of the New English Artegall. The Faerie Queene promises to save Irena from the tyranny which threatens the latter's rule (and, of course, her own as well), but she is actually seen to be threatening that stability in her premature recall of the means of implementing justice. The removal of Artegall mirrors Astrea's squeamish attitude to justice, particularly if

[25] Henley, *Spenser in Ireland*, 139–41; Jones, 'Spenser's Defense of Lord Grey'; Shire, *Preface to Spenser*, 63; McCabe, 'The Fate of Irena'. O'Connell, *Mirror and Veil*, 155–6, suggests, following Bennett (*Evolution of* The Faerie Queene, 194–5), that Artegall is a conflation of Grey and Sir John Norris in canto xii. See also J. W. Bennett, 'The Allegory of Sir Artegall in *The Faerie Queene*, V. xi–xii', *SP* 37 (1940), 177–200.

one bears in mind that the historical reason for the recall of Grey was the hostility generated by what was perceived to be his excessive use of violence.[26] Irena is shown to be dependent on Artegall/Grey and unable to function as a governor without his aid; the women are seen to arrange matters, but it is the men—Artegall and Talus—who actually try to resolve them, only to be prevented by the intervention of the Faerie Queene. The episode can be read as an attack on female rule, which is shown to be weak, capricious, and, worst of all, vacillating, negative qualities which are no earthly use when a 'salvage cuntry' like Ireland is concerned.[27]

Who, after all, is Irena? Graham Hough once remarked, rather impatiently, 'and heaven knows what Ireland his Irena signifies, for it seems to exclude the entire population of the land'.[28] Such a reading takes the book's narrative on trust and would appear to miss many of its numerous ironic complexities; the actual verses reveal a more paradoxical situation than mere propaganda. On the one hand, those living in Ireland are seen to flock to Irena, delighted to be free from Grantorto's tyranny; on the other, Irena's land/Ireland badly needs the services of Artegall and Talus to root out all subversive elements. When Artegall finally does leave, Irena returns to her state of distress so that the pacification of Ireland is shown to be prematurely aborted. It would seem odd were Spenser to be entirely ignorant of this problematic inconsistency, given the careful echoing of words and phrases throughout the narrative, continually forcing the reader to reconsider his or her judgements. The representation of Grantorto as an Irish foot-soldier would also seem to suggest that he is as much an enemy within as without, and that Talus' slaughter will have to be quite substantial.

In contrast are 'the people', those glad to be free of Grantorto, who make up the legitimate body politic of the land. It is most likely that these represent the colonial class of the New English whom Spenser was always keen to represent, in both a political and an aesthetic sense, in his writings. It was they who felt the distance of the queen's patronage and aid most keenly, constantly demanding military intervention so that a

[26] McCabe, 'The Fate of Irena', 122; Ellis, *Tudor Ireland*, 284.
[27] On contemporary attitudes to women's rule, see Constance Jordan, 'Woman's Rule in Sixteenth-Century British Political Thought', *RQ* 40 (1987), 421–51. On attitudes to women generally, see Linda Woodbridge, *Women and the English Renaissance: Literature and the Nature of Womankind, 1540–1620* (Brighton: Harvester, 1981); Ian McLean, *The Renaissance Notion of Woman: A Study in the Fortunes of Scholasticism and Medical Science in European Intellectual Life* (Cambridge: Cambridge University Press, 1980).
[28] *Preface to* The Faerie Queene, 192.

stable basis for their efforts to reform Ireland could be established. The discussion in *A View*, after all, finishes with the two speakers agreeing that Ireland needs to be reconquered and sorting out how this should be achieved so that the last third of the text is given over to military proposals concerning the exact requirements of the army which should be recruited to perform this Herculean task.[29] It is no coincidence that Lord Grey seems to have been as popular among the New English in Ireland as he was unpopular at the English court.[30]

Irena is, in effect, a cipher, an empty figure who stands for a blank Ireland which needs to be represented and defined by the New English colonists. At present she stands bereft as the Irish representative of the Faerie Queene, resembling the rather pathetic damsel in distress of Victorian cartoons, needing the martial maid Britannia to defend her from the Fenian menace.[31] If the requisite policies were to be carried out, then she would cease to be this parasitic ghost, a pale shadow who has nothing to do with the complex reality of Ireland; she would have to represent the people who flock to her who, at present, lack all voice and are unable to represent themselves, mirroring Irena as creatures lacking all substance.[32] In doing so, she would be transformed herself, fleshed out, and made into a substantial figure of government: the form would have to go beyond the content.[33] Irena may be depicted as 'true Leige and Princesse naturall' of Ireland, but the use of the word 'natural' is hard to take at face value, given the ironies developed in the proem and the first canto of Book V. Irena can only have a right to Ireland if she recognizes that it is more than likely that her rule depends upon the original conquest of her dynastic ancestors—or, rather, those who held the throne—in itself a fearful admission of arbitrariness, but without which Ireland can only be ruled by a pale slip of a girl, not the violent Arthurian hero the situation requires. Grantorto, the usurping Catholic tyrant, actually represents more of Ireland than Irena herself does, as the description of him indicates; she inherits the blind avoidance demonstrated by the marriage of the rivers in the previous book, and the refusal of Belphoebe to absorb the salvage man.

The discussion of justice within Book V is clearly framed by the

[29] See Brady, 'Spenser's Irish Crisis: Humanism and Experience', 30–3.
[30] Brady, *Chief Governors*, 292.
[31] See Liz Curtis, *Nothing But the Same Old Story: The Roots of Anti-Irish Racism* (London: Information on Ireland, 1984), 56.
[32] See, Karl Marx, *The Eighteenth Brumaire of Louis Bonaparte* (Moscow: Progress Publishers, 1954), 106; Said, *The World, the Text, and the Critic*, 123.
[33] Marx, *Eighteenth Brumaire*, 13.

question of Ireland. The main principle Spenser appears to wish to establish as vital to the government of the British Isles is that of equity, a concept largely associated with the writings of Jean Bodin, which demanded that the precepts of the code of law needed to be overridden by the representatives of the law when the foundations of the constitution or the authority of the monarch were under threat. Under such a legal system, magistrates were granted quite draconian powers in supposed defence of the centre; a simultaneously centripetal and centrifugal shift of power. In *A View*, Spenser's one citation of Machiavelli suggests this paradox, a detail which caught the eye of the republican John Milton, writing around the time of the execution of Sir Thomas Wentworth, earl of Strafford.[34] In *The Faerie Queene*, Book V, as in *A View*, Ireland provides the context for a defence of equity as a fundamental legal principle, forcing legislators to move beyond their experiences of the relatively ordered commonweal of England.

Artegall is a notably brutal governor, frequently employing Talus to perform his dirty work, precisely because the law is under threat and with it the very possibility of order. Hence the book contains a series of violent acts: Pollente has his head chopped off and placed on a pole (v. ii. 19); Murena has her hands and feet cut off and nailed on high (26); the Egalitarian Giant is thrown from a cliff (50) (three spectacularly violent deaths in one canto); Radigund has her head cut off by Britomart after her defeat in single combat (vii. 34); the Souldan is slain and his body so mangled and dismembered that all that remains of him are his shield and armour which are hung up (viii. 44–5); even less remains of Malengin after he is broken up into little pieces by Talus (ix. 19); the poet Malfont has his tongue nailed to a post for blaspheming against the queen (ix. 25–6); Arthur slays Geryoneo, another tyrant threatening Belge, having first disposed of his knights and seneschal (x–xi); finally, Grantorto is slain and his head is also cut off (xii. 23).[35] Talus is frequently more generally destructive when let loose upon the ordinary, unnamed population (vii. 35–6; xii. 7 and 26).

It would be an exaggeration to suggest that all such actions relate to incidents in Irish history; clearly the allegory of the Souldan relates to the defeat of the Armada and the figure of Geryoneo serves 'to justify

[34] See Willy Maley, 'How Milton and Some Contemporaries Read Spenser's *View*', in Bradshaw *et al.* (eds.), *Representing Ireland*, 191–208, at 195–6. On Strafford, see Hugh Kearney, *Strafford in Ireland, 1633–41: A Study in Absolutism* (Manchester: Manchester University Press, 1959).

[35] See Elizabeth Fowler, 'The Failure of Moral Philosophy in the Work of Edmund Spenser', *Representations*, 51 (Summer 1995), 47–76, at 54.

England's military intervention in the Low Countries'.[36] One can also divide the book up into three ever-widening sections: the first concerned with implementing the common law (i–iv); the second with the limitations of such law and the need for the legal system to adopt the principle of equity (iv–vii); and the third with 'the role of the queen's justice beyond the borders of England, in the conflict with Spain in the Netherlands, in Ireland, and, in the trial of Mary, Queen of Scots'.[37] But all such incidents are represented within the confines of a narrative which begins and ends in Ireland, setting the Irish question as Spenser's master subject; the Souldan and Geryoneo stand as images of Philip II, but in the final canto he appears like an Irish foot-soldier, blurring the two identities.

One should also be wary of relating the violent killings to Ireland; Tudor treason acts legislated for hanging, beheading, and mutilation, and frequently such acts were carried out in England.[38] Nevertheless, the landscape of dismembered figures and hideous slaughter can clearly be related to Ireland, which was almost continuously subject to rebellion and conflict in the later years of Elizabeth's reign, a reality reiterated throughout Spenser's writings. As I shall argue, the stubborn image of Ireland appears throughout Book V. The description of the aftermath of Pollente's death—a disturbingly harsh punishment given that Pollente's crime is extorting money from those who wish to pass over his toll bridge—would seem to place that action in an Irish setting:

> His corps was carried downe along the Lee,
> Whose waters with his filthy bloud it stayned:
> But his blasphemous head, that all might see,
> He pitcht upon a pole on high ordayned;
> Where many years it afterwards remayned,
> To be a mirrour to all mighty men,
> In whose right hands great power is contayned,
> That none of them, the feeble ouerren,
> But alwaies doe their powre within iust compasse pen.

(V. ii. 19)

Yet again, this description refers the reader back to an earlier one; this time, the marriage of the Thames and the Medway at the end of Book IV. One of the rivers represented was 'The spreading Lee, that like an Island fayre | Encloseth Corke with his deuided flood' (IV. xi. 44), so that

[36] Freeman, The Faerie Queene, 283–4; James P. Bednarz, 'Geryoneo', Sp. Enc., 331.
[37] O'Connell, 'The Faerie Queene, Book V', 281.
[38] Bellamy, Tudor Law of Treason, ch. 5; Williams, Tudor Regime, 375–80.

the journey of Pollente's headless trunk takes place around the city of Cork.[39] There is an even more significant echo, in that the river described next to the Lee is the 'balefull Oure, late staind with English blood'; Pollente's body stains the waters of the Lee with his 'filthy bloud'. The story that Spenser's narrator refused to tell at the wedding-feast—that of the 'saluage cuntreis'—is leaking out into the rest of the poem, colouring the Irish landscape with blood, and so changing Faerieland into a bloody Irish landscape. One problem remains: is Pollente an English extortionist, who is given his comeuppance by the impartial Artegall, pledged to uphold a blind system of justice? If the echo is careful and deliberate, the staining of the river with his blood may well be set against the more worthy spillage by Lord Grey's troops who were defeated on the banks of the Avonbeg (1580) during the Desmond Rebellion.[40]

The fate of the rest of Pollente's body, 'his blasphemous head', which is placed upon a pole *pour encourager les autres*, resembles the description given of the fate of Rory Oge O'More in John Derricke's *The Image of Ireland* (1581), a work which Spenser may well have known as it was published at the same time as Spenser's Irish career began, by a member of the Sidney circle, which also patronized Spenser.[41] Derricke places a lengthy narrative in the mouth of the executed rebel, so that his corpse is able to speak and take its place within the violent pagent of state power. The severed head looks down from the battlements and warns loyal subjects, 'Against the Crowne royall doe nothyng attempt, | For if against it, ye, falyng at odde, | Doe feele as I felt, the Strength of the Rodde'.[42] The sixth woodcut which accompanies the text shows the Lord Deputy, Sir Henry Sidney, setting out from Dublin Castle with the severed heads of rebels on poles. The verse attached reads: 'These trunkles heddes do playnly showe each rebelles fatal end, | And what a haynous crime it is the Queene for to offend.'[43]

The message given by the execution of Pollente is almost identical, and both give the viewer/listener the same message about state power and its effects. Nevertheless, Spenser's narration of the execution is far more

[39] Henley identifies Pollente as Sir John of Desmond, who was killed by Colonel Zouche and his head placed on Dublin Castle in the New Year of 1582: *Spenser in Ireland*, 139–40.

[40] *FQ*, p. 516.

[41] See Maley, *Salvaging Spenser*, ch. 1; id., *Spenser Chronology*, 90; *DNB* entry on Derricke.

[42] *Image of Ireland*, 97. See also Foucault, *Discipline and Punish*, 48–9. See above, Ch. 2 n. 61.

[43] *Image of Ireland*, woodcut 6. On Rory Oge O'More, see Bagwell, *Ireland Under the Tudors*, ii. 340–5.

ambiguous and disturbing; Derricke's representation of Rory Oge acts as an exemplum, albeit negative; Spenser's narrator defines the image of the dead Pollente as a 'mirrour', which encourages the reader to be rather more active in decoding the text, as well as placing the image within a sequence in the narrative, from Merlin's glass in which Britomart sees Artegall, to the extensive use of the metaphor in the proems to the queen, culminating in the lengthy discussion which opens Book VI.[44] It should further be noted that Pollente's crime is against the powerless and the image concludes that the sight of the headless corpse will urge them to 'their powre within iust compasse pen', a warning which recalls Spenser's citation of Machiavelli in *A View* (and Milton's reading) that the magistrate's abuse of power should incur draconian penalties. Equally, and in line with the sceptical representation of the queen's power in the poem, the message would seem to apply to her treatment of her less powerful subjects.

The implications of the killing of Pollente and the power relations inscribed therein are spelt out more clearly in a series of incidents later in the book, all contained within canto ix. This canto relates Talus' killing of Malengin, the nailing of Bonfont's tongue to the post, and concludes with the allegorized trial of Mary Queen of Scots in the Palace of Mercilla.[45] The link between the two cantos follows the defeat of the Souldan at the end of canto viii and the escape of his ferocious wife, Adicia, who flees into the forest at the start of canto ix:

> What Tygre, or what other saluage wight,
> Is so exceeding furious and fell,
> As wrong, when it hath arm'd it selfe with might?
> Not fit mongst men, that doe with reason mell,
> But mongst wyld beasts and saluage woods to dwell;
> Where still the stronger doth the weake deuoure,
> And they that most in boldnesse doe excell,
> Are dreadded most, and feared for their powre:
> Fit for *Adicia*, there to build her wicked bowre.
>
> (v. ix. 1)

The narrator directs us away from such sights to focus upon 'righteous *Artegall*', because, it is implied, Adicia can cause no harm because she 'wonne farre from the resort of men' (2). But the problem of Adicia cannot be so lightly dealt with, even if she does not return to haunt the Knight of Justice. Her fleeing into the woods recalls the stripping of

---

[44] See Herbert Grabes, 'mirrors', *Sp. Enc.*, 477–8; Williams, *Spenser's Faerie Queene*.
[45] For commentary see Northrop, 'Spenser's Defense of Elizabeth'; id., 'Mercilla's Court as Parliament', *HLQ* 36 (1973), 153–8; McCabe, 'The Masks of Duessa'.

Duessa, when Una persuaded Arthur to 'let her goe at will, and wander wayes unknowen' (I. viii. 49) because she had been exposed as the image of falsehood and could no longer be a danger. Duessa flees into 'the wastfull wildernesse apace' (I. viii. 50), only to return to threaten the union of Una and the Red Cross Knight, suggesting that Una's confidence was somewhat ill-founded. Duessa has not reappeared in the narrative—yet—but her role as the allegorical form of Mary Queen of Scots later in this canto would suggest that a very precise link between the two women has been forged. Adicia is portrayed at great length as a wild and dangerous savage—the word is used twice in the first canto. One can banish savagery to the woods and try to forget it is there, but, like a bad conscience, it will always return unless properly dealt with, a fear that is amply confirmed in the pastoral setting of Book VI. Artegall himself has to control his own savage nature, and his quest involves the rescue of Irena's 'saluage island'. Just as Error was defeated only to return as a more threatening and frightening figure when no longer a straightforward manifestation, so, it is implied, will the figure of Adicia.

In fact, this is precisely what happens. The lady they have rescued from the Souldan, Samient, who insists on leading them to Mercilla's palace—against their will (V. ix. 3)—warns them of a 'wicked villaine, bold and stout, | Which wonned in a rocke not farre away, | That robbed all the countrie there about, | And brought the pillage home, whence none could get it out' (4), that is, the sort of wilderness which Duessa and Adicia inhabit. The actions of Malengin, named in the next stanza, foreshadow those of the brigands at the end of Book VI, who hide their plunder on an inaccessible island, and also resemble the behaviour of the outlaws who terrify the lives of the shepherds in *Colin Clouts come home againe*. The description of Malengin marks him as specifically Irish, and echoes Spenser's depictions of the rebel Irish in mantles and glibs in *A View*, as has frequently been noted:

> Full dreadfull wight he was, as euer went
> Upon the earth, with hollow eyes deepe pent,
> And long curld locks, that downe his shoulders shagged,
> And on his backe an uncouth vestiment
> Made of straunge stuffe, but all to worne and ragged,
> And underneath his breech was all to torne and iagged.[46]

(v. ix. 10)

[46] On Malengin as Irish, see Hamilton, *Allegory in* The Faerie Queene, 190; Northrop, 'Spenser's Defense of Elizabeth', 281; Dunseath, *Spenser's Allegory of Justice*, 203; Hough, *Preface to* The Faerie Queene, 199; Harold Skulsky, 'Malengin', *Sp. Enc.*, 450.

Samient is left outside the rock as bait for Malengin, weeping and wailing as if she were a damsel (the word Spenser uses) in a romance or a saint's life (the legend of St George?), left as prey for him.[47] She stands as a type of Irena; a helpless sacrificial victim who needs male power to protect her. Malengin's reaction, when he discovers her presence, is to laugh (12), a reaction which prefigures that of Faunus when he sees Diana naked in Ireland in 'Two Cantos of Mutabilitie'. Such a '*Sardonain* smyle' serves to hide 'his false intent', so resembling the duplicity of Milton's Comus and his attempts to trap the lady; it is also the laughter of the powerless finally made powerful and having all his enemies at his mercy.

More threatening still is the direct challenge to the poetic order of allegory, and the political order which that allegory strives to represent, caused by the ability of Malengin to transform himself into any form he desires at will. When pursued by Artegall and Talus, he first turns himself into a goat, then a fox, a bird, a hedgehog, and, finally, a snake, before he is caught and killed by Talus. His actions bear a clear resemblance to those of Proteus, who transforms himself first into a mortal, then a faerie knight, a king, a giant, a centaur, and, finally, a storm, in his pursuit of Florimell (III. viii. 39–41).[48] Proteus has been tamed by the marriage of the Thames and the Medway, but the threat he poses to stability has been taken up by the rebellious Irish who exist beyond the boundaries and confines of the rule of law, haunting the English desire for civil stability with a world of constant flux in which truth cannot be fixed. That imperial union could not encompass the savage Irish, who now reappear as ghostly harbingers of chaos; the emaciated Malengin may well be one of the victims of the Munster famine Spenser apparently witnessed, 'Crepinge forthe . . . like Anotomies of deathe' (*View*, 158). Malengin points out the ambiguity in the phrasing of *A View*: 'anotomies of deathe' are not simply victims but threaten those who would establish the means of a proper life with their own terrible fate.

Eventually Malengin is caught by Talus, who destroys him with a psychotic ferocity:

[47] On the popularity of the legend of St George in Elizabethan England see Weatherby, *Mirrors of Celestial Grace*, ch. 2; Helen White, *Tudor Books of Saints and Martyrs* (Madison: Wisconsin University Press, 1963), ch. 9. If the allusion is deliberate, the Red Cross Knight's emergence as the English patron saint (I. x. 61) is now qualified by the telling of his story in an Irish context.

[48] Like Malengin, he eventually fails in his aim.

But when as he would to a snake againe
Haue turn'd himselfe, he with his yron flayle
Gan driue at him, with so huge might and maine,
That all his bones, as small as sandy grayle
He broke, and did his bowels disentrayle;
Crying in vaine for helpe, when helpe was past.
So did deceipt the selfe deceiuer fayle,
There they him left a carrion outcast;
For beasts and foules to feede upon for their repast.

(v. ix. 19)

Whereas the head of Pollente was displayed for all to see, the body of
Malengin is made to disappear, so that it can no longer provide any
message for others to read. Talus' destruction of Malengin repeats the
excessive action and reaction of Guyon destroying Acrasia's bower
(II. xii. 83), an episode which has frequently been read in both colonial
and Irish contexts by critics.[49] Just as Guyon's virtue is tested to the limit
by his confrontation with sexual beauty and the lure of the senses, causing
him to destroy beauty in the name of purity and truth, so Talus' part in the
legend of justice is enacted via his confrontation with Malengin.[50] Talus
can neither contain Malengin nor keep him at bay, and his only recourse
is absolute destruction, making the body of the Irish rebel disappear so
that it is reabsorbed into the landscape when eaten by beasts and
fowl. In a sense, the natural process mocks the failure of the human
imposition of law; the implication is that Malengin, like Error, has been
destroyed only for his legacy to become even more ghostly and terrifying
as it becomes part of the very landscape and, hence, virtually invisible
and even more protean than the 'human' figure.

This fear of uncontrollable chaos is reinforced if one returns and
rereads the aftermath of Guyon's righteous destruction of Acrasia's
bower, because that action also ends on an ominous note. After Guyon
has made 'the fowlest place' out of 'the fairest late' (II. xii. 83), the
knights who had been transformed into beasts by Acrasia are turned
back into their proper forms. However, there is one, named Grill, who
resists transformation and remains as a hog. Guyon comments, 'See
the mind of beastly man, | That hath so soone forgot the excellence | Of
his creation, when he life began, | That now he chooseth, with vile

[49] Greenblatt, *Renaissance Self-Fashioning*, ch. 4; Patricia Parker, 'Suspended Instruments: Lyric and Power in the Bower of Bliss', in id., *Literary Fat Ladies: Rhetoric, Gender, Property* (London: Methuen, 1987), 54-66.
[50] See Gilman, *Iconoclasm and Poetry*, ch. 3.

difference, | To be a beast'. His palmer agrees: 'The donghill kind |
Delights in filth and foule incontinence: | Let *Grill* be *Grill*, and haue his
hoggish mind' (87). Unable to effect a change, the two depart.

The incident, derived from the legend of Odysseus' encounter with
Circe, recalls New English criticisms of Old English 'degeneration' into
Irishness, notably Spenser's own account of the loss of self and identity
induced by the Irish environment on colonists: 'Is it possible that anye
shoulde so far growe out of frame that they shoulde in so shorte space
quite forgett theire Countrie and theire owne names that is a moste dangerous *Lethargie* muche worse then that of *messala Corvinus* whoe
beinge a moste learned man thorowe sicknes forgott his own name' (*A
View*, 115).[51] It further suggests that, however much one desires to transform unstable and hostile elements and incorporate them into a civilized
order, a certain stubborn, recalcitrant element will resist, remaining
beyond the boundaries and threatening to undermine the very notions
upon which such distinctions depend (Grill using the willpower which
defines him as human to become a beast, the Old English choosing to
throw off an English identity, Malengin using his power to transform
himself in order to undermine English attempts to transform Ireland).
The key problem for the civilized is that such wanton savagery defies
explanation. Talus destroys Malengin in the hope that he will not
return; we, as readers, know—or should know by now—that Talus'
hope is no more than a fantasy.

The second half of the canto, the visit of Artegall and Talus to Mercilla's Palace, is often read as the allegorical and political 'core' of the
book, laying out the concept of equity as Spenser felt it should be used in
Elizabethan polity, substantiated by the action of the last three cantos.[52]
What should not be forgotten is how tenaciously the ghost of Malengin
haunts the allegorical explication of justice at Mercilla's court, making
the narrative as much an attack on as a defence of Elizabeth. The
headnote to the canto glosses Malengin as 'Guyle'; the giant porter,
Awe, who guards Mercilla's porch has as his job 'To keepe out guyle,
and malice, and despight, | That under shew oftimes of fayned
semblance, | Are wont in Princes courts to worke great scath and hin-
drance' (v. ix. 22). Nevertheless, guile has entered into the court in the
guise of Bon/Malfont, the disgraced poet:

[51] See Hadfield and Maley's introduction to Bradshaw *et al.* (eds.), *Representing Ireland*, 9. The story of Grill derives from Plutarch, 'Odysseus and Gryllus', in *Moral Essays*,
trans. Rex Warner (Harmondsworth: Penguin, 1971), 159–75, not Homer.
[52] O'Connell, '*The Faerie Queene*, Book V', 282.

> There as they entred at the Scriene, they saw
> Some one, whose tongue was for his trespasse vyle
> Nayled to a post, adiudged so by law:
> For that therewith he falsely did reuyle,
> And foule blaspheme that Queene for forged guyle,
> Both with bold speaches, which he blazed had,
> And with lewd poems, which he did compyle;
> For the bold title of a Poet bad
> He on himselfe had ta'en, and rayling rymes had sprad.
>
> (v. ix. 25)

As a punishment, Bonfont is displayed like Pollente and his name inverted so that it 'was plainely to be red'. Nevertheless, even the altered name is somewhat unclear in terms of its precise significance, resulting, 'Eyther for th'euill, which he did therein, | Or that he likened was to a welhed | Of euill words, and wicked sclaunders by him shed' (26).[53]

Malfont is clearly related to the figure of Malengin, both representing a form of 'guile', a quality condemned at Mercilla's court, but it is by no means obvious that he deserves his punishment as richly as Malengin does. In some respects, the figure of Bon/Malfont serves as the type of a poet like Spenser, able to write what he likes in the borderlands of civilization adjacent to the dangerous wilderness inhabited by Malengin, but liable to harsh punishment when their work reaches the ears and eyes of the court. The depiction of Bon/Malfont is indeed grimly prophetic of a never-realized but possible history, given James I's dislike of this particular canto with its allegorical portrait of the trial of his mother, Mary Queen of Scots, and his insistence that Elizabeth have Spenser punished. In another, related, sense, the ambiguity surrounding the significance of the poet's name suggests that messages never have one single, clear meaning, which in itself points to the problem of treating language as a straightforward instrument which can be regarded as lacking guile. At a court where such a simplistic and draconian perception of writing persists, the poet will have to be duplicitous and skilled in guile, because he can always be misread and, simply through the act of writing, be seen to be undermining the stability of just truth, a point the ending of Book VI, with its plea that 'this homely verse' escape the 'venemous despite' of the Blatant Beast (VI. xii. 41), forcefully makes. It is by no means as easy as the English authorities imagine to make the

---

[53] On Bon/Malfont, see A. Leigh DeNeef, 'Bonfont, Malfont', *Sp. Enc.*, 101; Norbrook, *Poetry and Politics in the English Renaissance*, 133; Goldberg, *James I and the Politics of Literature*, 1–2.

ambiguity of guile disappear; Malengin and Malfont are related creatures and Spenser has to acknowledge that both inhabit his writing.

But if the 'meaning' of this incident is undeniably metaphysical on one
level, it is also straightforwardly political on another. As Artegall and
Talus proceed through the hall to reach 'the presence of that gratious
Queene' (27), they have to find a way through a large crowd which is
eventually silenced by Order (in itself a suggestion that disorder is
already within the court). The reaction of the crowd to the two knights
is recounted in detail:

> They ceast their clamors upon them to gaze;
> Whom seeing all in armour bright as day,
> Straunge there to see, it did them much amaze.
> And with unwonted terror halfe affray.
> For neuer saw they there the like array,
> Ne euer was the name of warre there spoken,
> But ioyous peace and quietnesse alway,
> Dealing iust iudgements, that mote not be broken
> For any brybes, or threates of any to be wroken.
>
> (v. ix. 24)

Superficially, this appears to be extravagant praise of Elizabeth's peaceful rule, but the point must be that the court is simply ignorant of the
realities of late Tudor rule, which involved heroic martial effort and
extreme violence in order to preserve the stability of the Crown,
nowhere more so than in Ireland.[54] Artegall and Talus have just defeated
a sinister threat in the form of Malengin, but are strangers at the queen's
court, where they are treated with contemptuous rudeness by the
courtiers whose soft lives their military struggles help, preserve and who
eventually betray them to their own cost.

The trial of Mary/Duessa reveals the queen to have a weak grasp of
the fundamental principles operating in the age of stone. She wishes to
spare the life of Duessa, a decision, as is implied by her past behaviour,
which will only result in her further trying to undermine the stability of
the realm. Significantly it is Artegall who has the final say and persuades
Mercilla, against her will, that she must have Duessa executed, and so
enforce the stern principles of equitable justice:

> But *Artegall* with constant firme intent,
> For zeale of Iustice was against her bent.
> So was she guiltie deemed of them all.

---

[54] For an overview, see Guy (ed.), *The Reign of Elizabeth I*.

> Then *Zele* began to urge her punishment,
> And to their Queene for iudgement loudly call,
> Unto *Mercilla* myld for Iustice gainst the thrall.
>
> (v. ix. 49)

As Richard McCabe has pointed out, Lord Grey was the one of the commissioners involved in the trial of Mary, and the most keen to see her executed, a reality reflected in his transformation into the figure of Zele, the word William Camden used when describing Grey's speech.[55] Mercilla is shown to understand far too little about the territories she rules, a pointed contrast to the likes of Lord Grey or Spenser himself. The problem is that, in telling the queen where she is going wrong, one risks having one's tongue nailed to a post.

The reality of Irish justice is the frightening figure of Talus, whose widespread slaughter is so repellent that he frequently has to be controlled by those in charge of him. After Britomart's victory over Radigund, Talus enacts a 'piteous slaughter' over the Amazon's followers, subjecting all 'that euer came within his reach' to his 'yron flaile' (V. vii. 35).[56] The narrator comments that 'the noble Conqueresse | Her selfe came in, her glory to partake', which would seem to suggest that Britomart intends to join in the slaughter. However,

> when she saw the heapes, which he did make,
> Of slaughtred carkasses, her heart did quake
> For very ruth, which did it almost riue,
> That she his fury willed him to slake:
> For else he sure had left not one aliue,
> But all in his reuenge of spirite would depriue.
>
> (v. vii. 36)

Artegall performs the same action in canto xii, restraining Talus' excesses after he has scattered bodies over the Irish landscape 'as thicke as doth the seede after the sowers hand' (xii. 7): '*Artegall* him [Talus] seeing so to rage, | Willd him to stay, and signe of truce did make' (8).

The last example perhaps serves as an attempt to distance Lord Grey from the effects of the violence at Smerwick and elsewhere.[57] But it also

---

[55] 'inflamed with a religious Zeal', cited in McCabe, 'Masks of Duessa', 239.

[56] For an exemplary reading of Radigund as an allegory of the Irish who feminize the English colonists, which further supports my general argument, see Carroll, 'The Construction of Gender and the Cultural and Political Other'. See also Henley, *Spenser in Ireland*, 141.

[57] McCabe, 'The Fate of Irena', 122.

raises questions concerning the very nature of power and justice, especially as we are granted an insight into the feelings of Britomart. The question which her sympathetic reaction to Radigund's followers forces the reader to consider is whether she is troubled by her hermaphroditic nature as a woman ruler, allowing her female heart to rule her male head and so failing like Mercilla (as happened with questions of sexual continence in her encounter with Malecasta); or whether she is correct that such unlicensed slaughter as Talus performs is a horrifying waste. Such a problem is not sorted out in *The Faerie Queene* and is an obvious defect of a system of *ad hoc* justice based on the notion of 'equity', which devolves power to the individual magistrates as representatives of the monarch. Britomart's reaction looks back to the lines accompanying the spectacle of Pollente's death, suggesting that his dismembered corpse be a 'mirrour to all mighty men', and that they 'alwaies doe their powre within iust compasse pen'. Whether this means general slaughter, as is sometimes required, or pardons and pacification, is a matter for the judgement of the individual. The penalties for error in such situations are frighteningly draconian. Book V might well be regarded as belonging to the genre of 'mirrors for princes', famously adapted in the middle of the sixteenth century into *A Mirror for Magistrates*, applied to English rulers in Ireland.[58] The age of stone requires that individuals who have to rule over chaotic lands like Ireland need to resort to violence; the problem is that they can never know when or if they are going too far.

Books V and VI, the discussions of justice and courtesy, are probably more closely linked than any other pairing of books in the poem. As Artegall is returning to the Faerie Court, he is attacked by 'Two griesly creatures' (v. xii. 28), Envy and Detraction, who are, like Malengin, represented as insubstantial, ghostly creatures waiting to prey upon the civilized:

> The one of them [Envy], that elder did appeare,
> With her dull eyes did seeme to looke askew,
> That her mis-shape much helpt; and her foule heare
> Hung loose and loathsomely: Thereto her hew
> Was wan and leane, that all her teeth arew,
> And all her bones might through her cheekes be red;
> Her lips were like raw lether, pale and blew,

---

[58] See Hadfield, 'Literature and History: *A Mirror for Magistrates*', in id., *Literature, Politics and National Identity*, ch. 3.

> And as she spake, therewith she slauered;
> Yet spake she seldom, but thought more, the lesse she sed.
>
> (v. xii. 29)

It is tempting to regard Envy as yet another victim of English policy in Ireland, emaciated and on the brink of death, silently biding her time to see if she can hit back at her oppressors.[59] Both Envy and Detraction try to represent Artegall in terms Spenser employs elsewhere in his writings to describe the condition of the New English under siege in a hostile Ireland: 'They both arose, and at him loudly cryde, | As it had bene two shepheards curres, had scryde | A rauenous Wolfe amongst the scattered flockes' (38). The clear irony is that it has been Artegall/Grey who has striven to defend the state of English Protestant Ireland from an international Catholic threat; Envy and Detraction are the real wolves.[60] In *A View*, Irenius makes a pointed contrast between the 'filthie Conuersacion' (p. 137) of the Catholic Irish and the 'good Conuersation' (p. 141) of the Protestant English colonists. Envy and Detraction's attacks on Artegall represent the triumph of the former over the latter, a further reminder that in the age of stone it is hard to recognize good let alone oversee its triumph, so perverted have language and value become.[61]

The poetry rapidly moves from a specific to a general problem. Detraction slanders Artegall's policies in Ireland, claiming that they have depended upon 'unmanly guile', and that he has stained the bright sword of justice with 'reproachfull crueltie': 'as for *Grantorto*, him with treacherie | And traynes hauing surpriz'd, he fouly did to die' (40). The point is that if Artegall has had to use 'guile' it is because, in implementing justice, he has to risk becoming what he opposes (which does not, of course, remove the suspicion or the fundamental problem); if what he has done appears 'unmanly', perhaps that is because he is in the service of a vacillating woman ruler who makes his task that much harder. The treachery used against Grantorto may also refer to the massacre at Smerwick; the general point is that Grantorto is by no

---

[59] On the iconography of Envy, see Aptekar, *Icons of Justice*, 201–5, 209–10; Nohrnberg, *Analogy of* The Faerie Queene, 688–96. See also Healy, *New Latitudes*, 97.
[60] On the representation of Catholics as wolves in English Protestant satire, see King, *Spenser's Poetry and the Reformation Tradition*, 37.
[61] Spenser is to a large extent following in the wake of John Bale in mapping a religious distinction onto a national one; see Hadfield, 'Translating the Reformation', in Bradshaw *et al.* (eds.), *Representing Ireland*, 43–59 and the frontispiece from Bale's *Vocacyon* representing 'The English Christian and the Irish Papist' reproduced on p. 116.

stretch of the imagination innocent himself and so deserves—and requires to be dealt with by—such measures as it takes to defeat him.[62] However, in the following stanza, the two hags unleash the Blatant Beast, and the allegorical significance of the episode becomes much broader. The beast, whose name derives from the Latin 'blatero', 'to babble in vayne' as a contemporary work glossed the word, 'began aloud to barke and bay, | With bitter rage and fell contention, | That all the woods and rocks nigh to that way, | Began to quake and tremble with dismay', a parody of Orpheus controlling and calming the natural world with his lyre.[63] The 'aire rebellowed againe. | So dreadfully his hundred tongues did bray' (41). We have been transported within the length of a stanza from an attack on English policy in Ireland to a figure who represents the problematic nature of language *per se*, so that a criticism of the former is shown to lead directly to the chaos which Book V struggles to hold at bay, a movement already implicit in the distinction between the good and filthy conversation described in *A View*. The dedicatory sonnets addressed to Grey and Ormond hope for a transformation of Ireland from barbarism to civilization; the ending of Book V makes it clear that this is unlikely to happen. The seemingly confident notion of 'truth' represented by Una in Book I is now even more clearly under threat.

In the first canto of Book VI, Calidore, the Knight of Courtesy, encounters Artegall slightly further on in his journey and asks him if he has seen the Blatant Beast. Artegall replies that he saw the 'Monster bred of hellishe race' on his return from the 'saluage Island' (VI. i. 7–9). The proem to Book VI and the opening stanzas of canto i provide a series of linguistic echoes which relate the problems of the book not only to those of the previous one, but also to the religious allegory of Book I. The implication is that comfortable English conceptions of 'truth' will be undermined if justice is not established throughout the queen's dominions.

Stanza 5 of the proem argues that courtesy has become so corrupted in the modern world that it has started to resemble its opposite: 'But in the triall of true curtesie | Its now so farre from that, which then it was, | That it indeed is nought but forgerie, | Fashion'd to please the eies of them, that pas, | Which see not perfect things but in a glas', lines which need to be placed alongside similar comments regarding the nature of

---

[62] Borris, *Spenser's Poetics of Prophecy*, 31.
[63] Ovid, *Metamorphoses*, 226, 246–8. On the significance of the Blatant Beast, see *FQ*, p. 618; Ronald B. Bond, 'Blatant Beast', *Sp. Enc.*, 96–8.

justice in the proem to Book V. In the same way the continuation of the metaphor of the mirror, which in this stanza is regarded as an imperfect instrument that distorts reality, and in the next as a means of praising Elizabeth, recalls the equivocal comments on the monarch at the same juncture in the previous book. The narrator suggests that no one can match the virtue of the queen as a model of courtesy, 'In whose pure minde, as in a mirrour sheene, | It [courtesy] showes, and with her brightnesse doth inflame | The eyes of all, which thereon fixed beene' (6). The verses are unsettling in a number of ways: first, it is by no means clear what mirrors show the viewer, especially in *The Faerie Queene*: whether they reflect the future, a type or antitype of the observer, or a fixed reality; second, because it is also unclear what form of courtesy the queen reflects in its perfect form—the good courtesy, which is a private rather than a public quality in this degenerate age, or the bad form of insincerity; third, it is not certain how and why the mirror of the queen 'inflames' her subjects.

But if the queen has an uncertain status as regards her courteous qualities, it soon becomes apparent that the virtue itself is a movable feast, a problem amply borne out by the narrative of the book that follows. Although courtesy is first described as a flower which grows on a 'lowly stalke' (4), the first stanza of canto i suggests otherwise: 'Of Court, men Courtesie doe call, | For that it there most useth to abound'. The same stanza, following Stefano Guazzo, defines it as the 'roote of ciuill conuersation'.[64] It is hardly surprising if Calidore is somewhat confused himself. Although 'he loathd leasing, and base flattery, | And loued simple truth and stedfast honesty' (3), a value system which relates him to Una in Book I, he has no idea how to start his quest or where to start looking for the beast, feeling that he has begun 'To tread an endlesse trace, withouten guyde, | Or good direction' (6), a complaint which recalls that of the narrator at the end of Book IV, doomed to the task of describing 'the seas abundant progeny': 'O what an endlesse work haue I in hand' (IV. xii. 1).[65] Calidore's quest not only 'leads to no fixed place'; it also starts from an uncertain point.[66] The journey is a circular one which folds back upon itself, because Calidore cannot discover the object of his quest, true speech, without discovering what this is in the world at large. The place in the narrative at which he starts must be

[64] Lievsay, *Stefano Guazzo*, 96–9.

[65] A statement which starts to undermine the confident union of Britain and the wider world in the previous canto (see above, pp. 142–5). See Goldberg, *Endlesse Worke*, 8.

[66] Cheney, *Spenser's Image of Nature*, 182.

the point at which he finishes, a stubborn reality which will either render the quest unnecessary or impossible. This is reflected in the seemingly etymologically based definition of the virtue in the final stanza of the proem: 'Then pardon me, most dreaded Soueraine, | That from your selfe I doe this vertue bring, | And to your selfe doe it returne againe' (7). Etymologies are, looked at one way, tautologies.[67] Just as we do not ever really grasp what the definition of 'courtesy' means as it hovers uneasily between public politeness and the deepseated truth found within the mind, neither do we ever reach the court of the Faerie Queene; the origin of courtesy is doubly hidden (lost), within and without the extant text.[68]

Calidore, like Artegall, fails to complete his quest, which—like the latter's—occupies relatively little of the book's overall narrative. However, whereas Artegall is hindered by the foolish intervention of his monarch, Calidore is simply unable to contain his foe even though he does manage to capture it:

> Thus was the Monster by the maystring might
> Of doughty *Calidore*, supprest and tamed,
> That neuer more he mote endammadge wight
> With his vile tongue, which many had defamed,
> And many causelesse caused to be blamed:
> So did he eeke long after this remaine,
> Untill that, whether wicked fate so framed,
> Or fault of men, he broke his yron chaine,
> And got into the world at liberty againe.

(VI. xii. 38)

The poem authorized in Spenser's lifetime ends with a dreadful vision of all linguistic acts being attacked by the beast regardless of merit, including *The Faerie Queene* itself: 'Ne spareth he most learned wits

[67] See Attridge, 'Language as History/History as Language', 98–104; Jonathan Culler, 'The Call of the Phoneme: Introduction', 2–4.

[68] There is extensive comment on the problematic nature of Book VI and its opening lines. See e.g. Humphrey Tonkin, *Spenser's Courteous Pastoral: Book VI of* The Faerie Queene (Oxford: Clarendon Press, 1972), ch. 2; id., '*The Faerie Queene*, Book VI', *Sp. Enc.*, 283–7; Fogarty, 'The Colonisation of Language', 92–6; Cain, *Praise in* The Faerie Queene, 174–9; Harry Berger, 'A Secret Discipline: *The Faerie Queene*, Book VI', in id., *Revisionary Play*, 215–42; O'Connell, *Mirror and Veil*, ch. 6; Michael C. Schoenfeldt, 'The Poetry of Conduct: Accommodation and Transgression in *The Faerie Queene*, Book 6', in Richard Burt and John Michael Archer (eds.), *Enclosure Acts: Sexuality, Property and Culture in Early Modern England* (Ithaca, NY: Cornell University Press, 1994), 151–69, at 152–6.

to rate, | Ne spareth he the gentle Poets rime, | But rends without regard of person or of time' (40).[69]

Calidore has frequently been blamed for his failure and the book has been read as an indication of Spenser's increasing frustration with his monarch and of a move from the hope for a public politics of literature towards private introspection, exemplified in Calidore's rejection by the Graces after he clumsily disturbs their dance.[70] One might extend this reading and suggest that Calidore's failure owes more to the problem of the ending of Book V, where the Blatant Beast is unleashed as a direct result of Artegall's inability to make Ireland governable. The chaos which spreads throughout Britain stems from the sovereign's lack of will in seizing the opportunity to impose an order upon Ireland when it is presented to her.[71] Artegall has difficulty not only in keeping disorder at bay, but also in discovering what constitutes a just rule and what does not. Nevertheless, by the end of the book, his realization that one can never discount arbitrariness in the natural order of things has started to lay the foundations of a workable polity. The untimely ending of his quest leaves Calidore with no chance to complete his own, because courtesy can have no effective significance as a virtue without the initial imposition of justice. The uncertain state and tragi-comic chaos of the opening of the book return throughout the narrative, notably when Calidore abandons his public quest and searches for his personal truth in the pastoral retreat through his discussions with Meliboe, an abdication of responsibility which might well recall that of Astrea.[72] Calidore is not simply lost at the start when he has to ask Artegall to help him; his quest remains the search for a ghostly 'endlesse trace'. The final stanza returns the poem to contemporary political problems with the narrator's fear that 'this homely verse' will not be able to escape the

[69] On the ending, see Richard Neuse, 'Book VI as Conclusion to *The Faerie Queene*', *ELH* 35 (1968), 329–53; Stanley Stewart, 'Sir Calidore and "Closure"', *SEL* 24 (1984), 69–86.
[70] Cain, *Praise in* The Faerie Queene, 175–6; O'Connell, *Mirror and Veil*, 178–88; Williams, *Spenser's* Faerie Queene, 196–7; Bernard, 'The Pastoral of the Self', in id., *Ceremonies of Innocence*, 163–85; Daniel Javitch, *Poetry and Courtliness in Renaissance England* (Princeton: Princeton University Press, 1978), ch. 5. See also Hadfield, *Literature, Politics and National Identity*, 190–3.
[71] Once the beast has escaped, it is notable that Spenser adds that 'long time after *Calidore*', Sir Pelleas and Sir Lamoracke, 'And all his bretheren borne in Britaine land' (39), also try and fail to capture it, making the problem a British one, a theme continued in 'Two Cantos of Mutabilitie'.
[72] See Williams, *Spenser's* Faerie Queene, 201; Tonkin, *Spenser's Courteous Pastoral*, ch. 5; O'Connell, *Mirror and Veil*, 175–6; Richard Mallette, 'Meliboe', *Sp. Enc.* 465; Bernard, *Ceremonies of Innocence*, 151–3.

'venemous despite' of 'wicked tongues' like those of the Blatant Beast, which will 'bring a mighty Peres displeasure' (41) (usually assumed to be Lord Burghley).[73] The symbiotic relationship between grand metaphysical speculation and current political problems, so frequently established at crucial junctures throughout *The Faerie Queene*, dictates the ending of the poem as it brings the reader back into the sphere of contemporary political problems, factional disputes, and the search for patronage.[74]

The second edition of *The Faerie Queene* establishes a series of parallels and patterns of reading which demands that the reader think through the questions raised in the first edition, as well as continually looking back at incidents and episodes which have just taken place.[75] The last three books observe a symmetry which centres such seemingly abstract forms around the question of Ireland. In Book IV, two opposing savage figures appear as harbingers of a problem which has to be dealt with; significantly, in Book V, Artegall's quest is to liberate the 'saluage island', but the book contains no actual representations of savages; in Book VI, they reappear with a vengeance, haunting the pastoral landscape in a manner which recalls *Colin Clouts come home againe*. The allegorical narrative shows that, if the problem of justice is followed through by 'the saluage knight', then savagery can be controlled and absorbed into the body politic of Britain, just as Artegall internalizes his own nature, instincts, and education.[76] The savage can be salvaged.[77] However, because the enterprise of justice fails, the savages reappear as a threat, resisting all attempts to make sense of their behaviour and origins. The landscape of Book VI is not *necessarily* that of rural Ireland; the problem is that it could equally be an England unable to contain hostile forces and challenges to its fragile civilized order, signifying a breakdown of the distinction between the two nations laid out in the other poem. Even when Ireland is not represented as a figure or series of figures within the text, it determines the conditions of representation.

---

[73] *FQ*, p. 709; O'Connell, *Mirror and Veil*, 184–5.

[74] Schoenfeldt, 'The Poetry of Conduct', 164.

[75] On this general process, see DeNeef, *Spenser and the Motives of Metaphor*, introduction; Alpers, *Poetry of* The Faerie Queene, ch. 1.

[76] As does Britomart as the Temple of Isis; see Graziani, 'Elizabeth at Isis Court'; Aptekar, *Icons of Justice*, ch. 6.

[77] See Giamatti, 'Primitivism and the Process of Civility in Spenser's *Faerie Queene*', 76.

In canto iv a 'saluage man' rescues Calepine from Turpine, having appeared 'by fortune, passing all foresight' (VI. iv. 2), the constant motif of action throughout the book which signifies the disorder of its wandering narrative (in many ways a return to the style of action in Book I).[78] He conforms to the figure of prelapsarian man in his peaceful, vagrant lifestyle, as he 'neither plough'd nor sowed, | Ne fed on flesh, ne euer of wyld beast | Did taste the bloud, obaying natures first beheast' (14). Unable to practise husbandry, he is, nevertheless, self-contained and self-sufficient. His inability to speak except through the use of 'rude tokens', such as 'kissing his hands, and crouching to the ground' to demonstrate compassion, serve further to link him to the state of nature of the 'good' savage, as Spenser makes clear:

> For other language had he none nor speach,
> But a soft murmure, and confused sound
> Of senselesse words, which nature did him teach,
> T'expresse his passions, which his reason did empeach.
>
> (VI. iv. 11)

The description of the salvage man particularly the important detail of the lack of speech, links him to countless accounts of such savages brought back by travellers and colonists, principally from the Americas.[79] He represents one extreme pole of the two diametrically opposed types of natural man, so that the poem does actually become for an instant the romance of empire described in the proem to Book II.[80] The only aspect of his behaviour which distinguishes the salvage man from a beast is his innate knowledge of good. Although he 'neuer till this houre | Did taste of pittie, neither gentlesse knew' (VI. iv. 3), when he hears Serena's cries and sees Calepine pursued by Turpine, he starts to feel compassion.

The role he plays in the narrative is wholly benevolent. He finds herbs which cure Calepine and make him whole again (although he is unable to cure Serena because her wound is 'inwardly unsound', (16)). He is able to chase Turpine away as his savage fury proves irresistible. In doing this, his 'mad mood' makes him 'Like to a Tygre that hath mist his

---

[78] Tonkin, 'The Faerie Queene, Book VI' 285; Gary Waller, English Poetry of the Sixteenth Century (London: Longman, 1986), 185.

[79] See e.g. First Three English Books on America, ed. Arber, 37, 150, 156, 385; Bartolomé de Las Casas, In Defense of the Indians, trans. Stafford Poole (Urbana: University of Illinois Press, 1974), 30–1; Hogden, Early Anthropology, 191–206; Porter, Inconstant Savage, ch. 14; White, 'The Noble Savage'.

[80] See Pagden, Fall of Natural Man, introduction; Hulme, Colonial Encounters, ch. 2.

prey', because 'The saluage nation doth all dread despize' (6), a description which qualifies the image of Adicia as a tiger after the killing of the Souldan. Later he is deemed worthy enough to fight alongside Arthur, before disappearing from the narrative in canto viii as suddenly as he appeared within it.[81] Unlike the satyrs or the savage man in Book IV he is useful and tractable, recognizing the benefits of civilization and responding to them positively by protecting Calepine and Serena from hostility. For him, language is straightforward in a way that Calidore's search demands it should be; the obvious problem is that unless we can forget our own sophistication we cannot return to the state of innocence which the salvage man represents. The paradox is that we inevitably have to affirm our difference from his goodness simply by dint of being able to observe and recognize it. In this way he stands as both a stage of innate primitive goodness which man must leave behind in order to advance, and the lost Golden Age referred to in the proem to Book V. The man without language is absorbed into the body of the civilized, yet, paradoxically, resists such inclusiveness by affirming his difference.

But the issue is more complex even than this because the narrator informs us that 'from his mothers wombe, which him did beare, | He was invulnerable made by Magicke leare' (4), which is why he is able to resist Turpine's spear-thrust and survive his fearless assaults on opponents with superior arms. This unreality within the fiction is further emphasized when we are told that, like Artegall and the Red Cross Knight, the salvage man is a changeling, so that his kind treatment of Serena, 'Yet shewd some token of his gentle blood . . . | For certes he was borne of noble blood, | How euer by hard hap he hether came; | As ye may know, when the time shall be to tell the same' (VI. v. 2).[82] The salvage man is 'undisciplyned' and has grown misshapen (like the satyrs), but he has 'gentle blood' so that he will 'at the last breake forth in his owne proper kynd' (v. 1).[83] The right time never arrives for us to discover the proper form and origin of the salvage man's noble lineage, so that he remains a fiction within a fiction, never part of the substantial narrative of Faerieland. The tailing off of his story is more than likely a deliberate device, one which has its place in a book where all stability and sense are

---

[81] For further comment on the role of the salvage man, see Cheney, *Spenser's Image of Nature*, 195–214; Norhnberg, *Analogy of* The Faerie Queene, 659–75; Roy Harvey Pierce, 'Primitivistic Ideas in *The Faerie Queene*', *JEGP* 44 (1945), 138–51, at 147–8.

[82] On the motif of the changeling in the poem, see Hume, *Edmund Spenser: Protestant Poet*, ch. 7; Rathborne, *Meaning of Spenser's Fairyland*, ch. 3.

[83] See the relevant debate in Baldesar Castiglione, *The Book of the Courtier*, trans. George Bull (Harmondsworth: Penguin, 1967), 54–5

under threat.[84] In contrast the fierce and hostile savages who take his place have more substance within the delicately private pastoral world of a book lacking both a narrative core and a central authority.

The aimlessly wandering Serena provides a narrative link between the salvage man who tries to cure her and the cannibalistic salvage nation who abduct her when, in canto viii, she is separated from Timias who is attacked by Disdain and Scorn (an episode which refigures the attack on Artegall by Envy and Detraction).[85] She is the only character in the poem who has encounters with both good and bad savages.[86] While the former fails to cure her, the latter almost destroy her.[87]

The 'saluage nation' are represented as the direct opposite of the salvage man, appearing at the moment in the narrative that the latter disappears (although, in keeping with the style of the book, there is no causal link between the two episodes). The first stanza which describes them invites a comparison between the two savages:

> In these wylde deserts, where she [Serena] now abode,
> There dwelt a saluage nation, which did liue
> Of stealth and spoile, and making nightly rode
> Into their neighbours borders; ne did giue
> Them selues to any trade, as for to driue
> The painefull plough, or cattell for to breed,
> Or by aduentrous marchandize to thriue;
> But on the labours of poore men to feed,
> And serue their owne necessities with others need.
>
> (VI. viii. 35)

Just as the salvage man does not work, neither do the saluage nation, but while the one lives on the fruits of the forest, the members of the

---

[84] One might also point to the unresolved narratives of the stories of Ruddymane (II. iii. 2), Timias, Coridon, or the death of Artegall (III. iii. 28) (see Evans, *Spenser's Anatomy of Heroism*, 21).

[85] Serena is attacked by the Blatant Beast when she wanders off after she and Calepine are surprised by Calidore (VI. iii. 24–7); the narrator comments that she 'Wandred about the fields, as liking led | Her wauering lust after her wandring sight' (VI. iii. 23), the repetition emphasizing her role and character.

[86] For details of Serena's role in the poem, see A. Leigh DeNeef, 'Serena', *Sp. Enc.*, 637.

[87] Comment on Serena has centred around her abduction; see, for example, Pierce, 'Primitivistic Ideas in *The Faerie Queene*', 150; Cheney, *Spenser's Image of Nature*, 104–16, 192–214; Waldo F. McNeir, 'The Sacrifice of Serena: *The Faerie Queene*, VI. viii. 31–51', in Bernhard Fabian and Ulrich Suerbaum (eds.), *Festschrift für Edgar Mertner* (Munich: W. F. V. Munchen, 1968), 117–56; Tonkin, *Spenser's Courteous Pastoral*, *passim*; Kenneth Borris, ' "Diuelish Ceremonies": Allegorical Satire of Protestant Extremism in *The Faerie Queene*, VI. viii. 31–51', *Sp. Stud.* 8 (1987), 175–209; Fogarty, 'Colonisation of Language', 100–1; A. Leigh DeNeef, 'Serena', *Sp. Enc.* 637.

other appropriate the fruits of other men's labours, behaviour which links them, yet again, to the description of the perils which face the New English settlers in *Colin Clouts come home againe* and, earlier in the poem, to the figure of Malengin (all live beyond the boundaries of civilization, in wastelands or deserts).[88] The salvage nation are carefully separated from civilized humanity by the narrator, owing to their practice of cannibalism:

> Thereto they usde one most accursed order,
> To eate the flesh of men, whom they mote fynde,
> And straungers to deuoure, which on their border
> Were brought by errour, or by wreckfull wynde.
> A monstrous cruelty gainst course of kynde.
> They towards euening wandring euery way,
> To seeke for booty, came by fortune blynde.
>
> (VI. viii. 36)

Once again, the element of chance is highlighted so that the capture of Serena—a woman who clearly does not know where she is going—by such creatures contains its own nemesis within the confines of the book's logic of disorder. The salvage nation represent an inversion of human nature, a jettisoning of reason so that the dictates of the body rule the head and all forms of order are cast aside, a state of affairs manifested in the random attacks on those unlucky enough to stray over the unseen borders (it was a motif of accounts of cannibals, from Herodotus to Columbus and beyond, that such people always lived just over the next hill, out of sight).[89]

In marked contrast is the description of the elaborate ritual prepared for the sacrifice of Serena, who is left naked before an altar ready for the priest's knife. The salvage nation listen to his charms and 'diuelish ceremonies' (45), then sound their bagpipes and horns, and shout so loudly that they make 'the wood to tremble at the noyce' (46), another parody of Orpheus which links their behaviour and its effects to that of the Blatant Beast. The priest is just about to plunge the knife into Serena's breast and 'let out loued life' (48), when Calepine, her lover, from whom she has been separated since the end of canto iv, stumbles upon the scene, 'by chaunce, more then by choyce' (46), and is able to save her.

---

[88] A recurring trope of savage cannibal peoples in descriptions dating from Herodotus onwards: see Herodotus' description of the 'androphogi', in *The Histories*, 277. On the importance of Herodotus see Hulme, *Colonial Encounters*, 20–1; Hogden, *Early Anthropology*, 22–8.

[89] Hulme, *Colonial Encounters*, 80–1.

The preparations for the sacrifice are narrated in great detail, as are the reactions of the cannibals to the sight of the naked Serena, creating a voyeuristic spectacle which has distressed (and fascinated) numerous readers owing to its graphic, pornographic, lingering over the helpless female body, making the connection between sex and male violence explicit.[90] The problem is that the langauge used to depict Serena's body uncomfortably resembles that of much Elizabethan poetry; Serena is undressed only to be wrapped up in conceits. The description culminates in the oft-quoted blazon:

> Her yuorie necke, her alablaster brest,
> Her paps, which like white silken pillowes were,
> For loue in soft delight thereon to rest;
> Her tender sides, her bellie white and clere,
> Which like an Altar did it selfe uprere,
> To offer sacrifice diuine thereon;
> Her goodly thighes, whose glorie did appeare
> Like a triumphall Arch, and thereupon
> The spoiles of Princes hang'd, which were in battel won.
>
> (VI. viii. 42.)[91]

Although the previous stanza has condemned the 'sordid eyes' and 'lustful fantasyes' (41) of the salvage nation, the reader is drawn into the pornographic gaze because the poetry used clearly originates from a 'civilized' quarter, not a savage one (we never hear the salvage nation speak—although they do shout a lot—which provides yet another link between them and the salvage man). As John Pitcher has pointed out, what should serve to separate cannibals and Elizabethan (male) readers, actually draws them closer together.[92]

On one allegorical level, Serena stands as yet another representation of Elizabeth, and also as a counterpart to Irena, both being connected by their links to the salvage nation, a verbal echo which would appear too strong to ignore. The characterless Irena has been transmogrified into the vulnerable, victimized Serena. While the former is unable to represent adequately or order the salvage nation over which she has nominal

---

[90] Useful comment is provided by Fogarty, 'Colonisation of Language', 100–1.

[91] I am indebted to a paper delivered by Ms Hannah Betts, who is completing a D.Phil. on the Elizabethan blazon at the University of Oxford, entitled 'Belphoebe's "Stately Mount": Admonitory Pornography in *The Faerie Queene*', at the London Renaissance Seminar Conference, '*The Faerie Queene*', Birkbeck College, University of London, 20 Apr. 1996.

[92] Pitcher, 'Tudor Literature', 89–90.

control, Serena is stripped naked and left helplessly terrified by the salvage nation who abduct her. Only the chance intervention of a knight
saves her, surely a comment on how perilously Elizabeth's power in Ireland (and, by implication, the rest of the British Isles) stood after her failure to support Grey's violent initiative, as well as being a reflection of
her own aimless wanderings in matters of subsequent policy. Neither
woman is represented as anything other than an empty, passive vessel,
subject to the control of the active males who surround her and dictate
what she must do. In effect, because she has refused to seize the initiative—in contrast to the warrior woman, Britomart—Elizabeth's
encounter with Ireland has reduced her to a pathetic creature, a problem
registered in the increasingly hostile representation of her throughout
the second edition of the poem, culminating in her exclusion from the
dance of the Graces (VI. x. 28).[93]

What, though, of the overtly voyeuristic style of the descriptions of
the naked Serena? Spenser carefully and deliberately draws readers into
the scene of 'scopic' desire for Serena's body because they will have to
confront the reality of her nakedness and its malign effects, especially if
they are New English colonists in Ireland.[94] The stripping of Serena—a
denuding which looks back to the stripping of Duessa in an equivalent
place in Book I (I. vii. 46–50)—is an explicit attack on the problems of
female rule in the sixteenth century, an iconic image which suggests
that, when confronted by a lawless territory like Ireland, only masculine
government which recognizes the one fundamental reality—the law of
conquest—can function, and does not fall back on notions of natural
rights (associated with the anemic and ineffective figure of Irena in the
poem) which will somehow be enforced. Serena is exposed to a male
gaze in a terrifyingly misogynistic *mise en scène*; the representation of
her body in terms of the Petrarchan poetry fashionable at court and fos-
tered by Elizabeth turns that poetry against the queen in the name of her
English colonial subjects in Ireland who were caught between the
incompetence of their central authorities and the savagery of the Irish.[95]

---

[93] On the Graces, see Stella P. Revard, 'Graces', *Sp. Enc.,* 338–9; Gerald Snare,
'Spenser's Fourth Grace', *JWCI* 34 (1971), 350–5; Wind, *Pagan Mysteries in the Renaissance,* ch. 2; Cain, *Praise in* The Faerie Queene, 175–6. The last woman of consequence in
the poem, Pastorella, is kidnapped by brigands and eventually retires to a monastery
(VI. xii. 23), leaving Calidore to fight the Blatant Beast alone, which could be read as
another criticism of Elizabeth; see Richard T. Neuse, 'Pastorella', *Sp. Enc.,* 532–4, at 533.
[94] On 'scopic' desire, see Fogarty, 'Colonisation of Language', 99.
[95] Marotti, ' "Love is Not Love" '. See also Berry, *Of Chastity and Power,* chs. 3–4;
Waller, *English Poetry of the Sixteenth Century,* 76–93.

The 'spoiles of princes', hung between Serena's legs, are no longer her trophies, but are reappropriated by the poem as signs of her tyrannical and perverse rule. Resembling allegory as defined by the letter to Raleigh, they are a 'dark conceit' which reveal as much as they hide; in this case Elizabeth's vagina, which, Spenser implies, has been the centre of her government, one whose power is now on the wane.[96] The great English fear of 'degeneration' is brilliantly evoked by drawing the reader into the savages' leeringly hostile gaze at the helpless woman/queen so that the two become united for a horrible moment, a point all the more powerfully conceived after the narrator's attempts to distance the two peoples earlier. Without proper—male—government the chaos of savagism will transform civilization rather than vice versa.

Serena's reaction to her ordeal is one of 'inward shame of her uncomely case' and she feels that, although 'the night did couer her disgrace', she cannot communicate her experience to Calepine until the next day. Once again, the narrative trails off into the void as the canto ends, 'The end whereof Ile keepe untill another cast' (51), one which, like the genealogy of the salvage man, never reaches the reader and so becomes part of the 'endlesses trace' of Calidore's quest as Serena disappears from the narrative. The effect is to lay the blame for her suffering squarely upon Serena's behaviour—her aimless wandering means that she was asking for it—as she is the one who has allowed the pastoral landscape to become menaced by the savages.

The dominance of such creatures is confirmed in the last episode of consequence in the book before Calidore's final encounter with the Blatant Beast: the destruction of the rural haven to which Calidore retreats after his fruitless search for his foe. After Serena's encounter with the cannibals it might still seem that there is a certain 'courtesy', a balance of words and things, in the two diametrically opposed representations of the savage within the book. Objects are easy enough to recognize in a provisional sense and the reader is thrust onwards into the narrative in the expectation of a final resolution satisfying the desire for a conclusion. This is a position Calidore appears to have come to accept in his conversations with Meliboe in the following canto (ix), keen to end his quest and sort out dilemmas, as well as believing that he can find a final truth.

---

[96] The lines are also a rewriting of the blazon which describes Belphoebe (II. iii. 26–8), a point made by Hannah Betts, 'Belphoebe's "Stately Mount" '. See also Montrose, 'Elizabethan Subject', 327–8. One might also note Eldridge Cleaver's remark cited in Toril Moi, *Sexual/Textual Politics: Feminist Literary Theory* (London: Routledge, 1985), 22.

Calidore begins to praise the simplicity of the shepherd's existence, believing that, unlike him, they lead the good life free from 'debate or bitter strife' of the wider world (18). Meliboe agrees and tells the story of the unhappy life he led at court before realizing that his place was in the fields. He concludes his account with the gnomic lines, 'But fittest is, that all contented rest | With that they hold: each hath his fortune in his brest' (29) and draws a traditional moral that 'It is the mynd, that maketh good or ill'. Calidore, who has been listening to the shepherd's words 'with greedy eare', has been 'rapt with double ravishment' at the 'melting mouth' of the shepherd whose 'pleasing tongue' turns him into 'one halfe entraunced' (26). Calidore hears what he wants to hear in Meliboe's speech, echoing the shepherd's condemnation of 'the worlds gay showes' (22, 27), and twisting the conclusion that each should follow his own role in life to mean that man can 'fashion his own lyfes estate' (31) so that he can leave the trials of the world behind for this pastoral idyll.[97]

Meliboe's words are more obviously interpreted—especially in the context of the book—to mean that Calidore should resume his quest.[98] The knight, however, does not seem to realize that his sojourn in the pastoral haven means that his quest has ground to a halt, a significance emphasized by the brutal events of the previous canto and the inconclusiveness of the narrative of the middle cantos (iv–viii) when Calepine becomes the substitute hero (although he too disappears from the end of canto iv until the end of canto viii, leaving the book without a knight).[99] The lines describing Calidore's sudden return at the opening of canto ix, 'Now turn againe my teme thou jolly swayne, | Backe to the furrow which I lately left' (VI. ix. 1), further emphasize the random nature of the narrative controlled by the narrator whose decisions may have an underlying purpose or may simply be purely arbitrary.[100] They also

---

[97] For further comment see Cheney, *Spenser's Image of Nature*, 219–21. Such problems are ubiquitous in pastoral literature; see e.g. the discussions in Bernard, *Ceremonies of Innocence*, ch. 1; Raymond Williams, *The Country and the City* (London: Chatto & Windus, 1973); Annabel Patterson, *Pastoral and Ideology: Virgil to Valéry* (Berkeley: University of California Press, 1987); Judith Haber, *Pastoral and the Poetics of Self Contradiction: Theocritus to Marvell* (Cambridge: Cambridge University Press, 1994).

[98] See Tonkin, *Spenser's Courteous Pastoral*, 116–18; Judith Anderson, *The Growth of a Personal Voice*: Piers Plowman *and* The Faerie Queene (New Haven: Yale University Press, 1976), 178–84. For alternative readings, see Williams, *Spenser's* Faerie Queene, 207–8; McCaffrey, *Spenser's Allegory*, 365–70.

[99] See William Blissett, 'Calepine', *Sp. Enc.* 127.

[100] The style is reminiscent of Ariosto's 'ordered multiplicity' in *Orlando Furioso*. See Peter V. Marinelli, 'Ariosto, Lodovico', *Sp. Enc.*, 56–7; Alpers, *Poetry of* The Faerie Queene, 160–99.

illustrate the lack of awareness that Calidore has of what is happening around him, in failing to intervene to save Serena from being bitten by the Blatant Beast or being attacked by the salvage nation.

Calidore is supposed to value 'simple truth' (VI. i. 3), but it is apparent here that this does not mean the absolute truth free from deception, as might be supposed, but rather the truth of simplicity at the expense of an overall truth. Put another way, one might judge that Calidore's love of truth, reflected in his trance at Meliboe's words, is the enthusiasm of a simpleton for the simple life. The vision of 'truth' promised at the start of Book I has become severely compromised and limited in scope. Calidore has transformed a particular, contingent 'truth' into a general one, something Meliboe warns him not to do. The sensual images describing his reactions to Meliboe's speech reveal that he has started to regard words as hedonistic; this suggests that he has regressed to the level of the captive knights in Acrasia's Bower who have become slaves to their senses. In obvious ways he has come to resemble Grill transformed by the Circean Acrasia, or the Old English described in *A View*, who were too weak to resist becoming Irish. Only Guyon's violent destruction of the Bower causes the men to cease to resemble beasts and resume their humanity (II. xii. 84–7).

Similarly, only the destruction of the pastoral retreat by a band of brigands who first try to sell the shepherds into slavery and then kill them after an argument—including Meliboe (VI. xi. 18), a clear refutation of Calidore's interpretation of his words—forces Calidore into action and eventually compels him to return to his pursuit of the Blatant Beast. The brigands who break up the shepherds' village bear a sinister resemblance to the salvage nation in that they are a 'lawlesse people' who 'neuer usde to liue by plough nor spade, | But fed on spoile and booty, which they made | Upon their neighbours, which did nigh them border' (x. 39). The same three details are repeated: the brigands do not work (specifically, practise tillage); they live by robbing their unfortunate neighbours; and they live just beyond the borders of civilization, into which they intrude in order to survive. The repetition of the characteristics of the salvage nation determines that the pastoral world is inhabited by bad rather than good savages, effectively cancelling out the figure of the salvage man.

The brigands do not live in a 'wylde desert' like the salvage nation, but

> Their dwelling in a little Island was,
> Couered with shrubby woods, in which no way

> Appeard for people in nor out to pas,
> Nor any footing fynde for ouergrowen gras.

> (VI. X. 41)

This would suggest that they are a threat much more obviously close to home both inside and outside the fictional world of the poem. They live within the forest, in a cunningly hidden retreat; the details of the description resemble those of a crannog (a fortified lake dwelling) used successfully by Hugh O'Neill in the Nine Years War.[101] Eventually, the brigands' lack of skill in rudimentary husbandry sows the seeds of their own downfall, as they allow Coridon and Calidore to tend their sheep after they pose as shepherds, 'For they themselues were euill groomes, they sayd, | Unwont with heards to watch, or pasture sheep' (VI. xi. 40). The disguised Knight of Courtesy is able to revenge the destruction of the pastoral idyll he was unable to prevent when he kills and scatters the brigands in a manner which recalls the actions of Talus ('all that nere him came, did hew and slay, | Till he had strowd with bodies all the way', (49)), rescues Pastorella, and makes off with all the 'spoyles and threasures' from their 'theeuish dens' (51).

Calidore has succeeded in overcoming the brigands, but only after the shepherds have all been killed and their settlement utterly destroyed, the fate that 'the shepheardes nation' feared in *Colin Clouts come home againe*. Had he pursued his quest or known exactly what sort of quest he was to pursue, such waste could have been avoided. The book ends with the fear that the tongue of the Blatant Beast will prevent the message of the poem from being heeded, perhaps that its contingent 'truth' will be absorbed into a general one, distorting it beyond its actual claims upon reality. The version of the poem published in Spenser's lifetime concludes with an urgent plea that refuses to separate the metaphysical from the everyday problems of government, both of which are located in the experience of reading an Irish landscape.

---

[101] Morton, *Elizabethan Ireland*, 39, 82. Many Irish castles were situated on lakes or waterways; see Nicholas Canny, 'Early Modern Ireland, *c.*1500–1700', in R. F. Foster (ed.), *The Oxford Illustrated History of Ireland* (Oxford: Oxford University Press, 1989), 104–60, plate facing p. 144.

'All shall changed be':
'Two Cantos of Mutabilitie' and the
Sense of an Ending

'TWO CANTOS OF MUTABILITIE', a fragment of an apparently never completed 'Legend of Constancie', first appeared in the 1609 folio edition of *The Faerie Queene*, published by Matthew Lownes, who had attempted to publish *A View* in 1598. Nothing is known of the date of composition of the cantos, whether they were a relatively early piece which was not incorporated into *The Faerie Queene*, or whether they were, as one critic has argued, 'Spenser's last testament of faith', composed in the final year of his life.[1] It is improbable that they were written before 1586, as Spenser refers to Arlo Hill, which he would have been unlikely to have known of before he took up his Kilcolman estate. The allusion to the Bregog and Mulla story told in *Colin Clouts come home againe* (lines 104–55), in VII. vi. 40, would suggest a date after 1590, and if the reference to Cynthia abandoning Ireland to wolves and thieves (VII. vii. 55) is a 'tactful reference to the rout of the English during Tyrone's rebellion', or the figure of Faunus is an allegorical depiction of Hugh O'Neill, a later date would be confirmed (at least, of the extant text).[2] It is quite possible that the cantos were discovered posthumously; equally, their publication by Lownes might suggest that they had come into his possession, perhaps via Spenser himself, at the same time as he

---

[1] Judah L. Stampfer, 'The *Cantos of Mutability*: Spenser's Last Testament of Faith', *UTQ* 21 (1951–2), 140–56. On the dating of the cantos, see Hackett, *Virgin Mother, Maiden Queen*, 269. Most critics believe they were a late composition, with the exception of Alice Fox Blitch; 'The Mutabilitie Cantos: "In Meet Order Ranged"', *ELN* 7 (1969–70), 179–86.

[2] Edmund Spenser, *The Mutability Cantos*, ed. Sheldon P. Zitner (London: Nelson, 1968), 2–4; Shire, *Preface to Spenser*, 64; Sheldon P. Zitner, 'The Faerie Queene, Book VII', *Sp. Enc.*, 287–9, at 287, 289. See also Russell J. Meyer, ' "Fixt in heauens hight": Spenser, Astronomy, and the Date of the *Cantos of Mutabilitie*', *Sp. Stud.*, 4 (1983), 115–29.

acquired the manuscript of *A View* that he attempted to have published. It must remain no more than the most tentative form of speculation, but it is conceivable that Spenser—or someone acting for him with or without his permission—was intending to make a stronger impact as a New English writer, a role he performed posthumously.[3]

The cantos can be read as a coda, a reinforcement of the fears surrounding the status of the court and its attendant virtue, courtesy, or else as a fable which encapsulates the fundamental message of the whole poem.[4] The ability of the court to transform nature and shape it (an Orphic function) has been continually challenged throughout the poem by the converse fear of a regression to an infinite relativization of difference which will engulf even the most seemingly stable centres of authority (a protean nightmare).[5] Here, on Arlo Hill, just outside Spenser's Irish estate in Kilcolman, the leader of the Gods, Jove, meets the challenge of the Titaness, Mutabilitie, for an argument to determine who holds sway over the universe. Mutabilitie's claim, which she substantiates at great length, is that Jove's exalted position is rightly hers because everything in the realm under the moon is subject to the perpetual change that she causes. Nature, who is appointed judge, grants that there is much reason behind Mutabilitie's allegations, but detects what she argues is a fatal flaw in Mutabilitie's arguments. It is true, Nature admits, that 'all things stedfastnes doe hate', the main point of Mutabilitie's speech on Arlo Hill, but:

> being rightly wayd
> They are not changed from their first estate;
> But by their change their being doe dilate:
> And turning to themselues at length againe,
> Doe worke their owne perfection so by fate:
> Then ouer them Change doth not rule and raigne;
> But they raigne ouer change, and doe their states maintaine.

(VII. vii. 58)

The canto ends on an apocalyptic note, with Nature asserting that Jove can continue to rule the universe because change is subject to change; Mutabilitie cannot escape the logic of her own premisses, and 'time shall

---

[3] Canny, 'Edmund Spenser and the Development of an Anglo-Irish Identity'; Maley, 'How Milton and Some Contemporaries Read Spenser's *View*'.

[4] Elizabeth Fowler argues that the cantos display 'a shift in register' in restating the fundamental legal problems which underlie the poem: 'Failure of Moral Philosophy', 49.

[5] John Guillory, *Poetic Authority: Spenser, Milton and Literary History* (New York: Columbia University Press, 1983), 48.

come that all shall changed bee, | And from thenceforth, none no more change shall see' (59).

These lines have often been interpreted as philosophical maxims, yet the neat caesura of the final alexandrine and the carefully signalled inversion of the chiasmus, might suggest that they are better read as metaphysical poetry than as philosophical speculation (metaphysics), comparable to Donne's 'Divine Meditation', 10. That sonnet concludes with the couplet, 'One short sleep past, we wake eternally, | And death shall be no more, Death thou shalt die'; the suppressed premiss of Nature's speech might be interpreted as 'Change thou shalt change'.[6] It clearly does not follow that, because change has to change, Jove can rule as a figure of constancy nominated by Nature. Nature herself is a shadowy figure about whom we learn little except that he or she is an elusive creature of disguise: 'Whether she man or woman inly were, | That could not any creature well descry: | For, with a veile that wimpled euery where, | Her head and face was hid, that mote to none appeare' (VII. vii. 5), recalling the troubling hermaphrodite figures of Books II and III. This remote figure becomes yet another type of Elizabeth in the following stanza:

> That some doe say [her veil] was so by skill deuized,
> To hide the terror of her uncouth hew,
> From mortall eyes that should be sore agrized;
> For that her face did like a Lion shew,
> That eye of wight could not indure to view:
> But others tell that it so beautious was,
> And round about such beames of splendor threw,
> That it the Sunne a thousand times did pass,
> Ne could be seene, but like an image in a glass.

> (VII. vii. 6)

The image of Nature's face as a reflection in a mirror recalls the descriptions in the proem to Book VI of courtesy as a shadowy virtue which could only be imperfectly realized and the queen's mind as a mirror of the apotheosis of that virtue. Nature, who judges this vital debate in

---

6 John Donne, *The Complete English Poems*, ed. A. J. Smith (Harmondsworth: Penguin, 1971), 313. For such judgements of the poem, see Zitner, 'Faerie Queene, Book VII', 288, where he describes the cantos as a 'celebration of life in process', a 'reconcil[iation] of the world of change and the unaltered spirit', 'eternal unchanging grace'. See also Kathleen Williams, ' "Eterne in Mutabilitie": The Unified World of *The Faerie Queene*', *ELH* 19 (1952), 115–30; J. E. Holland, 'The Cantos of Mutability and the Form of *The Faerie Queene*', *ELH* 35 (1968), 21–31; Robin Headlam Wells, *Spenser's* Faerie Queene *and the Cult of Elizabeth* (London: Macmillan, 1983), ch. 7.

Ireland, appears as remote from those who witness her performance as the queen did after she abandoned Ireland in Book VI. During the long silence that ensues before she makes her judgement, the expectant crowd of creatures try to gain clues from her face, but she keeps her eyes firmly on the ground (57). The mirror image of her face may well be splendid, but it is equally mysterious. Once the judgement has been delivered, 'was that whole assembly quite dismist, | And *Natur's* selfe did vanish, whither no man wist' (59). Like Astrea, and, in the 'Two Cantos of Mutabilitie', Diana, Nature abandons the world to live with her decisions, taking no further part in enforcing the order she wishes to affirm as right, consulting with no one and keeping her subjects waiting to find out her decision. The suggestion is that Mutabilitie may not be quite so easy to banish, partly because, Nature herself appears as a protean figure whose only existence is in the eyes and minds of those who observe her. It is by no means clear that she has the right or the power to defeat Mutabilitie.[7]

In the imperfect last canto (viii), which contains only two stanzas, the narrator appears to be quite impressed by Mutabilitie's arguments: 'When I bethinke me on that speech whyleare, | Of *Mutability*, and well it way, | Me seemes, that though she all unworthy were | Of the Heav'ns Rule; yet very sooth to say, | In all things else she beares the greatest sway' (VII. viii. 1).[8] The narrator attempts to offset such doubts with a metaphor: 'Then gin I thinke on that which Nature sayd, | Of that same time when no more *Change* shall be, | But stedfast rest of all things firmely stayd | Upon the pillours of Eternity' (2). All that remains to counter Mutabilitie's arguments is the comparsion, 'pillours of Eternity', a lack of substantial form which not only recalls the elusive figure of Nature herself, but also the problems of representing truth in the first place: Una, like Nature, wears a veil. Ideology, as Barthes recognized, is where the play of language stops and meaning is fixed by an authority.[9]

The problem with Nature is not the only irony haunting an affirmative reading of the poem. At the start of canto vi Mutabilitie is already described as having displaced Nature from the earth, 'That all which Nature had establisht first | In good estate, and in meet order ranged, | She did pervert, and all their statutes burst' (VII. vi. 5). The use of the

---

[7] See Harry Berger, Jr., 'The Mutabilitie Cantos: Archaism and Evolution in Retrospect', in id., *Revisionary Play*, 242–73, at 249; Guillory, *Poetic Authority*, 61–2.

[8] See Lewis J. Owen, 'Mutable in Eternity: Spenser's Despair and the Multiple Forms of Mutabilitie', *JMRS* 2 (1972), 49–68.

[9] *S/Z*, 100.

legal term, 'statutes' refers the cantos to the extensive discussion of the rule of law in *A View* (another reason, perhaps, to connect the two to Lownes?), a conjunction continued in the next stanza: 'Ne shee the lawes of Nature onely brake, | But eke of Iustice, and of Policie; | And wrong of right, and bad of good did make | . . . And all this world is woxen daily worse' (6). Such lines link the world of Mutabilitie to the state of the world left behind by Astrea at the start of Book V, implying that Mutabilitie stands as a figure of Ireland opposed to the figure of Elizabeth as Nature.[10]

Mutabilitie proceeds to challenge Cynthia for supremacy under the moon and forces the goddess down to face her. It is quite clear that Cynthia stands as yet another figure for Elizabeth, quite apart from the evidence of the letter to Raleigh which made such a connection explicit:

> Thence, to the Circle of the Moone she clambe,
> Where *Cynthia* raignes in euerlasting glory,
> To whose bright shining palace straight she came,
> All fairely deckt with heauens goodly story;
> Whose siluer gates (by which there sate an hory
> Old aged Sire, with hower-glasse in hand,
> Hight *Tyme*) she entred, were he liefe or sory:
> Ne staide till she the highest stage had scand,
> Where *Cynthia* did sit, that nuer still did stand.
>
> (VII. vi. 8)

The proximity of the figure of Time to Cynthia's throne, is a *memento mori*, an aggressively situated *dopplegänger*, like the poet Bon | MalFont outside the throne room of Mercilla, who points to the reality of Elizabeth's rule. Cynthia is described as never standing still, a double-edged reference to Elizabeth's inconstant policies and the mutability of her own body, which had been beyond childbearing age since the 1580s, leaving the succession uncertain.[11] The point is repeated towards the end of canto vii when Mutabilitie addresses Cynthia directly: 'Euen you faire *Cynthia*, whom so much ye make | *Ioues* dearest darling . . . | Then is she mortall borne, how-so ye crake' (50). Both stanzas are warnings to Elizabeth that, although she might appear invincible in her public role as a mighty empress, she is also subject to the ravages of time in her private person, a studied ambiguity which neatly reflects the paradox of the

---

[10] A resemblance strengthened if one recalls the mutable (Irish) figure of Malengin in V. ix.

[11] Hadfield, *Literature, Politics and National Identity*, 200.

queen's two bodies highlighted in the letter to Raleigh.[12] In itself such stanzas make it that much harder to read Nature's argument against Mutabilitie as anything other than a neat trick, as Mutabilitie's effects were available for all to see in the in the extra-fictional world to which the poem refers.

Both stanzas also link Cynthia's rule directly to the conquest of Jove, so that the description of Cynthia reigning in 'euerlasting glory' cannot but be ironic when placed alongside the account of the degeneration of the world from the age of Saturn whom Jove overthrew, especially given the echo strategically placed in stanza 6 that 'this world is woxen daily worse'. Cynthia's very status as a ruling goddess depends upon what she and Jove wish to deny, the very process of change and decay they are now forced to oppose. In Book V, Artegall was given the very sword, Chrysaor, which Jove used to defeat the Titans. With this he was remarkably successful until he was thwarted in his ultimate goal of pacifying Ireland. Mutabilitie is a Titaness, returning to claim her due revenge, because the forces appointed by Jove failed to finish their task. Once again, we are faced with the prospect that there is no just order in the universe, simply the law of conquest. Spenser's political vision might seem to verge on the Hobbesian. While Cynthia and Mutabilitie struggle in the heavens, a portent appears to 'the lower World', when the sky turns black and people worry 'least *Chaos* broken had his chaine' (14). Jove and Cynthia may not have natural justice on their side (the fact that the initial struggle is between a goddess and a Titaness could be a further attack on female rule), but if they are displaced the alternative could well be significantly more frightening.

The location of the debate between Jove and Mutabilitie (established at great length in vi. 36–55), lends further weight to demands that the cantos be read topically and politically, rather than as 'the comic minor plot' which foregrounds the major philosophical interest of the debate itself.[13] This takes place on Arlo Hill, Spenser's name for Galtymore, which overlooked his estate at Kilcolman and was 'a notorious resort of outlaws in Spenser's day'.[14] In *A View*, Irenius cites Arlo as one of the

---

[12] Hackett, *Virgin Mother, Maiden Queen*, 193.

[13] Zitner, '*Faerie Queene*, Book VII', 288; Richard N. Ringler, 'The Faunus Episode', *MP* 63 (1965–6), 12–19, at 12–13. For a reading of the cantos in terms of property rights, see Julia Reinhard Lupton, 'Mapping Mutability: Or Spenser's Irish Plot', in Bradshaw *et al.* (eds.), *Representing Ireland*, 93–115.

[14] See William Keach, 'Arlo Hill', *Sp. Enc.* 60. See also Henley, *Spenser in Ireland*, 87–8; Roland M. Smith, 'Spenser's Irish River Stories', *PMLA* 50 (1935), 1047–56, at 1049;

areas 'which lyinge neare unto anye mountaines or Irishe desertes had bynne planted with Englishe weare shortelye displanted and loste' (p. 57), after the chaos of the Wars of the Roses had reduced English government to disarray. Such intertextual connections establish the mutable nature of the geographical setting and also suggest that Arlo Hill is a borderland over which the savages of Book VI might well stray.[15]

The setting of the debate on a hill recalls Irenius' description of the Irish custom of assembling on a rath (hill) to debate 'aboute matters and wronges betwene Towneshipp and Towneshippe or one private persone and another' (p. 128), a practice which once expressed a rudimentary democracy when first established under English control, but which now leads to rebellion, anarchy, and murder:

But well I wote and trewe it hathe bene often times aproued that in these metinges manye mischiefs haue bene bothe practised and wroughte ffor to them doe Comonlye resorte all the scum of lose people wheare they maye frelye mete and Conferr of what they liste which else they Coulde not doe without suspicion or knowledge of others Besides at those parlies I haue diuerse times knowen that manye Englishemen and other good Irishe subiectes haue bene villanouslye murdered by movinge one quarrell or another amongest them. (pp. 128–9)[16]

In a crucial sense, the debate on Arlo Hill could be said to establish the borderland itself: the result could either affirm that there is a civilized order to the universe or allow matters to descend into chaos, depending on who actually wins the verbal battle. More immediately, and granted a potent irony in the light of the imminent destruction of the Munster Plantation—including Spenser's own estate—the encounter will establish either English or Irish hegemony. The stately dispute of gods and Titans might appear to some as an uncivilized squabble, a dangerous and absurd parody of proper debate. The other literary references of the poem, Chaucer's *Parlement of Foulys* and Ovid's *Metamorphoses*, which establish a native English and Classical heritage, only serve to throw the Irish context into starker relief.[17]

and, more generally, Rudolf Gottfried, 'Irish Geography in Spenser's *View*', *ELH* 6 (1939), 114–37, at 132–3.

[15] On the concept of the 'borderland' in early modern British history, see Steven G. Ellis, 'Crown, Community and Government in the British Territories, 1450–1575', *History*, 71 (1986), 187–204. See also Hechter, *Internal Colonialism*, pt. 1.

[16] For analysis, see Samuel Kliger, 'Spenser's Irish Tract and Tribal Democracy', *SAQ* 49 (1950), 490–7.

[17] Chaucer's work is explicitly mentioned at the start of canto vii (3–10); see Miskimin, *Renaissance Chaucer*, 35–41. On the Ovidian analogues of the poem, see Lupton,

The seemingly humorous incongruity of the situation is highlighted by the rhetorical question, 'Who knowes not *Arlo-hill*?' (VII. vi. 36), a question which recalls the similar interrogative form during the Dance of the Graces (VI. x. 16), 'who knowes not *Colin Clout*?'. The resemblance is underlined by the almost exact repetition of the structures of each line, with the question appearing in brackets after the mention of the name.[18] Both demand to be read ironically, rather than as affirmations of a stable identity, given that Galtymore/Arlo Hill was hardly likely to have been known to any but a few other Munster undertakers and officials concerned with the Plantation, especially in the light of the care with which Spenser appears to have established his New English persona as that of a neglected sage ignored by the metropolitan authorities.[19] Yet here is the very centre of the universe, the place where the fate of civilization will be decided, whatever more lofty minds might think.

The following stanza (37), signals that the setting of the debate within the Irish landscape—not Faerieland—is of a different order to the rest of the poem (whether the cantos themselves or the whole of *The Faerie Queene* is left unclear); either it is a passing interlude or an aetiological and etymological fable:

> And, were it not ill fitting for this file,
> To sing of hilles and woods, mongst warres and Knights,
> I would abate the sternenesse of my stile,
> Mongst these sterne sounds to mingle soft delights;
> And tell how *Arlo* through *Dianaes* spights
> (Beeing of old the best and fairest Hill
> That was in all this holy-Islands hights)
> Was made the most unpleasant, and most ill.
> Meane while, O *Clio*, lend *Calliope* thy quill.

> (VII. vi. 37)

The stanza is riddled with irony and ambiguity. The narrator claims that he would change his style to suit the narration of this episode, but that he cannot because his poem demands that he does not. It is not clear at this stage whether this means that he will not tell the story, or whether he will tell the story of Arlo Hill, but in a style fitting to the poem as it has

'Mapping Mutabilitie', 102–11; Ringler, 'Faunus Episode'; Michael Holahan, '*Iamque opus exegi*: Ovid's Changes and Spenser's Brief Epic of Mutabilitie', *ELR* 6 (1976), 244–70.

  [18] See Hadfield, *Literature, Politics and National Identity*, 171–2; Berger, 'Mutabilitie Cantos', 264.

  [19] For an alternative reading see Lupton, 'Mapping Mutabilitie', 110.

been narrated so far. Either way, the stanza becomes, retrospectively, an example of the trope of *occupatio*, defined by Abraham Fraunce as 'A kind of irony, a kind of pretended omitting or letting slip of that which indeed we elegantly note out in the very show of praetermission', because the story is actually told.[20] Indeed, the bare bones are outlined in stanza 37, namely the story of the fall of Arlo Hill from 'the best and fairest' on the island, to 'the most unpleasant, and most ill', a further suggestion that the subsequent story will be far from a tale of 'soft delights' and, in fact, exactly in keeping with what has gone before, particularly in the second half of *The Faerie Queene* (the ubiquitous story of the Fall recalls the abandonment of the world by Astrea, a narrative repetition which becomes more obvious as the canto continues). The final lines, which appear precise and in line with the change signalled at the start of the stanza, are similarly problematic. It is not clear why Calliope, the Muse of heroic poetry, should be more fitted than Clio, the Muse of history, to inspire the story, especially given that Calliope is presumably inspiring the story anyway (I, proem, 2).[21] The letter to Raleigh defines the poem, along Sidneyan lines, as 'an historicall fiction', further suggesting that any distinction made between Clio and Calliope, history and historical fiction, is an arbitrary one. However it is read, the stanza invokes the co-operation of the two Muses, drawing the reader's attention to the significance of the episode as a key to the mythology of the poem; in a sense, its myth of origin.

Stanza 38 starts the story proper, following on from the appellation of Ireland as 'this holy-Island', with a description of the land—significantly emphasized in capitals in the folio—as the most desirable part of Britain:

> Whylome, when IRELAND florished in fame
> Of wealths and goodnesse, far aboue the rest
> Of all that beare the *British* Islands name,
> The Gods then us'd (for pleasure and for rest)
> Oft to resort there-to, when seem'd them best:
> But none of all there-in more pleasure found,
> Then *Cynthia*; that is soueraine Queene profest
> Of woods and forrests, which therein abound,
> Sprinkled with wholsom waters, more then most on ground.
>
> (VII. vi. 38)

---

[20] *Arcadian Rhetoric* (1588), fo. 13, cited in Lee A. Sonnino, *A Handbook to Sixteenth-Century Rhetoric* (London: Routledge, 1968), 135–6.
[21] Assuming that this is how the lines should be read; see *FQ*, 720, 28. See also Berger, 'Mutabilitie Cantos', 256–7.

The stanza invokes a distant mythical time, presumably contemporary with the debate, although we are not actually told, when Ireland was the centre of the universe and was sought out by the gods, rather than neglected by them. Ireland was a pastoral *locus amoenus*, centred around Arlo Hill, a land of pleasure not work, akin to the garden of Adonis, or, more dangerously, the Bower of Bliss, rather than the hard anti-pastoral land observed now. Here nymphs and satyrs 'loue to play and sport' (39), a prelapsarian harmony exists before their names and identities become invested with significance, as they have in the earlier faerie landscape when they both harboured Una (I. vi. 7–33), or the satyrs practised a less harmless sport with Hellenore, Malbecco's estranged wife (III. x. 44–7).[22] There is a forecast of Ireland's current state in the description of Cynthia as 'soueraine Queene profest | Of woods and forrests' which becomes an ironic prophecy of Cynthia's (Elizabeth's) current rule over an ungovernable land of forests. Just as Ireland has fallen from its state of grace, so has the significance of the queen's mythological identity as Diana.[23]

However, there is a serpent in this Garden of Eden: Faunus, the 'Foolish God', 'though full many a day | He saw her clad, yet longed foolishly | To see her naked mongst her Nymphes in priuity' (42). To achieve this forbidden desire, he decides to bargain with one of her nymphs, Molanna. He will help her to satisfy her unrequited love for Fanchin if she will tell him where Diana bathes. The deal is made and Faunus sees Diana naked in a 'sweet spring' (45). However, he is unable to contain the 'great ioy' he feels at this sight and remain silent, so he breaks 'forth in laughter' and 'loud profest | His foolish thought' (46). Diana, suitably abashed and understandably a little cross, seizes him and discusses with her nymphs the exact mode of punishment to be inflicted upon the transgressor.[24] Various suggestions are made, but eventually Faunus is dressed like a stag and chased by their hounds, from whom he escapes, spurred on by fear. Molanna weds Fanchin, even though Diana knows of her complicity in Faunus' voyeurism.[25]

As a result, Diana decides that Ireland is no longer the place for her to reside, and 'full of indignation, | Thence-forth abandoned her delicious brooke', which had previously given her 'So much delight' (54). Instead, she leaves behind 'an heauy haplesse curse':

---

[22] Richard D. Jordan, 'satyrs', *Sp. Enc.*, 628.
[23] On Elizabeth as Diana, see Berry, *Of Chastity and Power*, ch. 3.
[24] Contrast Diana's reaction to Serena's (VI. viii. 50–1).
[25] On the historical and topological significance, see Smith, 'Spenser's Irish River Stories', 1052–6.

To weet, that Wolues, where she was wont to space,
Should harbour'd be, and all those Woods deface,
And Thieues should rob and spoile that Coast around.
Since which, those Woods, and all that goodly Chase,
Doth to this day with Wolues and Theues abound:
Which too-too true that lands in-dwellers since haue found.

(VII. vi. 55)

Ireland becomes the land that Cynthia rules in Spenser's time after she has fled the world like her other *alter ego*, Astrea.

The myth is a combination of three stories from Ovid's *Metamorphoses*, most importantly that of Actaeon (referred to in stanza 45) with the crucial alteration that whereas Actaeon is devoured by his own hounds, Faunus escapes from Diana's, making him into a figure like Duessa and the Blatant Beast, always likely to return.[26] The story of Faunus can be read as an allegory of English rule over Ireland, a counterpart to *A View*'s analysis of the helplessness of attempts to assert control unless viceregal authority is re-established (see above, Ch. 2). Ireland is the place where Elizabeth/Diana is seen naked, exposed like Serena before the salvage nation, the mysterious power of her regal body rendered helpless.

The incident has a precedent—quite apart from the blazon representing Serena's body—in the similar depiction of Belpheobe observed by Braggadocchio and Trompart hidden within the bushes (II. iii. 21–30). This episode, which contains the longest description of a female body in the poem, clearly refers back to the myth of Actaeon. Braggadocchio, inflamed with lust, attempts to assault her, but flees when she threatens him with her spear. Belphoebe runs off and subsequently disappears form the book (like Astrea, Diana, Serena, the Graces).[27] Braggadocchio and Trompart 'shrowd themselues from causelesse feare' (II. iii. 20); when Faunus hides in the bushes, the relationship is made explicit:

The simple maid [Molanna] did yield to him anone;
And eft him placed where he close might view
That neuer any saw, saue onely one;
Who, for his hire to so foole-hardy dew,
Was of his hounds devour'd in Hunters hew.

(VII. vi. 45)

---

[26] See Lars-Hakan Svensson, 'Actaeon', *Sp. Enc.*, 6–7; Ringler, 'Faunus Episode'; Holahan, '*Imaque opus exegi*'; Ovid, *Metamorphoses*, 77–80.
[27] Montrose, 'Elizabethan Subject', 328–9.

Actaeon has transgressed and seen what no one should see, the naked body behind the masks of power.

Other textual clues demand that the two incidents be read in terms of each other, quite apart from the letter to Raleigh informing us that Belphoebe is a type of Diana/Cynthia. At the end of the blazon, Belphoebe is compared to Diana who 'on *Cynthus* greene, | Where all the Nymphes haue her unwares forlore, | Wandreth alone with bow and arrowes keen' (II. iii. 31); this prefigures not simply the wandering of the nymphs on Arlo Hill, but also the description of Cynthia as '*Ioues* dearest darling, she was bred and nurst | On *Cynthus* hill' (VII. vii. 50), so that a direct link is made between the three separate figures; Belphoebe, Diana in Ireland, and Diana seen by Actaeon.

Such links strengthen the perception of a carefully constructed attack on the queen that the second edition of the poem activates what is latent within the first. The description of Belphoebe contains a missing halfline, the only one in the poem, which is of crucial significance:

> [she] was yclad, for heat of scorching aire,
> All in a silken Camus lylly whight,
> Purfled upon with many a folded plight,
> Which all aboue besprinckled was throughout
> With golden aygulets, that glistred bright
> Like twinckling starres, and all about the skirt about
> Was hemd with golden fringe
>
> Below her ham her weed did somewhat traine,
> And her streight legs most brauely were embayld
> In gilden buskins.
>
> (II. iii. 26–7)

The description moves from the skirt to the legs, not with undue haste, but, rather, leaving a gaping hole in the centre of Belphoebe's body, the elaborate account of the gorgeous clothes drawing attention to the absence at the centre. Appearing keen to hide the mystery of female power, as Serena's sex was wrapped up in a conceit, the narrator's loquaciousness simply draws our attention to it. We do and do not 'glimpse the naked goddess in her radical otherness'.[28] Such is the constant threat to the multiple guises of the Faerie Queene throughout the poem; by the end of the poem we can be in no doubt that the most significant challenge to her power comes from Ireland, where Actaeonfigures lurk, not yet picked off by the Crown forces.

---

[28] Montrose, 'Elizabethan Subject', 328.

Although Cynthia is waiting for her own body's demise at the end of the 'Two Cantos of Mutabilitie', the effect of Faunus' forbidden vision of the queen's vagina is the downfall of Ireland rather than his own demise. Cynthia/Diana preserves her power by retreating into an untouchable political void and Faunus remains at large. Those who suffer are the subjects of the queen who have to live in the dangerous pastoral world of Book VI and post-lapsarian Ireland. When Diana departs, Ireland falls both in terms of its physical landscape and etymologically; it ceases to be a 'holy island', a *locus amoenus* connoting concord, and becomes instead, the '*Banno* or *sacra Insula* takinge *sacra* for accursed' of *A View* (p. 145), the ordinary meaning of everyday usage having to give way to another root which reverses the normal understanding.[29] Language has split and become duplicitous so that one cannot trust exactly where words lead to or from, a problem which overshadows the allegorical narrative of the whole poem and which is here seen to result from the problem of governing Ireland.[30] 'Two Cantos of Mutabilitie' repeat what has developed into the fundamental political message of *The Faerie Queene*, that the queen's masks of power/authority are most in danger of slipping in Ireland and that her rule is threatened by her failure to intervene there, as much as it is by her own fading physical form, reliance upon which, at the expense of developing a durable public sphere, has also cost her subjects dear. Furthermore, the cantos transform that message into a myth of origins which is also the conclusion of the poem's allegorical content, physically, in terms of being appended as a fragment to what is already a fragment, and chronologically, both pre- and post-dating the time-scale of the poem's action.[31] The cantos announce an aporia, simultaneously describing how events came to be as they are (an etiological reading) and revealing the result of mistaken actions (a reading in terms of the historical allegory); they are both the end and the beginning of *The Faerie Queene*, haunting the poem like the banished, unhappy ghosts of 'A Brief Note'.[32]

[29] See also the note in *Variorum*, x. 372.

[30] See Martha Craig, 'The Secret Wit of Spenser's Language', in Paul Alpers (ed.), *Elizabethan Poetry: Modern Essays in Criticism* (Oxford: Oxford University Press, 1967), 447–72; Anderson, 'The Antiquities of Fairyland and Ireland'; Shire, 'Name-Concept and Name Conceit', in id., *Preface to Spenser*, 125–8; Goldberg, *Endlesse Worke*, ch. 1; Gross, *Spenserian Poetics*; Fogarty, 'Colonisation of Language', 83–90.

[31] See Geoffrey Bennington, 'Postal Politics and the Institution of the Nation', in Bhabha (ed.), *Nation and Narration*, 121–37.

[32] See Jacques Derrida, 'Passions: "An Oblique Offering" ', in David Wood (ed.), *Derrida: A Critical Reader* (Oxford: Blackwell, 1992), 5–35. On the concept of 'aporia', see

Although 'Two Cantos of Mutabilitie' can be read alongside *A View* as a demand for greater intervention in Ireland on the part of the Crown, and a demand that the voices of the disaffected New English be heard in court circles, they hint at a much more sinister reality, and one at odds with what has been asserted in that attempt to intervene in contemporary politics. The cantos also serve to undercut the ideal of transformation so vital to Spenser's political discourse. Nature might award Jove sovereignty over the universe, but she has no more implicit right to rule than Mutabilitie, the daughter of the Titans who fought Jove for mastery, but lost. The usurpation of Jove can, of course, be read as a parallel event to the Fall, which is linked specifically to Ireland, so that allegorically Jove's victory can be seen to be the counterpart to the triumph of Faunus in Ireland: mythical events overlap with each other and contradict themselves so that Mutabilitie's claim to hold sway over them appears to have been vindicated.[33] Jove's brief argument against Mutabilitie bears this problem out:

> Then thus gan *Ioue*; Right true it is, that these
> And all things else that under heauen dwell
> Are chaung'd of *Time*, who doth them all disseise
> Of being: But, who is it (to me tell)
> That *Time* himselfe doth moue and still compell
> To keepe his course? Is not that namely wee
> Which poure that vertue from our heauenly cell,
> That moues them all, and makes them changed be?
> So them we gods doe rule, and in them also thee.

(VII. vii. 48)

There are many ways in which the poem signals that we should not accept Jove's argument (it is worth noting the gap between Nature's eventual judgement and Jove's defence); but, most obviously, it is immediately undercut by Mutabilitie's reply. Jove claims that Time is subject to the power of the gods: Mutabilitie counters that his conclusion is based upon an assumption that what cannot be understood is caused by them: 'The things | Which we see not how they are mov'd and swayd, | Ye may attribute to your selues as Kings' (49). The problem is that this only appears to be the case and Jove is far too confident that everything is ordered by his power. Mutabilitie asks, 'what if I can proue, that euen

Christopher Norris, *Deconstruction: Theory and Practice* (London: Methuen, 1982), 49–50, 100; Madsen, *Rereading Allegory*, 126–7; Culler, *On Deconstruction*, 96. See also Paul De Man, 'The Rhetoric of Temporality', in id., *Blindness and Insight*, 187–228.

[33] See Hulse, Weiner, and Strier, 'Spenser: Myth, Politics, Poetry', 382–4.

yee | Your selues are likewise chang'd, and subiect unto mee?' (49), offer-
ing as her defence the example of Cynthia's decay and so moving the
allegory back from the general to the historically specific. The attack
works on two interrelated levels: on the one, Cynthia/Elizabeth has been
foolish to have placed her political faith in the wiles of her mutable
body; on the other, Jove, a usurper, who has elevated Cynthia/Elizabeth
to her current position of eminence, has to be wrong to claim that the
gods have power over Time.[34] He, and his main charge, both belong to
the world of change below the moon, however strenuously they attempt
to deny this stubborn state of affairs. Just as there was no natural law
which granted Irena easy sovereignty over the salvage land/Ireland, neither is there any which will keep rulers perpetually alive and in power.
Mutabilitie stands as yet another of Elizabeth's guises, a demonic inversion which reveals that she has become more like Duessa than Una, a figure of untruth rather than truth. This is the essence of Mutabilitie's
warning to Cynthia, one which short-circuits the fictional surface of the
text in order to address the monarch directly: 'her face and countenance
euery day | We changed see, and sundry forms partake, | Now hornd,
now round, now bright, now brown and gray: | So that *as changefull as
the Moone* men use to say' (VII. vii. 50, emphasis in text). Cynthia thinks
that she is defined as Jove's 'dearest darling', but time and her own fail-
ings have led her to become Mutabilitie's *doppelgänger*, a situation
which will cost her subjects dear unless the violent order of the masculine god can be re-established.

Jove, as the current leader of the gods, gains Nature's approval by
default, as he is not forced to make a convincing defence of his rule,
which implies that he could really be anyone, possessing no more inherent authority than that obtained through victorious conquest. Nature's
statement that things are not changed from their first state because they
turn 'to themselves at length againe' and 'worke their owne perfection
so by fate' (58), whatever its truth-value as an analysis of the nature of
matter, simply does not apply to the problem of Elizabeth's succession
or to the ghostly and substantial menace of Ireland threatening to
explode the desired unity of Britain and its attendant civilization. Once
again, taking Nature at face value is to take the writing as witty but
inconsequential metaphysical poetry.

In the same way, the Irish setting of the debate serves further to reinforce the fact that the real victory goes to Mutabilitie, whatever the

[34] Guillory, *Poetic Authority*, 63–4.

arguments used against her triumph by Nature, Jove, and Cynthia. If Ireland cannot be absorbed and fixed into a stable form, then the masks of power, the points at which interpretation has to stop and give way to an authority, will be thrust aside and the world of Proteus and Mutabilitie will take over. *The Faerie Queene* emerges as a desperate poem, the problem being that even seemingly fixed and abstract figures like Error, Grantorto, or Duessa easily revert into more subversive, mutable forms, threatening to reveal that the queen's robes of state are no more than the emperor's new clothes, so that the actual locus of power is merely a vacuum.[35] What is really dangerous is 'the blind and mobile flaw in the system' of the text, the problem that if the queen's authority has to be represented as a series of figures in order to confront and combat the multiplicity of enemies ranged against her, then that authority will also become fragmented.[36] The supposed unity of Book I will fail to escape from the difference it is defined against, an inescapable paradox.[37] In the end, only an irruption of violent action can solve matters, like that produced by Artegall, the salvage knight who bears an uncomfortable resemblance to those he is supposed to be subduing and civilizing. Only when a figure like Malengin can be made to disappear, an episode in the poem which has its counterpart in the apparent belief of Irenius that evil elements can be rooted out of Ireland without the slaughter of evil people, can Irena rule in peace and fulfil the meaning of her name, guaranteeing (and being guaranteed by) a subservient and transparent group of subjects. When these resist and demand a voice, power ceases to be monolithic, a state of affairs Spenser both recognizes and demands in his work, acknowledging that neither political nor literary representation can ever—or should ever—be pure. Words will never correspond exactly to things in the fallen world, so that allegory can never reach a straightforward, satisfactory conclusion; power must always be a diverse and complex phenomenon in the age of iron, which no one will ever fully control.

Ireland as represented in *The Faerie Queene* is a body of overlapping and conflicting texts which presents a whole series of figures: good and bad savages, pliable loyalists, disgruntled colonizers. The poem is a vast colonizing work trying to absorb all the representations it can and

---

[35] See the comments on Thomas More, in Greenblatt, *Renaissance Self-Fashioning*, 14.
[36] Barthes, *S/Z*, 36.
[37] Giamatti, *Play of Double Senses*, chs. 10–11; Goldberg, *Endlesse Worke*, ch. 1; Miller, *Poem's Two Bodies*, 16–17.

subject them to its own structure, familiarize and absorb the alien.[38] At the same time, there is a recognition that this is an impossible process (an endless work) and that the vast series of dichotomies produced— Una/Duessa, truth/error, savage/civil, queen/subjects, and so on—will never be held together at a final allegorical point. The teleological goal of the allegory is ultimately reduced to a series of inter- and intra-textual references which do not necessarily lead anywhere.

The Faerie Queene is caught within the paradox of announcing a political programme or definite allegorical message, and dealing with the problem of representation *per se*.[39] The text is as much a refusal of power, a surrender to the 'endlesse trace withouten guyde' which Calidore fears will be his lot, as it is a fashioning agent producing the gentlemanly reader or ideal queen. The fiction is an evasion of power, distanced from other discourses which have to induce action in an extratextual world or describe an external 'reality' (legal, political, medical, historical), so that it can contain all codes and none, refusing action as much as inciting it.[40] Ireland, as a literary representation, is both scattered throughout *The Faerie Queene* as series of traces and, in so far as it is the locus of chaos, represents what the allegory surrenders to (its content) and becomes dissolved by (its linguistic form), a relationship which demonstrates the symbiotic relationship between questions of everyday government and cosmic fate which the poem articulates.

'Two Cantos of Mutabilitie' articulate what a political tract like *A View* can never admit, that it may be impossible ever to control and govern Ireland, to transform it into a 'West England'; that Ireland is the place where chaos originates and which will absorb and consume all attempts to redeem it in the name of an Anglocentric civilization.[41] It is where (the English) language turns against itself and ceases to be able to transform its 'other'; the master tropes of *A View* have no privileged status in Faerieland, which adds a certain poetic justice to that text's failure to appear in the public sphere of print until 1633. Conquest is shown to be an arbitrary act devoid of distinction and significance (but no less necessary for that). The conclusion of *The Faerie Queene*, whether that be taken as the end of Book VI or includes the surviving ruins of

[38] Giamatti, 'Primitivism and the Process of Civility in *Spenser's Faerie Queene*'.

[39] A brilliant discussion of the problem of representation is contained in Kappeler, *The Pornography of Representation*.

[40] Attridge, 'Introduction: The Peculiar Language of Literature', in id., *Peculiar Language*, 1–16; Derrida, *Acts of Literature*, 37–43.

[41] On Ireland as a 'West England', see Hadfield and McVeagh (eds.), *Strangers to that Land*, 52.

Book VII, reiterates the experimental and inconclusive nature of that work, because, for Spenser, even the cruel power of Jove may be unable to halt the tide of endless change.

Lewis's charge that Ireland corrupted Spenser's imagination is truer than he meant. *The Faerie Queene* is a project of purported national focus which exposes the problematic nature of national identity and its implicit relationship with colonial expansion. *The Faerie Queene* moves from an English to a British context and, in doing so, has to confront the loss of its aesthetic and political unity because in the borderlands of the expanding and divergent English/British state there were numerous peoples who had no desire to fit easily into the narrow range of identities constructed for them by their would-be rulers. Spenser's writings catalogue the resistance of the Irish—in the 1590s, the most threatening opposition to the spread of English government—to the encroaching power of the hegemonic English monarch as well as the creation of a colonial class within the supposed boundaries of the state whose own English identity and loyalty to the Crown were challenged and eventually transformed by their experiences in trying to govern the Irish. *The Faerie Queene* is not a work which deals incidentally with Ireland but one which is framed by its author's own Irish experience, a fact registered in the development of both the form and the content of its allegorical design. The poem and its author ceased to be 'mere English' when both left England in the late 1570s or 1580 and were 'corrupted' by their relationship with Ireland. *The Faerie Queene* demands to be read alongside *A View of the Present State of Ireland*; while the latter proposes a solution to Spenser's fears of the apocalypse which he probably realized were too costly ever to be implemented,[42] the former would appear to recognize that the English could never govern Ireland properly or successfully and that the unhappy relationship between the two countries would permanently hobble England's political and moral hopes after the Reformation.

[42] Brady, 'Spenser's Irish Crisis: Humanism and Experience', 31.

Appendix:

Works mentioning Ireland in the title entered into the Stationers' Register during Elizabeth's reign

Entries without STC numbers have not been traced. Substantial analysis of those marked with an asterisk can be found in John Breen, 'Representing Exile: Ireland and the Formation of the English Nation (1558–1603)' (D.Phil. thesis, Queen's University, Belfast, 1995).

1580   'news out of Irelande', entered by John Aldee, 10 Dec. 1580 (STC 14257.5)

       'The true Reporte of the prosperous Succes which GOD gave unto the Englishe Souldiers againste the forraine bandes of our Romaine Enimyes arrived but soone inoughe to their Coste in Ireland in the yere 1580', entered by Edward White, 20 Dec. 1580 (STC 17124)

1582   'Receaved of him to printe *the Image of Ireland*', entered by Master Day, 8 July 1581 (STC 6734)

1583   'A ballade intituled, A brave encouragement made by A Soldier when he went into Irelande', entered by Henry Caree, 16 May 1583

1588   'Mendoza, a letter sent to Don Bernadin, with the advertisments out of Ireland', entered by John Woulfe, 23 Oct. 1588 (STC 15414)

1598   'a booke intituled A viewe of the present state of Ireland. Discoursed by way of a Dialogue betwene EUDOXUS and IRENIUS. uppon Condicion that hee gett further aucthoritie before yt be prynted', entered by Matthew Lownes, 14 Apr. 1598

1599   ' "Londons loathe to departe" to the noble E[a]rle of ESSEX E[a]rle mar-shall of England and Lord Generall of her maiesties forces against the TYERONishe Irishe Rebelles', entered by Thomas Purfoote, Snr. and Jr., 14 Apr. 1599 (STC 18632) *

       'A brief admonition to the seduced sort of Irish Rebelles', entered by Ric. Jones, 26 Apr. 1599 (STC 7434.7) *

1602   'All the newes out of Ireland with the yielding up of Chinsale', entered by Thomas Pavier and John Hardie, 22 Jan. 1602 (STC 7434) *

1602 'A boke called A Discourse occasioned upon the Defeate gyven to the Archrebells TYRONE and O'DONNELL by the Right honourable the Lord MOUNTJOY Lord Deputie of Ireland the 24th of December 1601/beinge Christmas Even/ And the Yielding up of Kinsale by Don JOHN to his Lordship', entered by Matthew Lownes, 19 Feb. 1602 (STC 3081) *

'A letter from A soldier of good place in Ireland to his frend in London touchinge the notable victory of her maiesties forces there againste the Spaniards and the yieldinge uppe of Kinsale and other places', entered by master Waterson, 24 Mar. 1602 (STC 7434)

1603 'A ballet called the joyfull welcome of the Right Honourable Mountjoy At his late comminge from Ireland', entered by Thomas Pavyer, 16 June 1603

Select Bibliography

The following list is not intended to be a comprehensive guide to works on Spenser and Ireland, simply works which guided my interpretation of material in this book and which may be useful for other readers. Most, but not quite all, have appeared in the footnotes. Those who require a fuller list of works should consult the entries for Willy Maley cited below.

PRIMARY SOURCES

ANON., ' "A Discourse of Ireland" (*circa* 1599): A Sidelight on English Colonial Policy', ed. David Beers Quinn, *PRIA* 47 (1942), sect. C, 151–66.

ANON., 'A Supplication of the blood of the English most lamentably murdered in Ireland, Cryeng out of the yearth for revenge' (1598), ed. Willy Maley, *Analecta Hibernica*, 36 (1994), 1–90.

ANON., 'A Treatise for the Reformation of Ireland, 1554–5', ed. Brendan Bradshaw, *The Irish Jurist*, 16 (1981), 299–315.

BEACON, RICHARD, *Solon his Follie, or a political discourse touching the reformation of commonweals conquered, declined or corrupted* (Oxford, 1594).

BODIN, JEAN, *The Six Bookes of the Commonweale*, trans. Ralph Knowles (London, 1606).

BRYSKETT, LODOWICK, *A Discourse of Civil Life* (London, 1606), ed. Thomas E. Wright, San Fernando Valley State College Renaissance Editions, 4 (Northridge, Calif., 1970).

CAMDEN, WILLIAM, *Britannia*, trans. Edmund Gibson (London, 1695).

CAMPION, EDMUND, *Two Bokes of the Histories of Ireland* (*c.*1570), ed. A. F. Vossen (Assen: Van Gorcum, 1963).

DERRICKE, JOHN, *The Image of Ireland* (London, 1581).

ERASMUS, DESIDERIUS, 'Dulce Bellum Inexpertis', in M. M. Phillips, *'The Adages' of Erasmus: A Study with Translations* (Cambridge: Cambridge University Press, 1964), 308–53.

—— *The Education of a Christian Prince*, trans. M. M. Cheshire and M. J. Heath, *Complete Works*, vol. xxvii, ed. A. H. T. Levi (Toronto: Toronto University Press, 1986), 199–288.

—— *The Complaint of Peace Spurned and Rejected by the Whole World*, ed. and trans. Betty Radice, in *Complete Works*, vol. xxvii, ed. A. H. T. Levi (Toronto: Toronto University Press, 1986), 289–322.

ERASMUS, DESIDERIUS, *The First Commentary on* The Faerie Queene, ed. Graham Hough (privately printed, 1964).

—— *The First Three English Books on America*, ed. Edward Arber (Birmingham, 1885).

GEOFFREY OF MONMOUTH, *The History of the Kings of Britain*, trans. Lewis Thorpe (Harmondsworth: Penguin, 1966).

GERALD OF WALES, *The History and Topography of Ireland*, trans. J. J. O'Meara (Harmondsworth: Penguin, 1951).

—— (Giraldus Cambrensis), *Expugnatio Hibernica (The Conquest of Ireland)*, ed. and trans. F. X. Martin and A. B. Scott (Dublin: Royal Irish Academy, 1978).

GERARD, WILLIAM, 'Notes of his report on Ireland, May 1578', *Analecta Hibernica*, 2 (1931), 93–291.

HADFIELD, ANDREW, and McVEAGH, JOHN (eds.), *Strangers to that Land: British Perceptions of Ireland from the Reformation to the Famine* (Gerrard's Cross: Colin Smythe, 1994).

HAKLUYT, RICHARD, *The Principal Navigations, Voyages, Traffiques and Discoveries of the English Nation* (1599), 8 vols. (London: Everyman, 1907).

HERBERT, WILLIAM, *Croftus Sive De Hibernia Liber* (*c.*1591), ed. Arthur Keaveney and John A. Madden (Dublin: Irish Manuscripts Commission, 1992).

HERODOTUS, *The Histories*, trans. Aubrey de Selincourt and A. R. Burn (Harmondsworth: Penguin, 1972).

HOLINSHED, RAPHAEL, *Chronicles of England, Scotland and Ireland* (1577, revised and expanded 1587), 6 vols. (London: J. Johnson, 1807–8), vol. vi, *Ireland*.

—— *Ireland under Elizabeth and James I*, ed. Henry Morley (London, 1890).

KEATING, GEOFFREY, *Foras Fease ar Éirinn: The History of Ireland*, ed. and trans. David Comyn and P. S. Dinneen, 4 vols. (London: Early Irish Text Society, 1902–13).

LIPSIUS, JUSTUS, *Sixe Bookes of Politickes or Civil Doctrine*, trans. W. Jones (London, 1594).

LUCIAN, *Toxaris, or Friendship*, in *The Works of Lucian*, ed. and trans. A. M. Harmon *et al.* 8 vols. (London: Heineman, 1913–67), v. 101–208.

MACHIAVELLI, NICCOLÒ, *The Arte of Warre*, trans. Philip Whitethorne (1560), repr. in The Tudor Translations 59, ed. W. E. Henley (London: David Nutt, 1905).

—— *The Discourses*, trans. Leslie J. Walker and Brian Richardson, ed. Bernard Crick (Harmondsworth: Penguin, 1970).

—— *The Prince*, trans. George Bull (Harmondsworth: Penguin, 1961).

—— *A Manuscript of the Stationers' Register, 1554–1640*, ed. Edward Arber, 5 vols. (London: privately printed, 1875–94).

MORYSON, FYNES, *An Itinerary Containing his Ten Yeeres Travell* (1617), 4 vols. (Glasgow: MacLehose, 1907).

—— *Shakespeare's Europe*, ed. Charles Hughes (London: Sherratt & Hughes, 1903).

MYERS, J. P. (ed.), *Elizabethan Ireland: A Selection of Writings by Elizabethan Writers on Ireland* (Hamden, Conn.: Archon, 1983).

OVID, *Metamorphoses*, trans. Mary M. Innes (Harmondsworth: Penguin, 1955).

PAYNE, ROBERT, *A Brief Description of Ireland* (1590), ed. Aquilla Smith (Dublin: Irish Archaeological Society, 1841).

POLYDORE VERGIL, *Polydore Vergil's English History, Vol. I, containing the first eight books*, ed. Sir Henry Ellis (London: Camden Society, 1846).

—— *The Anglia History of Polydore Vergil*, ed. Denys Hay (London: Camden Society, 1950).

RALEIGH, SIR WALTER, *The Discovery of the Large, Rich and Beautifull Empire of Guiana* (1595), in *Selected Writings*, ed. Gerald Hammond (Harmondsworth: Penguin, 1986), 76–123.

RICH, BARNABY, *A Short Survey of Ireland* (London, 1609).

—— *A New Description of Ireland* (London, 1610).

—— 'Rych's "Anatomy of Ireland" [1615], with an Account of the Author', ed. Edward M. Hinton, *PMLA* 55 (1940), 73–101.

SIDNEY, SIR PHILIP, *An Apology for Poetry*, ed. Geoffrey Shepherd (Manchester: Manchester University Press, 1965).

SMITH, SIR THOMAS, *De Republica Anglorum*, ed. L. Alston (Shannon: Irish Academic Press, 1972, rpt. of 1906).

SPEED, JOHN, *The Theatre of the Empire of Great Britain*, 2nd edn. (London, 1625).

SPENSER, EDMUND, 'A Brief Note of Ireland' (*c.*1598), in *Variorum*, x. 233–45.

—— *The Faerie Queene*, ed. A. C. Hamilton (London: Longman, 1977).

—— *The Mutability Cantos*, ed. Sheldon P. Zitner (London: Nelson, 1968).

—— *Poetical Works*, ed. J. C. Smith and E. de Selincourt (Oxford: Oxford University Press, 1912).

—— *A View of the Present State of Ireland* (*c.*1596), in *Variorum*, x. 39–232.

STARKEY, THOMAS, *A Dialogue between Pole and Lupset*, ed. Katherine M. Burton (London: Chatto & Windus, 1948).

—— *An Exhortation to the People, instructynge theym to unitie and obedience* (London, 1540).

WALSH, PETER, *A Prospect of the State of Ireland* (London, 1682).

WARE, SIR JAMES (ed.), *Ancient Irish Histories*, 2 vols. (Dublin, 1633).

WHITE, ROLAND, 'Roland White's "A Discourse Touching Ireland" (*c.*1569)', ed. Nicholas Canny, *IHS* 20 (1977), 439–63.

—— 'Roland White's "The Disorders of the Irishry" (1571)', ed. Nicholas Canny, *Studia Hibernica* 19 (1979), 147–60.

SECONDARY SOURCES

ALPERS, PAUL J., *The Poetry of* The Faerie Queene (London: Duckworth, 1967).
—— 'How to Read *The Faerie Queene*', *EC* 18 (1968), 429–43.
ANDERSON, BENEDICT, *Imagined Communities: Reflections on the Origins and Spread of Nationalism* (London: Verso, 1983).
—— 'Exodus', *CI* 20 (1994), 314–27.
ANDERSON, JUDITH H., 'The Antiquities of Fairyland and Ireland', *JEGP* 86 (1987), 199–214.
ANDREWS, K. R., *Trade, Plunder and Settlement: Maritime Enterprise and the Genesis of the British Empire, 1480–1630* (Cambridge: Cambridge University Press, 1984).
—— *et al.* (eds.), *The Westward Enterprise: English Activities in the Atlantic and America, 1480–1650* (Liverpool: Liverpool University Press, 1979).
ANGLO, SIDNEY, 'A Machiavellian Solution to the Irish Problem: Richard Beacon's *Solon his Follie*', in Edward Cheney and Peter Mack (eds.), *England and the Continental Renaissance: Essays in Honour of J. B. Trapp* (Woodbridge: Boydell & Brewer, 1990), 153–64.
APTEKAR, JANE, *Icons of Justice: Iconography and Thematic Imagery in Book V of* The Faerie Queene (New York: Columbia University Press, 1969).
ATTRIDGE, DEREK, *Peculiar Language: Literature as Difference from the Renaissance to James Joyce* (Ithaca, NY: Cornell University Press, 1988).
AVERY, BRUCE, 'Mapping the Irish Other: Spenser's *A View of the Present State of Ireland*', *ELH* 57 (1990), 263–79.
BAGWELL, RICHARD, *Ireland under the Tudors*, 3 vols. (London: Longman, 1885–90).
BAKER, DAVID, ' "Some Quirk, Some Subtle Evasion": Legal Subversion in Spenser's *A View of the Present State of Ireland*', *Sp. Stud.* 6 (1986), 147–63.
BARNARD, T. C., 'Crises of Identity among Irish Protestants, 1641–85', *P&P* 127 (1990), 39–83.
BARTHES, ROLAND, *Mythologies*, trans. Annette Lavers (London: Granada, 1973).
—— *S/Z: An Essay*, trans. Richard Miller (New York: Hill & Wang, 1974).
BARTLETT, ROBERT, *Gerald of Wales, 1146–1223* (Oxford: Clarendon Press, 1982).
BELLAMY, JOHN, *The Tudor Law of Treason: An Introduction* (London: Routledge, 1979).
BENNETT, J. W., *The Evolution of* The Faerie Queene (Chicago: Chicago University Press, 1942).
BENSON, PAMELA JOSEPH, *The Invention of Renaissance Woman: The Challenge of Female Independence in the Literature and Thought of Italy and England* (Philadelphia: Pennsylvania University Press, 1993).

BERGER, HARRY, JR., *Revisionary Play: Studies in the Spenserian Dynamics* (Berkeley: University of California Press, 1988).

BERNARD, JOHN D., *Ceremonies of Innocence: Pastoralism in the Poetry of Edmund Spenser* (Cambridge: Cambridge University Press, 1989).

BERRY, PHILIPPA, *Of Chastity and Power: Elizabethan Literature and the Unmarried Queen* (London: Routledge, 1989).

BHABHA, HOMI K., *The Location of Culture* (London: Routledge, 1994).

—— (ed.), *Nation and Narration* (London: Routledge, 1990).

BORRIS, KENNETH, ' "Diuelish Ceremonies": Allegorical Satire of Protestant Extremism in *The Faerie Queene*, VI. viii. 31–51', *Sp. Stud.* 8 (1987), 175–209.

—— *Spenser's Poetics of Prophecy in* The Faerie Queene, V, English Literary Studies, Monograph Series 52 (Victoria, BC: University of Victoria, 1991).

BOWIE, CHARLES MILLICAN, *Spenser and the Table Round: A Study in the Contemporaneous Background for Spenser's Use of the Arthurian Legend* (Cambridge, Mass.: Harvard University Press, 1932).

BRADBROOK, MURIEL, ' "No Room at the Top": Spenser's Pursuit of Fame', in id., *The Artist and Society in Shakespeare's England: The Collected Papers of Muriel Bradbrook*, vol. i (Brighton: Harvester, 1982), 19–36.

BRADSHAW, BRENDAN, 'Sword, Word and Strategy in the Reformation of Ireland', *HJ* 21 (1978), 475–502.

—— *The Irish Constitutional Revolution of the Sixteenth Century* (Cambridge: Cambridge University Press, 1979).

—— 'The Elizabethans and the Irish: A Muddled Model', *Studies*, 20 (1981), 38–50.

—— 'Edmund Spenser on Justice and Mercy', *Historical Studies*, 16 (1987), 76–89.

—— 'Robe and Sword in the Conquest of Ireland', in Claire Cross *et al.* (eds.), *Law and Government under the Tudors: Essays Presented to Sir Geoffrey Elton on his Retirement* (Cambridge: Cambridge University Press, 1988).

—— HADFIELD, ANDREW, and MALEY, WILLY (eds.), *Representing Ireland: Literature and the Origins of Conflict, 1534–1660* (Cambridge: Cambridge University Press, 1993).

BRADY, CIARAN, 'Faction and the Origins of the Desmond Rebellion of 1579', *IHS* 22 (1981), 289–312.

—— 'Spenser's Irish Crisis: Humanism and Experience in the 1590s', *P&P* 111 (1986), 17–49.

—— 'Spenser's Irish Crisis: Reply to Canny', *P&P* 120 (1988), 210–15.

—— *The Chief Governors: The Rise and Fall of Reform Government in Tudor Ireland, 1536–1588* (Cambridge: Cambridge University Press, 1994).

—— and GILLESPIE, RAYMOND (eds.), *Natives and Newcomers: The Making of Irish Colonial Society, 1534–1641* (Dublin: Irish Academic Press, 1986).

BREEN, JOHN, 'Imagining Voices in *A View of the Present State of Ireland*: A Discussion of Recent Studies Concerning Edmund Spenser's Dialogue', *Connotations*, 4 (1994–5), 119–32.

—— 'The Empirical Eye: Edmund Spenser's *A View of the Present State of Ireland*', *Irish Review*, 16 (Autumn/Winter 1994), 44–52.

BRENNAN, MICHAEL, 'William Ponsonby: Elizabethan Stationer', *Analytical and Enumerative Bibliography*, 7 (1983), 91–110.

BRINK, JEAN, 'Constructing *A View of the Present State of Ireland*', *Sp. Stud.* 11 (1990, publ. 1994), 203–28.

CAIN, THOMAS H., *Praise in* The Faerie Queene (Lincoln, Nebr.: University of Nebraska Press, 1978).

CAIRNS, DAVID, and RICHARDS, SHAUN, *Writing Ireland: Colonialism, Nationalism and Culture* (Manchester: Manchester University Press, 1988).

CALDER, ANGUS, *Revolutionary Empire: The Rise of the English-Speaking Peoples from the Fifteenth Century to the 1780s* (London: Cape, 1981).

CANNY, NICHOLAS P., 'The Ideology of English Colonisation: From Ireland to America', *William and Mary Quarterly*, 30 (1973), 575–98.

—— *The Formation of the Old English Elite in Ireland*, O'Donnell Lecture (Dublin: National University of Ireland, 1975).

—— *The Elizabethan Conquest of Ireland: A Pattern Established, 1565–76* (Hassocks: Harvester, 1976).

—— *The Upstart Earl: A Study of the Social and Mental World of Richard Boyle, First Earl of Cork, 1566–1643* (Cambridge: Cambridge University Press, 1982).

—— 'Edmund Spenser and the Development of an Anglo-Irish Identity', *YES* 13 (1983), 1–19.

—— 'Protestants, Planters and Apartheid in Early Modern Ireland', *IHS* 98 (Nov. 1986), 105–15.

—— *From Reformation to Restoration: Ireland, 1534–1660* (Dublin: Helicon, 1987).

—— 'Identity Formation in Ireland: The Emergence of the Anglo-Irish', in Nicholas P. Canny and Anthony Pagden (eds.), *Colonial Identity in the Atlantic World, 1500–1800* (Princeton: Princeton University Press, 1987), 159–212.

—— ' "Spenser's Irish Crisis": A Comment', *P&P* 120 (1988), 201–9.

—— 'Early Modern Ireland, c.1500–1700', in R. F. Foster (ed.), *The Oxford Illustrated History of Ireland* (Oxford: Oxford University Press, 1989).

—— 'The Marginal Kingdom: Ireland as a Problem in the First British Empire', in Bernard Bailyn and Philip D. Morgan (eds.), *Strangers Within the Realm: Cultural Margins of the First British Empire* (Chapel Hill: University of North Carolina Press, 1991), 35–66.

—— and CARPENTER, ANDREW (eds.), 'The Early Planters: Spenser and his Contemporaries', in Seamus Deane (ed.), *The Field Day Anthology of Irish Writing*, 3 vols. (Derry: Field Day Publications, 1991), i. 171–234.

CARPENTER, F. I., 'Spenser in Ireland', *MP* 19 (1922), 405–19.

CARROLL, CLARE, 'The Construction of Gender and the Cultural and Political Other in *The Faerie Queene* V and *A View of the Present State of Ireland*: The Critics, the Context, and the Case of Radigund', *Criticism*, 32 (1990), 163–91.

CAVANAGH, SHEILA T., ' "Such Was Irena's Countenance": Ireland in Spenser's Prose and Poetry', *TSLL* 28 (1986), 24–50.

—— ' "That Savage Land": Ireland in Spenser's Legend of Justice', in David Lee Miller and Alexander Dunlop (eds.), *Approaches to Teaching Spenser's Faerie Queene* (New York: MLA, 1994), 143–52.

—— *Wanton Eyes and Chaste Desires: Female Sexuality in* The Faerie Queene (Bloomington: Indiana University Press, 1994).

CHENEY, DONALD, *Spenser's Image of Nature: Wild Man and Shepherd in* The Faerie Queene (New Haven: Yale University Press, 1966).

CHIAPPELLI, FREDI (ed.), *First Images of America: The Impact of the New World on the Old* (Berkeley: University of California Press, 1976).

COUGHLAN, PATRICIA ' "Cheap and common animals": The English Anatomy of Ireland in the Seventeenth Century', in Thomas Healy and Jonathan Sawday (eds.), *Literature and the English Civil War* (Cambridge: Cambridge University Press, 1990), 205–23.

—— (ed.), *Spenser and Ireland: An Interdisciplinary Perspective* (Cork: Cork University Press, 1989).

COVINGTON, FRANK F., JR., 'Elizabethan Notions of Ireland', *Texas Review*, 6 (1921), 222–46.

—— 'Spenser's Use of Irish History in the *Veue of the Present State of Ireland*', *Texas Studies in English*, 4 (1924), 5–38.

CRAIG, MARTHA, 'The Secret Wit of Spenser's Language', in Paul Alpers (ed.), *Elizabethan Poetry: Modern Essays in Criticism* (Oxford: Oxford University Press, 1967), 447–72.

CULLER, JONATHAN, *The Pursuit of Signs: Semiotics, Literature, Deconstruction* (London: Routledge, 1981).

—— *On Deconstruction: Theory and Criticism after Structuralism* (London: Routledge, 1983).

—— (ed.), *On Puns: The Foundation of Letters* (Oxford: Blackwell, 1988).

CUMMINGS, R. M. (ed.), *Edmund Spenser: The Critical Heritage* (London: Routledge, 1971).

CUNNINGHAM, BERNADETTE, 'Seventeenth-Century Interpretations of the Past: The Case of Geoffrey Keating', *IHS* 25 (1986), 116–28.

DE MAN, PAUL, *Blindness and Insight: Essays in the Rhetoric of Contemporary Criticism*, 2nd edn. (London: Routledge, 1986).

DENEEF, A. LEIGH, *Spenser and the Motives of Metaphor* (Durham, NC: Duke University Press, 1982).

DERRIDA, JACQUES, *Of Grammatology*, trans. G. C. Spivak (Baltimore: Johns Hopkins University Press, 1976).

DERRIDA, JACQUES, *Margins of Philosophy*, trans. Alan Bass (Brighton: Harvester, 1982).

—— *Acts of Literature*, ed. Derek Attridge (London: Routledge, 1992).

—— *Spectres of Marx: The State of the Debt, the Work of Mourning, and the New International*, trans. Peggy Kamuf (London: Routledge, 1994).

DEWAR, MARY, *Sir Thomas Smith: A Tudor Intellectual in Office* (London: Athlone, 1964).

DOLLIMORE, JONATHAN, and SINFIELD, ALAN, 'History and Ideology: The Instance of *Henry V*', in John Drakakis (ed.), *Alternative Shakespeares* (London: Methuen, 1985), 206–27.

DUNSEATH, T. K., *Spenser's Allegory of Justice in Book V of* The Faerie Queene (Princeton: Princeton University Press, 1968).

EDWARDS, PHILIP, *Threshold of a Nation: A Study in English and Irish Drama* (Cambridge: Cambridge University Press, 1979).

ELLIS, STEVEN G., *Tudor Ireland: Crown, Community and the Conflict of Cultures, 1470–1603* (Harlow: Longman, 1985).

—— 'Crown, Community and Government in the British Territories', *History*, 71 (1986), 187–204.

ELLMANN, MAUD, *The Hunger Artists: Starvation, Writing and Imprisonment* (London: Virago, 1993).

FEATHER, JOHN, *A History of British Publishing* (London: Croom Helm, 1988).

FERGUSON, ARTHUR B., *Clio Unbound: The Perception of the Social and Cultural Past in Renaissance England* (Durham, NC: Duke University Press, 1979).

FINLEY, M. I., 'Colonies: An Attempt at a Typology', *TRHS* 26 (1976), 167–88.

FORD, ALAN, *The Protestant Reformation in Ireland, 1590–1641* (Frankfurt: Peter Lang, 1985).

FOSTER, ROY, *Modern Ireland, 1600–1972* (London: Penguin, 1988).

FOUCAULT, MICHEL, *Discipline and Punish: The Birth of the Prison*, trans. Alan Sheridan (Harmondsworth: Penguin, 1977).

FOWLER, ALASTAIR, 'Spenser and War', in J. R. Mulryne and M. Shewing (eds.), *War, Literature and the Arts in Sixteenth-Century Europe* (Basingstoke: Macmillan, 1989), 147–64.

FOWLER, ELIZABETH, 'The Failure of Moral Philosophy in the Work of Edmund Spenser', *Representations*, 51 (1995), 47–76.

GATES, HENRY LOUIS, JR. (ed.), *'Race', Writing and Difference* (Chicago: Chicago University Press, 1986).

GIAMATTI, A. BARTLETT, *Play of Double Senses: Spenser's* Faerie Queene (Englewood Cliffs, NJ: Prentice-Hall, 1975).

—— 'Primitivism and the Process of Civility in Spenser's *Faerie Queene*', in Fredi Chiappelli (ed.), *First Images of America: The Impact of the New World on the Old* (Berkeley: University of California Press, 1976), 71–82.

GILMAN, ERNEST B., *Iconoclasm and Poetry in the English Reformation: Down Went Dagon* (Chicago: Chicago University Press, 1986).

GOLDBERG, JONATHAN, *Endlesse Worke: Spenser and the Structures of Discourse* (Baltimore: Johns Hopkins University Press, 1981).

—— *James I and the Politics of Literature: Jonson, Shakespeare, Donne and their Contemporaries* (Baltimore: Johns Hopkins University Press, 1983).

GOTTFRIED, R. B., 'The Date of Spenser's *View*', *MLN* 52 (1937), 176–80.

—— 'Irish Geography in Spenser's *View*', *ELH* 6 (1939), 114–37.

GRAY, M. M., 'The Influence of Spenser's Irish Experiences on *The Faerie Queene*', *Review of English Studies*, 6 (1930), 413–28.

GRAZIANI, RENÉ, 'Elizabeth at Isis Court', *PMLA* 79 (1964), 376–89.

GREENBLATT, STEPHEN, J., 'To Fashion a Gentleman: Spenser and the Destruction of the Bower of Bliss', in id., *Renaissance Self-Fashioning: From More to Shakespeare* (Chicago: Chicago University Press, 1980), 157–92.

—— *Shakespearian Negotiations: The Circulation of Social Energy in Renaissance England* (Oxford: Clarendon Press, 1988).

—— *Marvelous Possessions: The Wonder of the New World* (Oxford: Clarendon Press, 1991).

GREENLAW, EDWIN A., 'The Influence of Machiavelli on Spenser', *MP* 7 (1909), 187–202.

—— 'Spenser and British Imperialism', *MP* 9 (1911–12), 347–70.

GREGERSON, LINDA, *The Reformation of the Subject: Spenser, Milton and the English Protestant Epic* (Cambridge: Cambridge University Press, 1995).

GRENNAN, EAMON, 'Language and Politics: A Note on Some Metaphors in Spenser's *A View of the Present State of Ireland*', *Sp. Stud.* 3 (1982), 99–110.

GROSS, KENNETH, *Spenserian Poetics: Idolatry, Iconoclasm, and Magic* (Ithaca: Cornell University Press, 1985).

GUILLORY, JOHN, *Poetic Authority: Spenser, Milton and Literary History* (New York: Columbia University Press, 1983).

HACKETT, HELEN, *Virgin Mother, Maiden Queen: Elizabeth I and the Cult of the Virgin Mary* (Basingstoke: Macmillan, 1995).

HADFIELD, ANDREW, 'English Colonialism and National Identity in Early Modern Ireland', *Eire-Ireland*, 28/1 (Spring 1993), 69–86.

—— 'Who knowes not Colin Clout?': The Permanent Exile of Edmund Spenser', in id., *Literature, Politics and National Identity: Reformation to Renaissance* (Cambridge: Cambridge University Press, 1994), 170–201.

—— 'The Naked and the Dead: Elizabethan Perceptions of Ireland', in Michèle Willems and Jean-Pierre Maquerlot (eds.), *Travel and Drama in Shakespeare's Time* (Cambridge: Cambridge University Press, 1996), 32–54.

HALE, D. G., *The Body Politic: A Political Metaphor in Renaissance English Literature* (The Hague: Mouton, 1971).

HAMILTON, A. C., *Allegory in* The Faerie Queene (Oxford: Clarendon Press, 1961).

HAMILTON, A. C. (ed.), *The Spenser Encyclopedia* (London: Routledge; Toronto: Toronto University Press, 1990).

HARPER, CARRIE A., *The Sources of the British Chronicle in Spenser's* Faerie Queene (Philadelphia: John C. Winston, 1910).

HAWTHORN, JEREMY (ed.), *Narrative: From Malory to Motion Pictures* (London: Edward Arnold, 1985).

HEALY, THOMAS, 'Civilisation and its Discontents: The Case of Edmund Spenser', in id., *New Latitudes: Theory and English Renaissance Literature* (London: Edward Arnold, 1992), 84–109.

HECHTER, MICHAEL, *Internal Colonialism: The Celtic Fringe in British National Development, 1536–1966* (Berkeley: University of California Press, 1975).

HEFFNER, RAY, 'Essex and Book Five of *The Faerie Queene*', *ELH* 3 (1936), 67–82.

—— 'Spenser's *View of Ireland*: Some Observations', *MLQ* 3 (1942), 507–15.

HELGERSON, RICHARD, *Forms of Nationhood: The Elizabethan Writing of England* (Chicago: Chicago University Press, 1992).

HENLEY, PAULINE, *Spenser in Ireland* (Cork: Cork University Press, 1928).

HINTON, EDWARD M., *Ireland Through Tudor Eyes* (Philadelphia: University of Pennsylvania Press, 1935).

HOGDEN, MARGARET, *Early Anthropology in the Sixteenth and Seventeenth Centuries* (Philadelphia: Pennsylvania University Press, 1971).

HOLAHAN, MICHAEL, '*Imaque opus exegi*: Ovid's Changes and Spenser's Brief Epic of Mutabilitie', *ELR* 6 (1976), 244–70.

HOUGH, GRAHAM, *A Preface to* The Faerie Queene (London: Duckworth, 1962).

HULME, PETER, *Colonial Encounters: Europe and the Native Caribbean, 1492–1797* (London: Methuen, 1986).

HULSE, CLARK, 'Spenser, Bacon, and the Myth of Power', in Heather Dubrow and Richard Strier (eds.), *The Historical Renaissance: New Essays on Tudor and Stuart Literature and Culture* (Chicago: Chicago University Press, 1988), 315–46.

—— WEINER, ANDREW D., and STRIER, RICHARD, 'Spenser: Myth, Politics, Poetry', *SP* 85 (1988), 378–411.

HUME, ANTHEA, *Edmund Spenser: Protestant Poet* (Cambridge: Cambridge University Press, 1984).

JENKINS, RAYMOND, 'Spenser with Lord Grey in Ireland', *PMLA* 52 (1937), 338–53.

JOHNSON, F. R., *A Critical Bibliography of the Works of Edmund Spenser Printed Before 1700* (Baltimore: Johns Hopkins University Press, 1933).

JONES, ANN ROSALIND, and STALLYBRASS, PETER, 'Dismantling Irena: The Sexualising of Ireland in Early Modern England', in Andrew Parker *et al.* (eds.), *Nationalisms and Sexualities* (London: Routledge, 1992), 157–71.

JONES, H. S. V., *Spenser's Defense of Lord Grey*, University of Illinois Studies in Language and Literature 5 (1919), 7–75.

—— *A Spenser Handbook* (New York: F. S. Crofts & Co., 1930).

JUDSON, ALEXANDER, *The Life of Edmund Spenser* (Baltimore: Johns Hopkins University Press, 1945) (*Variorum*, xi).

—— 'Spenser and the Munster Officials', *SP* 44 (1947), 157–73.

KANTOROWICZ, ERNST H., *The King's Two Bodies: A Study in Medieval Political Theology* (Princeton: Princeton University Press, 1957).

KAPPELER, SUSANNE, *The Pornography of Representation* (Cambridge: Polity Press, 1986).

KEARNEY, RICHARD, 'The Making of an English Empire', in id., *The British Isles: A History of Four Nations* (Cambridge: Cambridge University Press, 1989).

KENDRICK, T. D., *British Antiquity* (London: Methuen, 1950).

KING, JOHN, N., *Spenser's Poetry and the Reformation Tradition* (Princeton: Princeton University Press, 1990).

KLIGER, SAMUEL, 'Spenser's Irish Tract and Tribal Democracy', *SAQ* 49 (1950), 490–7.

KUPPERMAN, KAREN O., *Settling with the Indians: The Meeting of English and Indian Cultures in America, 1580–1640* (London: Dent, 1980).

LEERSEN, JOSEPH, *Mere Irish and Fíor-Ghael: Studies in the Idea of Irish Nationality, its Development and Literary Expression Prior to the Nineteenth Century* (Amsterdam: Benjamens, 1986).

LENNON, COLM, *Richard Stanihurst, the Dubliner, 1547–1618* (Dublin: Irish Academic Press, 1981).

LEVY, F. J., *Tudor Historical Thought* (San Marino: Huntington Library Publications, 1967).

LEWIS, C. S., *The Allegory of Love: A Study in Medieval Tradition* (Oxford: Oxford University Press, 1936).

LUPTON, JULIA, 'Home-making in Ireland: Virgil's Eclogue I and Book VI of *The Faerie Queene*', *Sp. Stud.* 8 (1990), 119–45.

MCCABE, RICHARD A., 'The Masks of Duessa: Spenser, Mary Queen of Scots and James VI', *ELR* 17 (1987), 224–42.

—— 'Edmund Spenser, Poet of Exile', *PBA* 80 (1991, publ. 1993), 73–103.

MCCAFFREY, ISABEL G., *Spenser's Allegory: The Anatomy of Imagination* (Princeton: Princeton University Press, 1976).

MACCARTHY-MORROGH, MICHAEL, *The Munster Plantation: English Migration to Southern Ireland, 1583–1641* (Oxford: Clarendon Press, 1986).

MCNEIR, WALDO F., 'The Sacrifice of Serena: *The Faerie Queene*, VI. viii. 31–51', in Bernhard Fabian and Ulrich Suerbaum (eds.), *Festschrift für Edgar Mertner* (Munich: W. F. V. Munchen, 1968), 117–56.

MADSEN, DEBORAH L., *Rereading Allegory: A Narrative Approach to Genre* (Basingstoke: Macmillan, 1995).

MALEY, WILLY, 'Spenser and Ireland: A Select Bibliography', *Sp. Stud.* 9 (1991), 227–42.

MALEY, WILLY, *A Spenser Chronology* (Basingstoke: Macmillan, 1994).

—— 'Spenser's Irish English: Language and Identity in Early Modern Ireland', *SP* 91 (1994), 417–31.

—— *Salvaging Spenser: Colonialism, Culture and Identity* (London: Macmillan, 1997).

MALTBY, WILLIAM, *The Black Legend in England: The Development of Anti-Spanish Sentiment, 1558–1660* (Durham, NC: Duke University Press, 1971).

MAROTTI, ARTHUR F., ' "Love is Not Love": Elizabethan Sonnet Sequences and the Social Order', *ELH* 49 (1982), 396–428.

MARTIN, WILLIAM C., 'The Date and Purpose of Spenser's *Veue*', *PMLA* 47 (1932), 137–43.

MEMMI, ALBERT, *The Colonizer and the Colonized*, trans. Howard Greenfield (New York: Orion Press, 1965).

MIKICS, DAVID, *The Limits of Moralising: Pathos and Subjectivity in Spenser and Milton* (Lewisburg: Bucknell University Press, 1994).

MILLER, DAVID LEE, *The Poem's Two Bodies: The Poetics of the 1590* Faerie Queene (Princeton: Princeton University Press, 1988).

MONTROSE, LOUIS A., 'The Elizabethan Subject and the Spenserian Text', in Patricia Parker and David Quint (eds.), *Literary Theory/Renaissance Texts* (Baltimore: Johns Hopkins University Press, 1986), 303–40.

MOODY, T. W., MARTIN, F. X., and BYRNE, F. J. (eds.), *A New History of Ireland*, iii, *Early Modern Ireland, 1534–1691* (Oxford: Clarendon Press, 1976).

• MORGAN, HIRAM, 'The Colonial Venture of Sir Thomas Smith in Ulster, 1571–5', *HJ* 28 (1985), 261–78.

—— 'Mid-Atlantic Blues', *Irish Review*, 11 (Winter 1991), 50–5.

—— *Tyrone's Rebellion: The Outbreak of the Nine Years War in Tudor Ireland* (Woodbridge, Suffolk: Royal Historical Society/Boydell Press, 1993).

MORTON, GRENFELL, *Elizabethan Ireland* (London: Longman, 1971).

NICHOLLS, KENNETH, *Gaelic and Gaelicized Ireland in the Middle Ages* (Dublin: Gill & Macmillan, 1972).

NOHRNBERG, JAMES, *The Analogy of* The Faerie Queene (Princeton: Princeton University Press, 1976).

NORBROOK, DAVID, '*The Faerie Queene* and Elizabethan Politics', in id., *Poetry and Politics in the English Renaissance* (London: Routledge, 1984), 109–56.

NORTHROP, DOUGLAS A., 'Spenser's Defense of Elizabeth', *UTQ* 38 (1969), 277–94.

O'CONNELL, MICHAEL, *Mirror and Veil: The Historical Dimension of Spenser's* Faerie Queene (Chapel Hill: University of North Carolina Press, 1977).

ONG, WALTER J., 'Spenser's *View* and the Tradition of the "Wild" Irish', *MLQ* 3 (1942), 561–71.

O'RAHILLY, ALFRED, *The Massacre at Smerwick (1580)* (Cork: Cork University Press, 1938).

PAGDEN, ANTHONY, *The Fall of Natural Man: The American Indian and the Origins of Comparative Ethnology* (Cambridge: Cambridge University Press, 1982).

—— 'The Savage Critic: Some European Images of the Primitive', *YES* 13 (1983), 32–45.

—— *European Encounters with the New World: From Renaissance to Romanticism* (New Haven: Yale University Press, 1993).

PARKER, JOHN, *Books to Build an Empire: A Bibliographical History of English Overseas Interests to 1620* (Amsterdam: New Israel, 1965).

PARKER, PATRICIA, 'Suspended Instruments: Lyric and Power in the Bower of Bliss', in id., *Literary Fat Ladies: Rhetoric, Gender, Property* (London: Methuen, 1987).

PATTERSON, ANNABEL, 'The Egalitarian Giant: Representations of Justice in History/Literature', *JBS* 31 (1992), 97–132.

PAWLISCH, HANS, *Sir John Davies and the Conquest of Ireland: A Study in Legal Imperialism* (Cambridge: Cambridge University Press, 1985).

PHILLIPS, JAMES E., 'Renaissance Concepts of Justice and the Structure of *The Faerie Queene*, Bk. V', *HLQ* 33 (1970), 103–20.

PIERCE, ROY HARVEY, 'Primitivistic Ideas in *The Faerie Queene*', *JEGP* 44 (1945), 138–51.

POCOCK, J. G. A., *The Ancient Constitution and the Feudal Law: A Study of English Historical Thought in the Sixteenth Century*, rev. edn. (Cambridge: Cambridge University Press, 1987).

PORTER, H. C., *The Inconstant Savage: England and the North American Indian, 1500–1660* (London: Duckworth, 1979).

PRALL, STUART E., 'The Development of Equity in Tudor England', *American Journal of Legal History*, 8 (1964), 1–19.

QUILLIGAN, MAUREEN, *Milton's Spenser: The Politics of Reading* (Ithaca, NY: Cornell University Press, 1983).

QUINN, DAVID BEERS, 'Sir Thomas Smith (1513–77) and the Beginnings of English Colonial Theory', *PAPS* 89 (1945), 543–60.

—— *The Elizabethans and the Irish* (Ithaca, NY: Cornell University Press, 1966).

—— 'The Munster Plantation: Its Problems and Opportunities', *JCHAS* 71 (1966), 19–40.

RAAB, FELIX, *The English Face of Machiavelli: A Changing Interpretation, 1500–1700* (London: Routledge, 1965).

RAMBUSS, RICHARD, *Spenser's Secret Career* (Cambridge: Cambridge University Press, 1993).

RATHBORNE, ISABEL E., *The Meaning of Spenser's Fairyland* (New York: Columbia University Press, 1937).

RICHTER, MICHAEL, *Giraldus Cambrensis and the Growth of the Welsh Nation* (Aberystwyth: National Library of Wales, 1972).

RICHTER, MICHAEL, *Medieval Ireland: The Enduring Tradition* (Basingstoke: Macmillan, 1983).

RINGLER, RICHARD N., 'The Faunus Episode', *MP* 63 (1965–6), 12–19.

ROWSE, A. L., *The Expansion of Elizabethan England* (London: Macmillan, 1955).

SAID, EDWARD, *The World, the Text and the Critic* (London: Faber & Faber, 1983).

—— *Culture and Imperialism* (London: Vintage, 1993).

SHEEHAN, BERNARD W., *Savagism and Civility: Indians and Englishmen in Colonial Virginia* (Cambridge: Cambridge University Press, 1980).

SHEPHERD, SIMON, *Spenser* (London: Harvester, 1989).

SHIRE, HELENA, *A Preface to Spenser* (London: Longman, 1978).

SILBERMAN, LAUREN, *Transforming Desire: Erotic Knowledge in Books III and IV of* The Faerie Queene (Berkeley: University of California Press, 1995).

SILKE, J. J., 'The Irish Appeal of 1593 to Spain: Some Light on the Genesis of the Nine Years War', *Irish Ecclesiastical Record*, 5th ser., 92 (1959), 279–90.

—— *Ireland and Europe, 1559–1607* (Dundalk: Dundalgan, 1966).

SINFIELD, ALAN, *Faultlines: Cultural Materialism and the Politics of Dissident Reading* (Oxford: Clarendon Press, 1992).

SKINNER, QUENTIN, *The Foundations of Modern Political Thought*, 2 vols. (Cambridge: Cambridge University Press, 1978).

SMITH, ROLAND M., 'Spenser's Irish River Stories', *PMLA* 50 (1935), 1047–56.

—— 'The Irish Background of Spenser's *View*', *JEGP* 42 (1943), 499–515.

—— 'Spencer, Holinshed and the *Leabhar Gabhála*', *JEGP* 43 (1944), 390–401.

TONKIN, HUMPHREY, *Spenser's Courteous Pastoral: Book VI of* The Faerie Queene (Oxford: Clarendon Press, 1972).

WALLER, GARY, *English Poetry of the Sixteenth Century* (London: Longman, 1986).

WILLIAMS, KATHLEEN, *Spenser's Faerie Queene: The World of Glass* (London: Routledge, 1966).

WILLIAMS, PENRY, *The Tudor Regime* (Oxford: Clarendon Press, 1979).

WRIGHT, LOUIS B., *Middle-Class Culture in Elizabethan England* (Chapel Hill: University of North Carolina Press, 1935).

YATES, FRANCES A., *Astrea: The Imperial Theme in the Sixteenth Century* (London: Routledge, 1975).

YEATS, W. B., 'Edmund Spenser', in id., *Essays and Introductions* (London: Macmillan, 1961), 356–83.

Index

Pollente 148, 157, 158–60, 163,
165, 168; Paridell 134–6, 138 n.
71; Proteus 142, 144, 162, 186,
200; Radigund 119, 157, 167–8;
Red Cross Knight 89, 116, 124,
125–6, 128, 129, 130, 137, 161, 162
n. 47, 176; Rheusa 145; Ruddymane 177 n. 84; sa(l)vage man
139–2, 175–7, 183; sa(l)vage nation
132–3, 136, 137, 177–81; Samient
161–2; Sansloy 130; Saturn 148,
150, 151, 190; Satyrane 131, 136 n.
65, 137–8, 140, 142; satyrs 130–7,
141, 176, 194; Scorn 177; Scudamore 119, 129, 138, 140; Serena
133, 142, 175, 176, 177–81, 183,
194 n. 24, 195, 196; Slieve Bloom
mountains 145; Souldan, the 157,
158, 160, 161, 176; Sylvanus
130–1, 140; Talus 138, 148, 150–1,
154, 155, 157, 160, 162–3, 164, 166,
167–8, 184; Thames 142–5, 158,
162; Thaymis 137; Therion 137;
Timais 177; Time 189; Timon
89; Titans 148 n. 10, 150, 151, 186,
190, 191, 198; Trompart 195;
Troynouvant 134; Turpine 175,
176; Una 89, 124, 125–6, 129,
130–4, 135, 137, 138, 152, 161, 170,
171, 188, 194, 199, 201; Venus 131,
139; Zele 167–8
The Shepheardes Calender 15, 68
A View of the Present State of Ireland 3,
5, 9, 11, 18, 22–3, 29–32, 42, 50–84,
85–112, 114–15, 132, 134, 137–8,
146, 148, 151, 152, 156, 157, 160,
161, 162, 164, 169, 170, 183, 185–6,
189, 190–1, 195, 197, 198, 202
censorship of (alleged) 79
manuscripts of 42, 79, 83–84, 186
names in: Eudoxus 22, 23, 53, 64–5, 67,
71, 84, 85, 98, 101, 108, 134, 146;
Irenius 18, 22, 23, 24, 29, 30, 32,
53, 64–65, 67, 84, 85, 96, 98, 100,
101, 108, 132, 146, 151, 169, 191,
200

Spenser, Peregrine 19
Spenser, Sylvanus 21
Spenser, William 21
Stanley, Sir William 36
Stanihurst, Richard 24, 97, 103
Starkey, Thomas 72
State Papers 82

Stationers' Register 19, 52, 78–84
Strabo 86, 101, 105, 107, 110
Strachey, William 141
Strafford, earl of, *see* Wentworth, Sir
Thomas, earl of Strafford
Strongbow (Richard FitzGilbert de Clare)
95
Suetonius 39
'Supplication of the blood of the English'
48–9
Swift, Jonathan 69

Tacitus 101, 103, 105
tanistry 96
Tasso, Torquato 115
Thames, river 142–5
Throckmorton, Elizabeth 140 n. 77
Tilbury (Elizabeth's speech at) 115
Tipperary 4
transhumance, *see* farming
transplantation 40
treason 158
Trim, Co. Meath 62
Troy 134, 135
Tudors 12, 88, 92, 95, 96, 108, 109, 110,
158, 166
Turks 27, 54, 55
Tyrone, earl of, *see* Hugh O'Neill, second
earl of Tyrone
Tyrone's Rebellion, *see* Nine Years War

Ulster 19, 103
Utopia, Utopian 10

vagina 181, 197
Venus 131, 139, 141
Vere, Edward de, earl of Oxford 116
Vergil, Polydore 88, 99, 100
Vespucci, Amerigo 92
viceroy, viceregal 39, 40, 150, 195
Virgil 115
Virginia 109, 141, 142

Wace 110
Wales 41, 92, 110
war 54–5
Wars of the Roses 191
Ware, Sir James 5, 79, 85, 92, 99
Waterford 109 n. 82
Wentworth, Sir Thomas, earl of Strafford
157
West Indies, West Indians 36, 91
Westminster 20

Westminster Abbey 20
Wexford 18, 24
White, John 142
'wild men of the woods' 137–8
William the Conqueror 76
William of Malmesbury 110
William of Newburgh 95

Woodhouse, A. S. P. 129
World War I 1
World War II 52

Yeats, W. B. 5

Zouche, Colonel John 159 n. 39